I0802480

# Solidarity or Service

## Composition and the Problem of Expertise

John Trimbur

Boynton/Cook Publishers
HEINEMANN
Portsmouth, NH

Boynton/Cook Publishers, Inc.
361 Hanover Street
Portsmouth, NH 03801–3912
www.boyntoncook.com

*Offices and agents throughout the world*

© 2011 by John Trimbur

All rights reserved. No part of this book may be reproduced in any form or by any electronic or mechanical means, including information storage and retrieval systems, without permission in writing from the publisher, except by a reviewer, who may quote brief passages in a review.

The author and publisher wish to thank those who have generously given permission to reprint borrowed material:

"Articulation Theory and the Problem of Determination: A Reading of *Lives on the Boundary*" by John Trimbur from *JAC* 13.1, pages 33–50. Copyright © 1993 by *JAC: A Quarterly Journal of Rhetoric, Culture, and Politics*. Reprinted by permission of the publisher.

"Agency and the Death of the Author: A Partial Defense of Modernism" by John Trimbur from *JAC* 20.2, pages 283–298. Copyright © 2000 by *JAC: A Quarterly Journal of Rhetoric, Culture, and Politics*. Reprinted by permission of the publisher.

"The 'Communication Battle,' or Whatever Happened to the 4th C?" by Diana George and John Trimbur from *College Composition and Communication* Vol. 50, No. 4, pages 125–141. Copyright © 1999 by the National Council of Teachers of English. Reprinted by permission of the publisher.

*Credit lines continue on page 224.*

**Library of Congress Cataloging-in-Publication Data**

Trimbur, John.
Solidarity or service : composition and the problem of expertise / John Trimbur.
p. cm.
Includes bibliographical references and index.
ISBN-13: 978–0–86709–603–3
ISBN-10: 0–86709–603–9
1. English language—Rhetoric—Study and teaching (Higher). 2. English language—Rhetoric—Study and teaching—Social aspects. 3. Expertise. I. Title.
PE1404.T778 2011
808'.042071173—dc22 2011001834

*Editor*: Charles I. Schuster
*Production*: Victoria Merecki
*Typesetter*: Aptara®, Inc.
*Cover design*: Steven Schirra
*Manufacturing*: Steve Bernier

Printed in the United States of America on acid-free paper
T & C Digital

*for Lundy*

# Contents

# Acknowledgments

Thanks, Chuck—for encouraging this project. I deeply appreciate Charles I. Schuster's interest in this collection. I treasure his friendship and editorial ability in this project and earlier ones.

Thanks, Diana and Lundy. Two of the essays included here were adapted from those originally cowritten—"The 'Communication Battle,' or Whatever Happened to the 4th C?" with Diana George and "Popularizing Science: At the Boundaries of Expert and Lay Knowledge" with Lundy Braun. Thanks to NCTE and the University of Pittsburgh Press for permission to reprint these essays.

Thanks to Southern Illinois University Press, *JAC*, and NCTE for permission to reprint other essays.

# Introduction

# Expertise in U.S. College Composition

The essays gathered in this collection explore the role of expertise and the problem of professionalization in U.S. college composition. From various angles, the essays seek to understand how institutions set boundaries between professionals and ordinary people, how ideologies organize expert and lay knowledge into cognitive and cultural hierarchies, and what the implications of these actual and symbolic economies of expertise might be for teachers, theorists, and program administrators who believe that writing instruction should promote rhetorical agency and popular participation in public life.

Taken as a whole, these essays begin with the necessary recognition that since the rise of corporate capitalism and the expansion of the white-collar workforce at the turn of the twentieth century, the professions of law, medicine, engineering, civil service, academia, and so on consolidated monopolies of expertise based on credentials, meritocratic frameworks, professional associations, accrediting agencies, licensing exams, mentoring relations, and social networks. These monopolies of expertise endowed credentialed specialists—or what Richard Ohmann calls the "professional-managerial class"—with the social and cultural authority to determine what counts as justified knowledge, standard practices, and prudent public policy. By the same token, this regime of expertise represented laypeople as naïve, dependent, and deferential, disqualified from knowledge production yet educated sufficiently to acknowledge the need for highly trained professionals to manage the complexities of modern society. According to its own self-portrait, the professional-managerial class is entitled to speak and act on behalf of a public interest located above politics and business, in the name of a farsighted rationality that transcends the immediate passions of public opinion or the profit motive of the marketplace. If anything, the very idea of the expert became a touchstone in defining what it means to be modern, rational, and scientific.

Questions about the mission of the professional-managerial classes have been raised, to be sure, in critiques of expertise that include, for example, John Dewey's *The Public and Its Problems* (1946), C. Wright Mill's notion of the "crackpot realism" of Cold War technocrats (1958), Jurgen Habermas' (1972) understanding of the limits of "instrumental rationality," and Ulrich Beck's rewriting of modernity in *Risk Society* (1992). Furthermore, it is important to acknowledge how the terms of professional authority started to shift in the final decades of the twentieth century, with the growing pressures of neoliberalism to recast (and to privatize) professional expertise as a form of human capital in the global expansion of free markets and an emergent knowledge economy rather than a vocational calling to serve the public interest. In turn, the inability of late capitalism to provide for the common good has provoked a popular reaction against the professional-managerial class (known more commonly on Fox News and talk radio as the "liberal elite") and a loss of credibility on the part of laypeople, disenchanted and disoriented by the failures of the professionals in charge to make good on their promises of a better life for all.

The essays in this collection add to this understanding of the current status of professionalized expertise an effort to imagine how the relationship between professional and popular knowledge might be changed, remade, and transformed by connecting the expertise of specialists to the experience and practical understandings of ordinary people, as part of a common undertaking to mobilize the available intellectual resources in order to produce socially useful knowledge. The intention is neither to abandon expertise and professional knowledge in the name of some unproblematically more authentic popular knowledge, nor to suppose expertise can be brought, in direct and unmediated ways, by professionals to serve their clients. These essays rather seek to redefine expertise and to rearticulate it to popular aspirations. This is the meaning I hope to signify by the title of the collection *Solidarity or Service*, which is taken from a distinction Raymond Williams (1989a) draws between "social conscience" and "social consciousness." He divides participants in the adult education movement of postwar Britain between those, like himself and others, for whom teaching and producing knowledge were matters of solidarity with ordinary people, with the aim of jointly developing an active social consciousness, and those for whom teaching adult education was imagined as a public service and an act of social conscience, brought to deprived sectors of the population under the auspices of middle-class self-improvement.

* * * * *

I want to admit at the outset the risk of making the essays contained in this collection seem more programmatic than they actually are. The essays were originally published as articles or chapters in the spirit of the occasional essay, as forays into the moment of their history in the annals of U.S. college composition, with its shifting issues, debates, interests, and appetites. At their inception, the essays were acts of alignment and division, often written with the self-conscious goal of promoting a tendency in the study and teaching of writing (e.g., the social turn, cultural studies, postprocess, or modernism's "unfinished business"). I do not want to disclaim the partisanship of the essays or their alliance with such intellectual/political compatriots as Patricia Bizzell, Lester Faigley, Bruce Horner, Min Zhan-Lu, Joseph Harris, Tom Fox, Diana George, Paula Mathieu, the late James Berlin, and many others. What I find striking, though, in retrospect, now at a remove from the contentions of the time, is that even when I thought I was writing about something else how compulsively I kept returning to the problem of professional work, its contradictions, and its relation to popular forms of knowledge, drawing on sources in rhetoric, critical theory, and Marxism to gain some traction on a set of issues I apparently could not shake.

There would be limited justification for this collection, of course, if the problem of expertise, professionalism, and the popular were simply an idiosyncratic fixation on my part. I believe, however, that a case for the timeliness of this book can be made given how deeply engrained the idea of expertise is in U.S. college composition, what it has highlighted in the study and teaching of writing, and what it has obscured.

The notion of *expertise* appears, for example, as a central organizing term in composing research and writing theory: in expert-novice studies of composing and revising by Nancy Sommers (1980), Sondra Perl (1980), and Linda Flower and John R. Hayes (1981); in representations of how undergraduates learn academic writing, such as David Bartholomae's idea of "inventing the university" (1985) and Kenneth A. Bruffee's notion of collaborative learning as the reacculturation involved in joining new discourse communities (1984); and in rhetorics of inquiry that investigate how novices learn particular disciplinary discourses, such as research by Carol Berkenkotter and Thomas N. Huckin (1995), Dorothy Winsor (1996), and many others. The idea of expertise keeps popping up as the commonsense target of writing instruction in longitudinal studies, such as Nancy Sommers' at Harvard (Sommers and Saltz 2004); in work on transferability; and in Douglas Downs and Elizabeth Wardle's recent proposal to turn the first-year composition course into an "Introduction to Writing Studies" (2007). And it also appears in ostensibly left alternatives, such as cultural studies approaches to composition, where writing assignments prompt students to emulate the denaturalizing rhetorics of Roland Barthes, John Berger, and other expert critics. In all these examples, expertise carries its own self-explaining warrant, for if the aim of composition teachers is to help students crack the code of various discursive practices and write with consequence in a range of rhetorical situations, then it seems to make sense to identify the expertise of experienced writers and to teach it to students.

For the most part, the *expertise* invoked by such expert-novice configurations has been treated as a neutral and technical term that identifies particular kinds of proficiency as the goal of writing instruction, making the learning of writing, in effect, an apprenticeship in the ways of experienced practicing writers. The usefulness of the idea has more or less been taken for granted, and the issues of contention have typically involved how to represent and research expertise in writing, whether as a type of problem-solving activity that can be examined through protocol analysis of expert practitioners imported from cognitive psychology or as a situated practice that requires ethnographic investigation and textual analysis of how writers learn the local rhetorics of particular discourse communities. This is the now familiar argument in the taxonomy wars of the 1980s and early 1990s that counterposed cognitivist and social theories of composing, along with attempts by Michael Carter (1990), Cheryl Geisler (1994), and others (including Linda Flower (1994), the *bête noir* of cognitivism in the social camp's view) to synthesize the two in a sociocognitive approach.

At any rate, the point to emphasize is that even the sharpest attacks on cognitivism's notion of expertise as a technocratic figure of thought, such as James Berlin's in "Rhetoric and Ideology in the Writing Class" (1988), left the very idea of expertise intact, seeking to redefine it from a social perspective rather than to problematize the conceptual and practical work it does in the study and teaching of writing. For example, in his final work, *Rhetoric, Poetics, and Cultures,* Berlin (1996) presents methods of analysis from cultural studies, such as binary oppositions, narrative codes, preferred reading positions, and subject formation, in a course designed for students to apply expert knowledge to their own lived experience as readers, viewers, spectators, workers, and consumers, but without interrogating the grounds of that expertise or the way its critical apparatus shapes the consciousness of critics and their relationship to ordinary people.

The notion of expertise also appears in U.S. college composition in a different light as the body of expert knowledge that enables the field to claim professional standing and disciplinary legitimacy. In this regard, the idea of expertise is closely related to the monopolies of knowledge and services that professions seek to establish and maintain as the material conditions of their existence. Such connections between expertise and the formation of the modern professions have been developed in the history and sociology of the professions (cf. Abbott 1988; Bledstein 1976; Bourdieu 1977; Collins 1979; Freidson 1986; Larson 1977) and brought into composition studies by Richard Ohmann (1987, 2003) in his evolving notion of the professional-managerial class. The results of the professionalization of composition studies are well known: the proliferation of graduate programs, journals, book series, conferences, and symposia; the heightened recognition within academia of composition as a legitimate field of study; the rise of freestanding writing programs and departments at the graduate and undergraduate level; the internationalization of composition, with consultancies in writing on the part of U.S. composition specialists in Europe, Asia, Latin America, and Africa; and perhaps, above all, the fact that, at least before the 2008 economic crash, 70 percent of rhetoric and composition PhDs were getting tenure-track jobs compared to about 40 percent of literature PhDs.

The contrast between these two representations of expertise is instructive. When expertise is viewed as a type of highly skilled but conventionalized performance, as in expert-novice studies and apprenticeship models of writing instruction, it appears to isolate something enabling for students and something teachable for instructors. On the other hand, when expertise is linked to the professionalization of U.S. college composition, something quite different happens. There is little of the taken-for-granted value of the term found in the realms of research and course design. Instead, expertise in its institutionalized form, precisely to the extent the study and teaching of writing has been professionalized, becomes the source of intellectual ambivalence and conflicted emotions. Sentiments range from an energized and sometimes uncomfortably triumphant sense of composition's newly won academic status (especially in regard to literary studies) to concerns about the normalization of intellectual work and fears of becoming just another careerist and trendy discipline (like literary studies) to a residual nostalgia for the bad old days when composition was a smaller, marginalized operation in English departments but a purer one where everybody (unlike the faculty in literary studies) shared the goal of serving students, opening access to higher education, and building a literate democracy.

To my mind, the way that these meanings of expertise have spread across U.S. college composition is not a problem that can be fixed by defining terms. In fact, I don't consider the range of meanings to be a problem at all. The task rather, at least as I see it, is to examine the pressures and limits that these various representations of expertise and its professionalization might exert on each other.

The first sense of expertise, for example, found in expert-novice research and course design, could benefit from the heightened sense of social consequence found in composition's anxieties and identity crises about its own professionalization. Certainly writing theory and ethnographic studies of how novices enter new discourse communities have examined some of the cultural and linguistic stresses and strains of this process, the conflicting social allegiances at the individual level between professional ways of being, on the one hand, and home communities, political commitments, and subcultural identities on the other. But it is rare that such work explores how the acquisition of expertise on the part of individuals, in the formation of a professional consciousness, reproduces the professional authority that divides specialists from laypeople and official from popular knowledge. As far as I can tell, this structural dimension is missing in expert-novice studies and apprenticeship models of writing instruction. In turn, the danger is that professional authority appears to be a personal accomplishment achieved through individual effort instead of a social fact that requires explication.

By the same token, the worries and woes in some quarters about the professionalization of U.S. college composition might be mitigated by a heightened appreciation of the rhetorical possibilities of expertise not only to produce exclusive and hyperspecialized disciplinary discourses but also to expand the domain of public deliberation and participation in civic and intellectual life. Recent attention to public writing, popular literacies, and activist rhetorics offers a way to recast professional practices by linking them in active relation to the experience and understanding of ordinary people and the prospects of counterpublics and grassroots literacies. Instead, compositionists often express their suspicion of professionalism in the name of a genial amateurism that wishes to preserve the pleasures of writing and the possibilities of a common language uncontaminated by specialized jargon and the instrumental logic of the technocrats. The problem is that by designating the essay of reflection, observation, and experience as the primary defense against the esoteric theorizing of small coteries of intellectuals, the essayist wing of U.S. college composition often misses the point that the essay itself is as class-inflected as any professional discourse. With its roots in late eighteenth- and early nineteenth-century belletristic rhetorics, the essay became a key discursive vehicle in the emergent middle classes' bid for the moral and cultural authority to explain their own and everybody else's experience (cf. T. Miller 1997).

In this sense, what was known briefly as the "theory war" between Gary Olson and the late Wendy Bishop (and that continues a subterranean existence in the identity split within composition between "reflective writer-teachers" and "theorists") might be seen as counterposing two styles of essay writing and claims to rhetorical authority, with Bishop based in the plain style of Anglo-American essayist tradition, familiarly voiced to enhance the personal presence of a discriminating observer; while Olson, on the other hand, comes from the critical tradition of an intellectual vanguard in the continental style, for whom the essay is a vehicle of dissection.

* * * * *

If this sounds like a stalemate left over from the taxonomy wars, there are significant efforts within composition to break the gridlock and imagine a critical perspective on expertise and its professionalized discourses. Let me mention two that I find particularly illuminating. Joseph Harris' interrogation of expertise in "The Other Reader" (1992), for example, begins by noting how cultural critics (he singles out Janice Radway and Tania Modleski but his case can be extended more widely) too often set up the "other reader" as a cultural dupe who falls for the lure of soap operas, advertising, romance novels, rock music, and so on. In contrast, "the figure of the critic" is posed as someone "who can read (and often even enjoy) popular works without being injured or seduced by them" and yet who "doubts that others can do the same" (228). As Harris sees it, there is little "reciprocal exchange" between expert critics and ordinary readers. Rather, the "ideological analysis of the scholar subsumes the views of the ordinary reader" and the "actual words of non-academics rarely find their way into the writings of even the most political critics." This disqualification of the insights of ordinary people is, of course, one of the central props of professional authority and a deeply antidemocratic impulse that Harris proposes to counter by imagining "a kind of cultural criticism in which the comments of ordinary readers (or students) function not only as material to work with and explain . . . but also as checks against the bias" of the critic's reading (229). The work that follows is "to set up classrooms where students can talk about their responses to popular texts as mixed rather than simple, where they can write as people who are at once rock fans *and* intellectuals" (233).

This important recognition of how professional and popular knowledges might be brought into contact as pedagogical resources can be found as well in the work of Patricia Bizzell. Bizzell is commonly identified as one of the leading proponents of academic discourse in the 1980s, and the 1985 Conference on College Composition and Communication

(CCCC)'s debate, when she and Bruce Herzberg engaged Lil Brannon and Cy Knoblauch on the merits of teaching academic discourse explicitly, is one of the defining moments for composition in that decade. There is no question that Bizzell argued strenuously for the value of academic discourse, in part to refute the view of basic writers as limited by cognitive deficiencies and to see these students instead as altogether educable but lacking a familiarity with the academic ways of knowing that are unequally distributed in a racialized and gendered class society. At the same time, it is crucial to note that, despite charges she was trying to inculcate students with academic discourse in a unidirectional socialization process, Bizzell's view of the discursive practices of academia and how they are acquired and used was never a monolithic one but rather acknowledged that the production of knowledge is overdetermined by social, cultural, personal, and political forces and, thereby, open to the infiltration of external voices.

Bizzell's remarkably frank (and sometimes confessional) introduction to the essays she wrote during this period, collected in *Academic Discourse and Critical Consciousness* (1992), explains her growing misgivings about seeing academic discourse as causal in promoting a critical detachment that would "more or less automatically" bring "insight into social injustices and the will to correct them" (20). Further, Bizzell began to doubt that Paolo Freire's notion of critical consciousness—or, as she says, "*any* critical method" for that matter (20)—could guarantee certainty in demystifying the dominant social order and setting an agenda for collective liberatory action. As a result, in a move that has great pertinence to this discussion of expertise, Bizzell turned to rhetoric. This involved questioning her own stance "as a privileged advocate for marginalized basic writers" (29), an expert in the ways of academic and intellectual life who could bring to students in some direct way the resources needed to acquire critical consciousness. Instead, she realized her own beliefs and values concerning social justice would have to be negotiated *with* students, that she would, in effect, have "to find some way"—some rhetorical authority based not on method but on persuasion—"to achieve direction without playing the expert" (29).

By framing the question of expertise as a topic of investigation instead of the grounds of teaching, in subsequent work Bizzell has gone on to examine and to argue for the validity of "mixed" or "hybrid" forms of academic writing on the part of scholars and students alike, where popular and professional discourses interpenetrate and create new rhetorical possibilities (1999, 2000, 2002). This shift, moreover, is indicative of an undercurrent in U.S. college composition, still in an emergent phase, which has challenged the older commitment to teaching students how to "code-switch" between vernaculars and Standard English by recognizing language differences in the first instance as available resources of writing (instead of presumptive "errors"). *Alt Dis: Alternative Discourses and the Academy*, which Bizzell coedited with Christopher Schroeder and Helen Fox (2002), was instrumental in thematizing attention to the rhetorical effects of merging rather than separating codes and discourses, professional and popular registers, to expand the identities and interests that can be articulated to academic writing. More recently "code-meshing" and "translanguaging," as developed in the work of Suresh Canagarajah (2006) and Vershawn Ashanti Young (2009), has continued this emphasis on language and discourse differences as the available semiotic resources to make new meanings in an era of multilingualism and World Englishes rather than "interference" with the metropolitan standard. The aim of such a "translingual" approach is not to reject Standard English or the academic genres, but as Bruce Horner and Min Zhan-Lu have argued, to put them on display as malleable codes and discourses in order to rework them, from the inside, to expand the prospects of rhetorical agency, in light of the full range of a writer's linguistic resources (Horner and Lu 2007; Horner et al. 2011).

* * * * *

Patricia Bizzell's decision to decline the role of the expert is understandable as a matter of resisting the foundational certainties of professionalism to bring about a more just social order. I don't think she gives herself enough credit, however, on another score: namely, how she, along with others such as Mina Shaughnessy, Kenneth A. Bruffee, and David Bartholomae, brought their professional training in graduate literary studies and New Critical close reading to the work of ordinary writers in composition classrooms during the era of open admissions and basic writing in the 1970s. To my mind, this is one of the formative moments in U.S. college composition, when a cadre of writing teachers, many of them recent literature PhDs, linked their expertise as sophisticated readers to the goal of democratizing higher education—and a sign of how professional knowledge can be articulated to popular energies for social change. I realize there were many mistakes and muddled understandings at the time, but what seems critical to recognize is how this decisive step in the professionalization of U.S. college composition involved not just the exercise or transmission of expertise but its redirection and redefinition, as socially conscious writing teachers invented theories and pedagogies to join their work to mass pressure from below, on the part of trade unions and the civil rights movement, to open higher education to minorities, the poor, and working-class students who had formerly been excluded and whose talents and intelligence had been squandered by selective admissions.

I want to hold on to this legacy and, in a sour time of retrenchment, fiscal crisis, privatization, and corporatization in higher education, to imagine once again how writing teachers, theorists, and program administrators might make literacy a popular and socially useful resource of participating in intellectual life and of activating the kinds of public deliberations needed for a more just and inclusive social future.

* * * * *

This collection is grouped into three sections, each of which has an introduction that locates the essays at their time of writing and suggests how they might be linked to each other and to the themes of the book. Part One, "Terms and Frameworks," looks at the theoretical orientations that have shaped my understanding of expertise. Part Two, "Professionalization of U.S. College Composition," examines the origins, contradictions, consequences, and prospects of the professionalization of the study and teaching of writing. Part Three, "Expert and Lay Knowledges," focuses on the relationships between specialized and popular knowledges and how this relationship might be rearticulated.

Three of the essays, "Writing Instruction and the Politics of Professionalization" (Chapter Four), "Popularizing Science: At the Boundary of Expert and Lay Biomedical Knowledge" (Chapter Six), and "Changing the Question: Should Writing Be Studied?" (Chapter Five) have been revised and updated. "Popular Literacy and the Resources of Print Culture" (Chapter Seven) is the complete version of a manuscript that had to be cut for publication in *College Composition and Communication*. The other essays appear with minor editing and corrections. The volume ends with a new essay, "The Crisis of Expertise," as an Afterword.

# PART ONE

# Terms and Frameworks

The essays in this section indicate some of the key terms and conceptual frameworks I have found useful in developing an understanding and critique of expertise in U.S. college composition. This is not to say that the terms and frameworks are part of a methodical research program that I've been pursuing over the past thirty-five years. The path is more digressive than systematic. But I don't think the line of inquiry is accidental either. If the essays in this section have a direction, it's because of a tangent I've been on since I started teaching basic writing in inner-city community colleges in Philadelphia and Baltimore in the mid-1970s. With an undergraduate history degree from Stanford and a graduate education in American Studies at SUNY–Buffalo, I was utterly unschooled in rhetorical theory or composition research, and the only question I could imagine to ask at the time was how do the lives of the students I was teaching and writing go together in the racialized and gendered realities of late capitalism?

It's probably not surprising that I didn't publish much until the late 1980s, though I acquired a good deal of practical experience directing writing programs and writing centers, starting peer tutoring and writing across the curriculum programs, and running local and regional conferences. Then the "social turn" in composition made the things I knew from history, social theory, and four years in a small Trotskyist group appear to be interesting to colleagues in composition. The simple and naïve question I had asked in Philadelphia and Baltimore about the relationship between lives and writing suddenly seemed to be relevant.

The late 1980s were a time of the taxonomy wars between the expressivists, cognitivists, and social constructionists. At the time, I was fully enrolled in the social camp, due in part to my own predilections and in part to the influence of my mentor Ken Bruffee and my solidarity with the work of James Berlin, Patricia Bizzell, David Bartholomae, and Lester Faigley. (I actually used to say "Writing is a social act," as though that proved something.) But I also stayed in touch with Peter Elbow, another key influence on what I was imagining writing instruction to be, and felt he was being oversimplified as a token of an expressivist position he had never claimed to espouse. In any case, by the early 1990s, I was experiencing a cognitive dissonance that led me to suspect that the taxonomies, which initially had seemed so clarifying, were in other ways constraining a proper understanding of how lives and writing go together, to the extent that the taxonomic categories had ordered the relation of ideas, interests, and social locations to each other in logical and necessary correspondences.

With the arrival of British cultural studies in U.S. college composition, conceptual frameworks, such as Stuart Hall's notion of articulation (1986), made available alternative means of linking lives and writing to the social formation—only not in advance, based on an ideological reading of preset positions on a taxonomic grid. Instead, in Hall's "Marxism without guarantees" (1983), the connection is located conjuncturally, at specific moments in history, based not on an essential belonginess of ideas and class interests but on how people link ideas to class interests through actual practice.

I draw on Hall in the essay, "Articulation Theory and the Problem of Determination: A Reading of *Lives on the Boundary*" (Chapter One), to come to terms with the way Mike Rose uses an edifying coming-of-age narrative but diverts it from conventional associations with individual self-fashioning and rags-to-riches entrepreneurial values to affirm the educability of ordinary people (1990). Through Rose's textual labor and Hall's explanatory framework, I started to see that discourses and cultural practices, including the discourse and practices of professional expertise, might be rearticulated, away from predictable connections to the status quo and dominant ideologies and toward popular aspirations and the interests of the many. From this perspective, the political valence of how lives and writing go together cannot be inferred ahead of time in taxonomic determinations but depend rather on how people make sense of and respond to the rhetorical situations that arise at particular conjunctures in the history of the contemporary. In other words, I was relearning one of Marx's fundamental lessons—that people make their own history, only not in conditions of their own making.

Articulation theory led me further to reconsider the notion of agency and the possibilities of consequential action, both of which had seemed to be so thoroughly unsettled by poststructuralist accounts of the "death of the author" and postmodern "incredulity" as an influential structure of feeling. Like many people in U.S. college composition, I had been instructed in the 1980s by the continental theory of Foucault, Derrida, Barthes, and Lyotard and the peculiarly American antifoundationalism of Thomas Kuhn, Stanley Fish, and Ricard Rorty that Kenneth A. Bruffee (1984) brought forward as the theoretical grounds of "social construction."

Chapter Two, "Agency and the Death of the Author: A Partial Defense of Modernism" was, in certain respects, my attempt to come to terms with this intellectual legacy and to explain my growing concern that antifoundationalism and postmodernism were hardening into a kind of orthodoxy in the "theory" wing of U.S. college composition that rejected the grand metanarratives of enlightenment and liberation from intellectual and material scarcity and began to use *modernist* and *modern* as terms of dismissal without fully registering what I took to be the political consequences. Accordingly, "Agency and the Death of the Author" offers a corrective counterhistory by picturing a popular Enlightenment of partisans and pamphleteers to stand against the "great books" tradition of the Enlightenment *philosophe*s that had so thoroughly scandalized the postmodernists and virtually brought them into being with its claims about rationality and a Universal Subject. My project here in the most immediate sense was to preserve the viability of the "author" against those who had proclaimed its death, with Walter Benjamin's (1986) notion of the "author as producer" as a primary instance of modernity's still vital intellectual and political legacy.

In a wider sense, this "partial defense" of modernism also expresses my skepticism about the breathless claims that started circulating in the mid-1990s, holding that postmodernism (or post-Fordism, postindustrialism, fast capitalism, or globalization) constituted a radical rupture with the past and the emergence of a new historical epoch. To my mind, this postmodern fever, with its vehement denunciations of modernism and modernity, amounted to a deviation from the revolutionary legacy and emancipatory projects of the modern era that took late capitalism's triumphal self-description of a new world order too seriously. I knew that it was hard, particularly after the fall of the Soviet Union and the other Stalinized workers states, to talk about the "historical mission of the proletariat" with a straight face, but I didn't want to give in altogether to the ironic detachment and overriding sense of contingency that marked the post-Marxist cultural left in the United States. That's why, the defense of modernism here is "partial," in the sense of "limited, unfinished, and partisan."

## Chapter One

# Articulation Theory and the Problem of Determination

## A Reading of *Lives on the Boundary*

The narrativity of an individual life is a literary trope that figures across a range of genres. From memoirs, biography, the journalistic profile, and the celebrity story to the autobiographical novel and *bildungsroman*, the narrativity of a life is a familiar and apparently altogether consumable literary convention, turning up in award winners such as Patti Smith's *Just Kids* (2010) and popular magazines such as *People*. Other forms of writing, too—popular psychology books such as Gail Sheehy's *Passages* (1977) and the gamut of self-help and popular advice tracts that line bookstore shelves—seem to take it for granted that an individual life not only can be narrated but that such narration can make a life intelligible and thereby subject to control and change.

Harvey Kail suggests that composition theory and textbooks likewise rely on the narrativity of a Student Writer's life by projecting mythic quests for students to take on their road to advanced literacy. In "Narratives of Knowledge: Story and Pedagogy in Four Composition Texts" (1988), Kail argues that we can read out the plots of standard textbooks such as Young, Becker, and Pike's *Rhetoric: Discovery and Change* (1970), Ann E. Berthoff's *Forming, Thinking, Writing* (1983), William E. Coles Jr.'s *Teaching Composition* (1974) and *The Plural I* (1978), and Kenneth A. Brufee's *A Short Course in Writing* (2007) in order to identify their underlying narratives and the tales they tell of the formation of a personality through emergence into literacy. According to Kail, these narratives are familiar ones, based on Christian and social traditions deeply rooted in American culture, such as the search for identity, salvation, self-improvement, and knowledge. By paying attention to these narratives, moreover, Kail suggests an alternative way to represent composition studies, not just as a series of discrete theoretical positions on a taxonomic grid (Becker, Young, and Pike are "cognitivists"; Berthoff, a "neo-Cassirerean"; Coles, an "expressivist"; Bruffee, a "social constructionist") but as a series of conjunctures that link scholarly and pedagogical discourses and practices to culturally sanctioned narratives, to the interests, institutions, and identities these narratives call up, and to the way these narratives make the meanings of reading and writing intelligible to students and teachers alike.

By and large, however, composition studies has paid relatively little attention to its own narrativity, to the way in which composition theory and practice are articulated to the master narratives that charter belief and action in American culture. This may appear to be surprising because the notion that knowledge is invariably authorized by its narrativity has become something of a commonplace in postmodern thought. Richard Rorty (1979), Jean-Francois Lyotard (1984), and others, for whatever differences may otherwise divide them, seem to agree that what we have traditionally called knowledge is in fact a "fiction," a manufactured account that legitimizes itself precisely to the extent it holds its readers in the thrall of persistent and unexamined metaphors and metanarratives.

There has, of course, been a recent turn toward narrative in composition studies, in part following Jane Tompkins' (1988) call to "unlearn" the critical essay and write in a more personal and autobiographical style. In the work of Donald McQuade (1992), Nancy Sommers (1992), and others, however, narrative remains separate from "thesis-driven" exposition. It figures as an academically devalued genre capable, its advocates hold, of redeeming prose by replacing the authoritarian, masculinist, and hierarchical strategies of arguing for a position with the immediacy and authenticity of lived experience rendered narratively. This turn to narrative, thus, has largely limited itself to counterposing narrativity as a way of knowing to argumentative strategies, instead of probing for the connections between narratives and other discursive forms and cultural practices—or, as Kail (1988) might put it, how the discourse of composition studies joins together with available culturally authorized narratives and the social contexts in which these narratives arise.

In this essay, I want to suggest the usefulness of investigating the conjunctures at which discourses and practices in the field of composition studies are linked to discourses and practices outside of it. I will be looking in particular at how the narrativity of an individual life in Mike Rose's *Lives on the Boundary* (1990) is articulated to wider cultural narratives. I have chosen to focus on *Lives on the Boundary* in part because it makes its own narrativity so explicit by relying on autobiography to tell the story of what the book's subtitle calls the "struggles and achievements of America's educational underclass." But I am also interested in *Lives on the Boundary* because its use of such a popular genre to narrate its concerns makes the book more problematical than has usually been acknowledged.

## The Problem of Narrativity in *Lives on the Boundary*

Since *Lives on the Boundary* appeared in 1989, it has been hailed as the book composition studies was waiting for. Addressed to the general public, as well as to education and composition specialists, *Lives on the Boundary* seemed to do the kind of cultural and ideological work needed in the Reagan/Bush era of educational retrenchment by providing an eloquent and moving case for expanded educational opportunity, multicultural curricula, enlightened pedagogy, and the educability of all Americans. At last, it appeared that someone had succeeded in translating the hard-won experience and expertise of writing teachers, and especially of basic writing teachers in open admissions programs, into a popular idiom capable of affecting public opinion. *Lives on the Boundary* was greeted as the book to give composition studies a public voice and visibility to counter bestsellers such as E. D. Hirsch's *Cultural Literacy* (1987) and Allan Bloom's *The Closing of the American Mind* (1987) and commission reports from William Bennett, Diane Ravitch and Chester Finn, and Lynne J. Cheney.

To bring his case to a broad audience, Rose has chosen to devote a substantial part of the book to his own life. Rose tells the story of his "passage from South Vermont [the working-class neighborhood where he grew up] to Loyola," where Rose was an undergraduate and, as he puts it, "entered the conversation" (67). We follow Rose on a kind of pilgrim's progress, from his struggles as a high school student who arises, miraculously, from the slough of Voc-Ed despond, through college and the temptations of literary studies in graduate school, to his redemptive work as a teacher of the neglected and underprepared. This narrative, of course, possesses enormous cultural resonance, recalling such autobiographies as Richard Wright's *Black Boy* (1945) and Richard Rodriguez's *Hunger of Memory* (1983). But because the tale of a poor or working-class youth rising from his humble origins is such a familiar one, it also contains some political risks I think have not been adequately accounted for. To put it as directly as I can, the risk is that readers will take *Lives on the Boundary* to be another comforting American success story of an individual who, through the power of education and the guidance of more experienced teacher-mentors, takes the predictable road to self-improvement and upward mobility, from the mean streets of Los Angeles to the halls of UCLA. Such a narrative, furthermore, fits in to what Harvey Graff calls the "literacy myth" (1991): the moral consensus that has dominated the meanings of literacy since the mid-nineteenth century by representing the ability to read and write as a social explanation of success and failure in class society, a token of middle-class propriety, and a measure to divide the worthy from the unworthy poor.

The issue I am concerned with here is whether Rose's decision to use the narrativity of a life backfires on him. Despite Rose's obvious intentions to argue for fundamental reforms in American education, the question needs to be asked whether the autobiographical impulse in *Lives on the Boundary* inevitably locates the book for its readers within what Kristin Ross (1988) calls the "exemplary bourgeois cultural project" of narrating a life, individualizing a person's fate, and positioning readers as witnesses to an edifying tale of individual initiative and the transformative powers of education and literacy. But before I consider whether Rose's life history is absorbed, inadvertently or not, by the cultural narrative it articulates, I want first to define more precisely the notions of conjuncture and articulation I will be using to read *Lives on the Boundary*.

## Taxonomies and Conjunctures

For the most part, literature reviews and histories of writing instruction have used a taxonomic strategy to order composition by dividing and classifying its various pedagogies, rhetorics, and research programs into categories, with perhaps the discontinuity of a Kuhnian paradigm shift to demarcate one approach from another. Like any rhetorical strategy, taxonomies both enable and constrain their users, bringing some things to light while suppressing others. Taxonomies, in other words, need to be seen not just in terms of whether they are accurate classifications but also in terms of their uses and what they make possible.

The standard taxonomies in the field, such as James A. Berlin's (1988) expressionistic, cognitivist, and social-epistemic rhetorics, Lester Faigley's (1986) expressive, cognitive, and social views of composing, and Stephen North's (1987) division of the field into researchers, historians, scholars, and practitioners, are useful for the ordering functions they perform and the differences, both practical and theoretical, they bring to the surface. Particularly for a young and emerging field such as composition studies, taxonomies can codify positions that might appear otherwise to arise spontaneously from the pressures of practice. In this regard, Berlin's and Faigley's taxonomies especially have contributed to the professionalization of the field by giving it a shape, by identifying central issues, and by lifting the study and teaching of writing from the shared activity of a few like-minded individuals at the margins of English departments into the realm of scholarly controversy where a set of standard positions defines the context of issues and establishes the terms of ongoing discussion. From this perspective, we might say that without taxonomies it would be difficult to think and speak composition studies at all. By dividing and classifying, taxonomies create a unity of differences as the terrain of composition studies.

At the same time, such division and classification tend to make instances of intellectual work into a token of trends and currents in the field. The work of David Bartholomae, for example, and in particular his essay "Inventing the University" (1985), is often cited as a founding statement of a social constructionist, academic discourse approach to writing instruction. As Carolyn C. Ball (1992) argues, however, this conventionalized view may actually ignore or suppress the recognition of so-called expressivist or cognitivist currents in Bartholomae's writing. If anything, this reification of "Inventing the University" in terms of a monovocal taxonomic category seems virtually to be called for by the generic function of the literature review and the scholarly convention of locating one's work in relation to prior work, as the ground to validate new inquiries or a foil to establish countertendencies.

However, as Susan Miller says of North's division of composition studies into humanistic "scholars" and empiricist "researchers," taxonomies are based not on "logical, but political, differences" (*Rescuing the Subject* 1989, 37). Taxonomic categories need to be seen not just as the formal defining terms of a field of study but as the result of particular conjunctures that ascribe certain cultural meanings and political valences to ideas and practices. Unlike the categories of a taxonomy, which reside in the space of logic, conjunctures are located in actual historical time. A conjuncture designates those moments when ideas (whether in the form of theories or narratives or other genres) are joined to other ideas, practices, institutions, interests, and subjectivities. Conjunctures constitute the temporal and temporary moments at which ideas take on particular social weight, cultural meaning, and rhetorical effect not because of their intrinsic or essential identities (as specified categorically) but because of the way these ideas are articulated concretely by specific men and women and take on specific identities in specific historical settings and social contexts.

To give a brief example: from a conjunctural perspective, the emphasis on the value of personal voice and individual sincerity in the work of Peter Elbow cannot be reduced simply to a category of expressivist rhetoric that distinguishes it, say, from the emphasis on academic discourse and the kind of imitative ventriloquy Bartholomae notes in students' efforts to appropriate the institutional voices of the university. The sincerity of self-revelation that Elbow struggled to teach young men writing statements of conscientious objection during the Vietnam War carries a quite different political meaning from the usual practice of sincerity in expressivist rhetorics. Berlin, correctly I think, sees these rhetorics as critical of "the dehumanizing effects of industrial capitalism" but at the same time indebted to "the entrepreneurial values capitalism most admires: individualism, private initiative, the confidence for risk taking, the right to be contentious with authority (especially the state)" (1988, 487). The point here is that apparently identical ideas and practices can take on quite different cultural meanings and political valences depending on the conjuncture at which (and to which) they are articulated. The rhetorical effect of ideas and practices is produced not only by reference to their logical features but also by the practical joining together of discourse, institutions, and interests that social utterances and performances inevitably enact. When sincerity of expression is linked to mass movements against war, as occurred during the Vietnam War, or invoked as a means to give voice to those who have been systematically silenced, as during the Black Expressionist movement of the 1960s (see Leroi Jones/Amiri Baraka's classic essay "Expressive Language" [1966]), an expressivist rhetoric can indeed be oppositional in effect. At other times, however, in "normal" classrooms of middle-class students, expressivist rhetoric may well serve simply as a form of personal protest that, as Berlin notes, is "easily coopted by the very capitalist forces it opposes" or, at best, a limited means of "creative realization of the self" (1988, 487).

What I am suggesting is that there is no way to derive the meaning of an utterance on the basis of a taxonomic categorization or to predict with certainty its rhetorical effects. Unlike the categories in a taxonomy, which are meant to have a predictive value, the notion of a conjuncture suggests that nothing can be guaranteed ahead of time strictly according to formal or textual qualities alone. Rather, effective meaning is a matter of what happens: practice takes place in historical time and social space.

## Stuart Hall's Theory of Articulation

The notion of a "conjuncturalist" approach to the relationship between ideas, practices, and social formations might be seen as an attempt to formulate a neo-Marxist model of determination. As Raymond Williams notes, "No problem in Marxist cultural theory is more difficult than that of determination" (1977, 83). Part of the difficulty may be attributed in the first place to the writings of Marx and Engels, which seem at times to presuppose a fixed correspondence among the existing stage of material production, social relations, and consciousness. In *The German Ideology*, for example, Marx and Engels state quite clearly that the "mass of productive forces accessible to men determines the conditions of society" (1970, 18). There is a tendency in Marx and Engels' writings to see human activity and historical development as governed by scientific laws of determination, a tendency that objectifies the social process and, as Engels indicates in a letter to Bloch in 1890, reads human will and agency out of history. "The historical event," Engels writes, may "be viewed as the product of a power which works as a whole unconsciously and without volition. For what each individual wants is obstructed by everyone else, and what emerges is something that no one willed" (1890, 476). At the same time, of course, one can also find equally authoritative passages that seem to affirm the creativity of human agency, even if it operates within particular constraints. Probably the best-known statement of this view is Marx's famous remark that "people make history but in conditions not of their making."

According to Williams, the confusion surrounding the problem of determination results in part from the "extraordinary linguistic complexity" of the term *determine* (1977, 84). While the term has certainly been colored in its uses within the Marxist tradition by scientistic biases and a typically nineteenth-century positivist quest for certainty, the root sense of *determine*, Williams says, refers not only to an external force or authority—whether history or God—that decides or controls the outcome of an action but also to the way limits are set and pressures exerted by the momentum of the social process itself. According to the latter sense of the term, Williams says, "Society is then never only the dead husk which limits social and individual fulfillment," as it sometimes appears in orthodox Marxisms that hold to an abstract determinism based on isolated and autonomous forces acting upon the social formation from outside. Instead, for Williams, society "is always also a constitutive process with very powerful *pressures* which are both expressed in political, economic, and cultural formations and, to take the full weight of constitutive, are internalized and become individual wills" (1977, 87; emphasis added).

Perhaps the fullest exploration of the problem of determination in contemporary Marxist thought occurs in Stuart Hall's theory of articulation (1986). Like Williams, Hall wants to develop a model of determination based not upon the implacable and predictable laws of history but upon the limits and pressures of specific historical, social, and cultural conjunctures. Situating his theory of articulation within past and current critical discourses, Hall has attempted to formulate a model of determination that avoids, on the one hand, the traditional Marxist view of a fixed and necessary correspondence between cultural practices and social structures and, on the other, more recent poststructuralist views of the indeterminancy or necessary noncorrespondence and incommensurability of discourses, practices, and structures. By looking at how particular ideas, discourses, and practices are linked—or articulated—to particular conjunctures in the social formation, Hall has sought to define a "Marxism without guarantees," a guide to action that relies not on the predictive certainties of classical Marxist theory but on a reading of those linkages and how they articulate, at specific times and places, interests, subjectivities, and social forces.

Hall's theory of articulation was developed as part of a larger project to define the meaning of cultural studies in relation to what Hall calls "culturalist" and "structuralist" paradigms of critical thought. Cultural studies is often seen as the effort of the Birmingham (UK) Centre for Contemporary Cultural Studies, under Hall's directorship, to balance the culturalist work of Williams, Richard Hoggart, and E. P. Thompson from the late 1950s and early 1960s (the period of the emergence of the British New Left) against the impact of more recent poststructuralist and postmodernist trends on Marxist thought in the 1970s and 1980s, as embodied above all in the influence of Althusser's structuralist Marxism. The usual version holds that a balancing act between the two paradigms was achieved by turning to Gramsci and his notions of hegemony and a war of positions in civil society, to account, on the one hand, for the empirical specificity characteristic of Williams and, on the other, the importance of difference that emerges from Althusser. This is a fair portrayal in a general sense but somewhat unnuanced. Cultural studies, at least in Hall's representation of it, is not so much an effort to locate a middle ground between the two paradigms as to use the two paradigms themselves as limits and pressures on each other, to hold them in dynamic tension as forms of reciprocal interrogation. To see how Hall's theory of articulation derives from this dynamic tension, we need now to look more closely at the way Hall reads the two paradigms against each other and the effect of this reading on Hall's model of determination.

First of all, the culturalist work of Williams, Hoggart, and Thompson registers a break from the reductionist economic determinism of orthodox Marxism in the direction of a Marxist or socialist humanism that emphasizes the creativity of cultural practices and the authenticity of working-class experience. In various ways, Williams, Hoggart, and Thompson argued that the popular culture of the working class is not simply a form of false consciousness imposed from above in the interest of ruling elites but rather is a way of life and shared subjectivity that resists as much as it accommodates the dominant order. According to this view, precisely because the formation of subjectivities is linked to class position, the lived experience of the working and subordinate classes offers a grounds to measure the distorting effects of ideology against reality. The culturalist paradigm, in other words, severs the ties of the left to the mechanical materialism of traditional Marxism but preserves a necessary correspondence among class position, cultural practices, and forms of consciousness as the framework of determination.

In contrast, the structuralist paradigm argues that there is no essential subjectivity at the center of experience, but rather that experience of the "real" is itself made available and intelligible only as an effect of ideology, already preshaped by the categories, classifications, and frameworks of culture. In this sense, the structuralist paradigm loosens the ties in culturalism between cultural practice and social position by thinking of the social formation as a unity, which is constructed through the differences of relatively autonomous practices rather than an expressive totality of corresponding practices. In Hall's view, Althusser's notion of the social formation as a structure in dominance of relatively autonomous practices and institutions that cannot be reduced to a system of homologous correspondences typifies the structuralist paradigm. These structures, as Althusser has it, "hail" or "interpellate" subjects by creating subject positions that speak and place individuals in capitalist social relations. Subjects, as Hall says, are by this account "bearers of structures" rather than "active agents" in making their own history.

Hall's strategy is to use these two paradigms as limits and pressures on each other. Hall takes Althusser and the structuralist paradigm as a way to reread Williams and the culturalists, to retain the creative subject by turning it into a subject positioned not by an essential class location but by mediating social and cultural forces, a subject in ideology who lives, as Althusser puts it, in and through imaginary relations to the real and contradictory conditions of existence. Althusser's understanding of the social formation as a complexly overdetermined structure instead of a simple or monolithic one allowed Hall, as he says, "to live in and with difference," to imagine a social formation determined by a totality of relatively autonomous institutions and practices (in, say, education, culture, mass media, the rituals of everyday life, and so on), which can be reduced neither to forms of each other nor to reflexes of the economic order but which still cohere as a unity in difference. For Hall, there is no necessary correspondence between cultural practices and social structures that can be referred to the determinations of class position or authentic experience.

At the same time, Hall also wants to put a break on certain post-structuralist tendencies, arising in part from Althusser but certainly exceeding him, to think that there is not only no necessary correspondence but rather that there is a necessary noncorrespondence that makes it analytically impossible to relate practices, beliefs, discourses, identities, and institutions to each other in determinate ways. According to Hall, Foucault and others take the emphasis on difference in Althusser's relative autonomy of overdetermined practices in the direction of a radical heterogeneity, incommensurability, and the absolute autonomy of practices that refuses to think of determination as anything other than local and specific contingencies. In other words, Hall is prepared to follow the poststructuralists by thinking that cultural and social practices can be read as if they were textual or linguistic events. But by reaching back to the culturalist emphasis on lived experience, Hall also wants to resist what he sees as the typically postmodern abandonment of any appeal to the "real" or to experience outside of discourse. Hall holds on to the Marxist project of theorizing a complex unity of the social formation—but not by relating base to superstructure or latent to manifest content in a structure of necessary correspondence. Instead, Hall is proposing a fractured or articulated totality in which people make their own history, only under conditions not of their making.

Hall's theory of articulation conceptualizes the conjunctures at which people knit together disparate and apparently contradictory practices, beliefs, and discourses in order to give their world some semblance of meaning and coherence. Articulation theory, in other words, describes how people make a unity that is neither necessary nor previously determined. So, if Hall uses Althusser to set limits on the essentialism of class identity in the culturalist paradigm, by the same token he uses Williams and draws upon Gramsci to put pressure on what he calls the "creeping functionalism" in Althusser's structuralism, the tendency to see ideology as performing the function required of it by reproducing the social relations of production without countertendencies. In Hall's view, Althusser's "ideological state apparatus," the famous ISA, collapses the state and civil society, precisely the gap through which Hall sees the pressures of ideology from below running, in the tensions and conflict between the people and the ruling bloc. This domain of the popular is not strictly imposed from above but rather is negotiated in a contested arena where the struggle for hegemony and consent takes place. By using Gramsci's theory of hegemony and Ernesto Laclau's argument that the political connotation of ideological elements has no necessary belongingness to class or social location, articulation theory, Hall says, "enabled us to think how an ideology empowers people, enabling them to make some sense or intelligibility of their historical situation, without reducing those forms of intelligibility to their socio-economic or class location or social position" (1986, 53). The point for Hall is that one can connect cultural practices to the social formation—only not in advance. Articulation is always a matter of struggle in a war of positions where nothing is certain ahead of time but rather a matter of practice. No outcome can be guaranteed, as it is in orthodox Marxism, by the laws of history but must be determined concretely at specific conjunctures of history.

By refusing the scientistic metanarrative of orthodox Marxism and denying the necessary correspondence between practice and class location, Hall poses instead the quite practical yet crucial analytical question: "under what circumstances can a connection be forged or made" among particular ideologies, political subjects, cultural practices, and social movements and institutions? The double meaning of articulation—to put into words and to yoke together physically—offers both "a way of understanding how ideological elements come, under certain conditions, to cohere together within a discourse, and a way of asking how they do or do not become articulated, at specific conjunctures, to certain political subjects" (1986, 53). The workings of articulation, as Hall describe them, are simultaneously discursive and social: articulation names those historical moments at which certain ideas are uttered and combined (sometimes by severing ideological elements from their conventional uses and recombining them with other elements) into material forces capable of binding subjects together in social identities and movements.

## Articulating *Lives on the Boundary*

From the perspective of articulation theory, the question to ask of *Lives on the Boundary* is how Rose puts into words the narrativity of his own life and how this articulation is thereby linked to other discourses, practices, subjectivities, and institutions. Rose has chosen to narrate his life history, as a student and a teacher, both to indict an educational system that wastes the intellectual curiosity of young people and adults and to demonstrate the possibilities of individual growth and development within America's educational underclass. Rose wants readers to see, and to feel, how such class-based educational practices as testing and tracking produce the desire of poor and working-class students not to excel and get ahead but to be "average," to distance themselves emotionally from a reward system that neglects their talents and potential. And he wants readers to understand how the intervention of caring teachers can mobilize and cultivate the intellectual resources of nonmainstream students. This is a story worth telling, especially at a moment in our collective history when "reform" movements in education are calling for higher standards, national testing, teacher accountability, discipline, and a return to a canonical curriculum. It is a story to break the prevailing silence in public discourse about education by speaking of democratic aspirations to increase access, to open opportunity, and to remove educational barriers to the poor and working class.

The problem, though, is whether the narrativity of a life in *Lives on the Boundary* is adequate to Rose's purposes, whether it can adequately represent the social processes of illiteracy and school failure in contemporary America and project a compelling vision of needed change. As I have already suggested, as a coming-of-age narrative, *Lives on the Boundary* might be read as an instance of the "exemplary bourgeois cultural project" of narrating a life. What makes the narrativity of a life so "exemplary" as a class-based tale is the fact that just to have a life—to experience oneself as possessing a life that can be narrated in the first place—is itself a particular historical development, inseparable from the emergence of individualism and the authority and autonomy ascribed to the bourgeois subject in class society. The narrativity of a life, in other words, is not something that is naturally given but rather is a strategic trope for what C. B. Macpherson (1962) calls the ideology of "possessive individualism," in which the individual emerges as a social subject by taking on a proprietary relationship to his or her own life. The autobiographical impulse to narrate a life, therefore, is not a straightforward one but rather the result of a particularly bourgeois cultural project of making and owning a sovereign and inalienable life, free from the ascriptions of birth, status, and social obligation in traditional society.

The classic coming-of-age narrative, however, tends to naturalize this struggle to fashion a self-created life and an individual personality by representing the passage from youth to maturity not as the formation of a particular kind of subjectivity in class society but as a timeless biological and psychological process. The rhetorical effect is an ostensibly Universal Subject whose life is narratable because its meanings transcend historical circumstance by expressing general laws of development and human nature. What is disguised or mistaken to be a natural desire to tell one's own story is, in fact, a critical moment in the bourgeoisie's growing self-consciousness and cultural self-confidence, as it entitles its members to author their own life histories and to inscribe the formation of the bourgeois personality in literature and popular culture as the normative story of growing up.

Such a coming-of-age narrative has a fairly predictable and formulaic narrative pattern. The plot typically recounts the adventures and crises of an alienated youth and how these youthful exploits and the wisdom of older and more experienced adults enable the youth to reconcile his or her identity to the constraints of class society. Readers are often offered a vicarious experience of the transgressions and marginality of youth, but only so that such disruptions of adult order and common sense will enable readers more surely than ever to define the boundaries of the normal. In this sense, what we call the *coming-of-age narrative* enacts not only a rite of passage from youth to maturity but also a ritual of inversion that permits formulaic moments of violation in order to contain their subversive force within the hierarchical patterns of mature order and authority.

According to Marxist critics such as Georg Lukács (1971) and Jean-Paul Sartre (1965), the classic coming-of-age narrative tells how the disruptive desires and the turbulence of youth are contained by class society as the central character achieves maturity by taking on a professional calling and joining the adult world of full-fledged citizens. An atmosphere of calm typically pervades the narrative, the result of what Lukács sees as the social optimism of the rising bourgeoisie and the narrative transformation of a troubled youth into a well-adjusted and idealized bourgeois subject. For Sartre, this calm is a matter of the distanced lucidity of the narrator who represents the desires of youth as an "adventure" and a "brief distraction which is over with" (1965, 134). As the turbulent events of youth are situated narratively at the remove of time, they are relieved of their convulsive energies by the narrator's achieved stability and maturity. For this reason, the formation of a personality, as Sartre says, "is told from the viewpoint of experience and wisdom; it is listened to from the viewpoint of order" (134).

For Lukács and Sartre, the subject is shaped not only archetypally by the passage from youth to maturity and innocence to experience, but also practically by reconciling his or her youthful desires to the alienated adult world of work. In a typical coming-of-age narrative, a youth will wander through bohemia, want to be a writer or a painter, experiment with drugs and sexuality, travel to exotic places—and then settle down by choosing a profession, a calling, a *métier*. In other words, in the classic tale of the formation of a bourgeois personality, a youth comes into maturity by internalizing the necessity of work in the capitalist division of labor as a matter of personal choice, and the narrative represents this choice as a moral lesson learned from the errors and enthusiasms of youth. As Sartre says, "Neither the general nor the doctor impart their memories in a raw state: they are experiences that have been distilled, and we are warned as soon as they begin to speak that their story has a moral" (1965, 134).

Readers will recognize the classic features of the coming-of-age narrative in *Lives on the Boundary*. The book does indeed narrate a rite of passage, from a turbulent adolescence in South Los Angeles through a youthful flirtation with Beat culture and a brief literary romance with graduate studies in English to Rose's mastery of the secrets of the academy brought about by his acquisition of an identity and professional expertise as teacher and researcher. Rose's struggle, for himself and his students, to crack the code of the university appears in this narrative both as an affirmation of the (adult) authority of academic discourse and its institutions and as an act of benevolence toward the underprepared, from whose ranks Rose has risen. The question then is whether, or to what extent, *Lives on the Boundary* enacts the kind of reconciliation to the party of order and maturity that Lukács and Sartre find characteristic of the classic coming-of-age narrative.

The question of the social allegiances of *Lives on the Boundary*, I believe, hinges on the problem of determination I have been concerned with in earlier sections of this essay. Lukács and Sartre link the coming-of-age narrative, historically and culturally, to the formation of the bourgeois subject as the owner and operator of an exemplary life, an act of self-creation that culminates in the moralization of professional work as an explanation of success and failure in class society. From this perspective, the cultural practice of narrating a life seems to fit neatly with class location, and one might therefore postulate a necessary correspondence between the genre and the reproduction of capitalist social relations. There are, of course, other ways of narrating a life, as Sartre's admiration for Jean Genet in *St. Genet* indicates, that hold on to a position of marginality, criminality, and transgression that will not be reconciled to the dominant order. Mike Rose's book, however, is not written from such an outsider's perspective. But it is not written from the inside, either. Rather, as the title tells us, the book is located at the boundary of the dominant culture, at the points of intersection where the lives of the dispossessed encounter an educational system that sorts individuals into a capitalist division of labor, allotting life chances by separating mental from manual labor, the upwardly mobile from those stuck in place.

*Lives on the Boundary* is more than just an account of how Rose slips through the system, more than a tribute to the initiative (and luck) of the few who make it. What allows Rose to evade the class-bound limits of the self-made coming-of-age narrative—and what distinguishes his book from Wright's and Rodriguez's autobiographies—is his refusal to separate himself from the lives on the boundary and to take on the kind of distanced lucidity that Sartre finds characteristic of the genre. For Wright and Rodriguez, the cultural trajectory of personal development alienates them from their indigenous communities. In a very real sense, each confirms the adage that you can't go home again, that you can only look back. Wright and Rodriguez become professional writers, men of letters, and take on cosmopolitan identities that lead them to view their places of origin in terms of a cultural deficit, a lack of sustaining social and intellectual resources. Rose, however, despite his journeys into the wider world and his standing as a successful professional, never quite leaves his neighborhood or his youth behind. He remains open to the pressures of the milieu in which he grew up—the frustrated aspirations and ambitions of the people he knew along the way. As Rose discovers through his interactions with underprepared students and adult learners, the narrativity of his own life is articulated in terms of other lives. The veterans Rose teaches in a special program at UCLA figure as his "Voc-Ed comrades reincarnated" (1990, 137), and his work with Concepcion Baca (a student who drops out of UCLA, goes to work, and then returns to complete her degree and go on to graduate studies) causes him to register "how much of myself I saw in her" (204). Rather than calling attention to the distance between himself and America's educational underclass, as Wright and Rodriguez do, Rose repeatedly uses the story of his own personal success as a sign of the educability of all those others who have fallen through the systemic cracks in American schools.

The point is that Rose does indeed use a conventionalized and formulaic coming-of-age narrative, but he diverts it from the usual pattern of the self-made success story and the edifying tale of maturity to articulate another set of social, cultural, and educational interests that offer a democratic vision of education for all. In this sense, Rose rearticulates one of the most basic of American myths by severing the cultural meaning of personal success and professional achievement from its usual conservative functions. Rose's own professional expertise appears in *Lives on the Boundary* not as a reconciliation to work in class society or an exemplary lesson in maturity but as a practice that links his own labors to those of students and adult learners at the margins of the educational system and to the popular pressures from below that have struggled to extend educational opportunity. Like Mina Shaughnessey and Kenneth A. Bruffee in the days of open admissions at CUNY and David Bartholomae and Patricia Bizzell, Rose remakes himself as a teacher and researcher, joining his expertise in close reading to the social force of protest movements of the late 1960s and early 1970s that fought to open higher education to those who had been excluded and, in effect, created the historical conjuncture from which the figure of the basic writer arises in composition studies.

By the account I offer here, Rose's professional expertise is not just the result of individual initiative, the accumulation of credentials, and the creation of a career. Instead, professional expertise is articulated with and to political subjectivities and social movements. Expertise is certainly coded by the cultural narratives of maturity and distanced lucidity as a particular determination of consciousness and class position. If professional practices and discourses typically represent the dispossessed as a client population in need of the intervention of expert benefactors, the political valence and cultural meaning of professional work nonetheless cannot be guaranteed in advance as an accommodation to the dominant culture and its division of specialists and laypeople. Professional expertise, as I believe *Lives on the Boundary* demonstrates, can also articulate a sense of solidarity with the aspirations and purposes of the dispossessed. It all depends on practice.

## Rearticulating Literacy

But if the effects of professional work depend on practice, it is not the case that professional practices are themselves offered freely; nor can they be enacted simply by an act of will. While the conditions of professional work are not predetermined in a final and fixed sense, they are determinate—the result of how they are joined together with other practices in an ensemble of overdetermined social relations and cultural realities. This point is worth mentioning because one of the dangers of professionalism is its tendency to generalize the conditions of its own work into causal factors that determine success and failure in class society. On one hand, the relative autonomy of professional work—what professionals experience daily as a series of individual decisions and responsibilities—can lead them to cast success and failure as a matter of volition and individual effort. On the other hand, professionals, especially in education, often make the forms of literacy they have mastered into causal factors that explain the fate of individuals and social formations.

Rose comes close to this occupational hazard of professionalism for a moment when he claims that his work with veterans made him realize that "education has the power to equalize things" (1990, 137). One might justifiably worry that Rose has slipped into the peculiarly American view of education as a social panacea—the great American literacy myth that the ability to read and write determines the outcome of people's lives. At least according to revisionist currents in literacy studies, this might well appear to be exactly what Rose has done.

From Lévi Strauss in *Tristes Tropiques* (1977) to J. Elspeth Stuckey's provocatively titled *The Violence of Literacy* (1991), revisionist critics have held that literacy is not primarily a means of intellectual development and upward mobility. Instead, as Lévi Strauss says, the "only phenomenon with which writing has always been concomitant is the creation of cities and empires, that is the integration of large numbers of individuals into a political system, and their grading into castes or classes" (1977, 337). Stuckey is even more direct when she says that "literacy is a system of oppression that works against entire societies as well as against certain groups within given populations and against individual people" (1991, 64). From this perspective, to speak of the transformative powers of literacy for the individual, as Rose does, at best is naïve and at worst reproduces a discourse of equal opportunity and predictably unequal results, thereby turning systematic inequality into the result of differences in individual effort and talent, not of social determinations.

Stuckey is right to emphasize the connections between literacy and the way individuals are ranked in an unequal social order. At the same time, however, she seems to argue that there is a necessary correspondence between the cultural practices of literacy and social structures. According to Stuckey, people like Rose fail to see how the "violence of literacy is the violence of the milieu it comes from, promises, recapitulates. It is attached inextricably to the world of food, shelter, and human equality" (1991, 94). Literacy, for Stuckey, is determined by—or "attached inextricably" to—the reproduction of class relations in advanced capitalist society. Literacy has a locked-in, guaranteed-in-advance class character.

In contrast, Rose avoids the mechanical determinism in Stuckey's account by offering a sense of how literacy is articulated in variable and sometimes unpredictable ways to the social formation. In *Lives on the Boundary*, we do see the violence of literacy Stuckey describes. Rose's profile of the adult learner Millie and her struggle with a multiple-choice reading comprehension test demonstrates how schooled literacy disconnects underprepared students from their practical knowledge of the world and leads educators thereby to label them as cognitively deficient (216–20). Literacy does indeed function, as Rose shows, as an instrument to pathologize subjects. But, for Rose, literacy can also function in a variety of other ways that evade the surveillance of a class-based educational apparatus. "Consider the sources of literacy," Rose says, "among the children of El Monte: shopkeepers' signs, song lyrics, auto manuals, the conventions of the Western, family stories and tales, and more" (1990, 236). What Rose sees here is how literacy is not only a tool of a class-based ranking system but also a cultural resource embedded in and persistently available through the "pop cultural flotsam" that pervades the American landscape—"television and *People* magazine," "the Bible and . . . American media illusion" (237). For Rose, literacy is a matter not simply of the limits of an oppressive social order. It is also a quite concrete pressure and sensuous activity that surrounds all Americans and can be tapped for the purposes of human development and liberation. Whether that happens or not, I have tried to suggest throughout this essay, depends not on a fixed or necessary correspondence between literate practices and the social formation but rather on how individuals and groups articulate literate practices to institutions and subjectivities.

In this regard, Rose's sense of how "education has the power to equalize things" can be useful precisely to the extent it is detached from its usual political meaning of giving everyone an equal chance (when unequal class-based outcomes can be predicted in advance) and rearticulated as a political pressure to change the standards and practices that are used to evaluate and rank students in the first place. Investing education with "the power to equalize things" can avoid being simply another version of the literacy myth to the extent it articulates redefined standards and practices of literacy that are capable of promoting a more equal social order. Rose's account of the popular and everyday sources of literacy begins imagining such a redefinition and thereby contests not only the traditional view of what makes a person literate but also the current neoconservative monopoly of the public discourse on educational standards. What Rose suggests is that it is not enough just to change or expand our sense of literacy to include noncanonical and unauthorized forms of writing—and then continue to evaluate and rank students in the same old ways. Rose also wants to appropriate the "literacy crisis" from the Reagan/Bush camp, to rearticulate it as a matter not of whether standards are high enough but rather of how standards can be reconceived to serve popular aspirations and democratic goals.

*Lives on the Boundary* takes a lot of risks. To recount his life, Rose turns to the familiar coming-of-age narrative that has historically and culturally been encoded with the entrepreneurial values of individual initiative, professional maturity, and personal success. Rather than presenting a critical analysis to demystify the genre (as radical theorists typically do), Rose has sought to rearticulate the narrative from the inside—to disconnect its cultural meanings and political valence from its usual ideological function of reproducing capitalist social relations and instead to join together the narrativity of his own life to the ongoing struggle for democracy and social justice. In this regard, Rose's use of such a popular genre as autobiography not only allows him to speak to the public as well as to specialists; it also allows him, strategically, to locate *Lives on the Boundary* in the current cultural wars of position to secure popular consent and social allegiance. In *Lives on the Boundary,* Rose has chosen to speak in the idiom of what Gramsci calls the "national-popular," the constellation of common sense, ideological elements, and everyday practices that shape the subjectivities of civil society. What Rose thereby seems to suggest is that the task of radical democracy is not just to speak as critics against the master narratives of American culture but to speak as rhetors through them—to rearticulate the social and ideological force of the American mythos in the name, the voices, and the interests of the many.

## Chapter Two

# Agency and the Death of the Author

## A Partial Defense of Modernism

There is a story circulating in rhetoric and composition that some time in the late 1970s the author died—or maybe just dissolved into the semiosis of intertextuality. The story has its weak and strong versions. The strong version asserts that no author was there in the first place, only an ideology of authorship, an inscription of the cultural practices and social institutions that organize and regulate the production of writing. This author-effect is written, as it were, into the public record by the attribution of forms of writing to their composers, copyright law, the emergence of a literary marketplace, careers in writing, the rise of criticism, and so on. In contrast, the weak version asserts that indeed there was at one time an author or, stated more precisely, a historical project of locating the source of written works in the producer. This version upholds a labor theory of value based on the productive work of the author. It runs from, say, the Romantics (with their emphasis on originality and creativity) through the high modernists (with their emphasis on the composition of the difficult text). In either case, however, the idea is that the author—along with all the other characteristic figures of modernity (the Freudian ego, the transcendental subject, the possessive individual, the revolutionary proletariat)—has now passed away, having been made obsolete and irrelevant, fragmented and decentered by changing relations of writing and reading in the era of postmodernism.

In composition studies, the death of the author was greeted as a theoretical breakthrough, hitting the street with the force of an ideological rectification. The critique of authorship was energizing because it seemed to create a conceptual space in which new work could take place, a space where composition theory could replace the outmoded modernist notion of the author with an updated version of agency more adequate to the postmodern condition. In short, although the author was apparently dead, people nonetheless felt that there was still something left to talk about. A number of initiatives therefore were forthcoming:

- In the study and teaching of writing, theorists started to assign as much (or more) agency to readers and critics as to writers in the production of texts.
- People started to grow suspicious of notions of personal voice and expressivist rhetorics as hopelessly implicated in the author-effect.
- People started to say things like "the writer is written by as much as writes the text."
- Cognitivist notions of writing as purposeful action began to seem, at best, inadequate to the sheer surplus writing enacted through the writer and, at worst, a hopeless bid for control over the conditions of textuality controlling the writer.
- The act of writing itself was refigured: it was no longer viewed as the productive art of making meaning and expressing a self but instead as an unending play of signifiers, as an unstable negotiation by which writers position and reposition themselves in relation to other subjects, discourses, social institutions, and cultural practices.
- People gave up on a unitary representation of the composer as the person doing the work of writing and started to think of the writer instead as "always already"—not an originating author-source but a relay point in the circulation of discourses of race, class, gender, nationhood, sexual orientation, ethnicity, age, religion, region, and so on.

Now, the point of this sketch of the shifting fortunes of the author is not to distance myself from the initiatives I've listed—which, after all, I've participated in with many other people whose work I admire and to whom I am indebted. The point is that in composition studies, the death of the author (and the intellectual practices that followed) mobilized allegiances in a way similar to the earlier slogan "process not product." For example, the Elbow-Bartholomae debate about whether voice is authentic or constructed offers a familiar instance of how assumptions about authorship align teachers to student writers—to facilitate a disclosure of subjectivity (Elbow) or to locate the cultural logics of subjectivity (Bartholomae).

This debate—and all the others like it—is conventionally located in composition theory at an epochal divide, where postmodernists draw a line in the sand, putting on one side the old bad Cartesian self, the phallocentric author, the Enlightenment notion of a Universal Subject (all of the things that are retrograde about modernism) while putting on the other side the new good decentered nomadic textual self (as a figure of all that's vital and interesting about postmodernism). In other words, the story of the death of the author that I've recounted briefly (and, no doubt, simplistically) carried with it an edifying mission: namely, once we get rid of the mystifying figure of the author, then we can rehabilitate the notion of agency. We can fill in the space left vacant by the death of the author with a theory of agency that transcends the illusions of the past and clarifies our tasks in the present.

There is, however, an odd twist to the story. The exhilaration that accompanied the burial of the author turned almost immediately into a sense of anxiety, a feeling that postmodern theorists had reached a certain impasse. As Lester Faigley observes in *Fragments of Rationality,* there was a growing suspicion that despite its critique "of discourses that pretend to contain truth and serve to justify practices of domination," postmodern theory "does not supply a theory of agency" (1992, 20). This was a sobering moment, for the intellectual tools we had used to dismantle the figure of the author seemed to leave us unequipped to find an adequate replacement.

From my vantage point, the story of the death of the author has simply brought us back to the problem of agency as Marx posed it when he said that people make their history but not in conditions of their own making. What Marx is getting at here (at least the Marx I want to separate from the mechanical determinism of the Second International and the Stalinized state orthodoxies of the Third International) is that agency refers to the practical logic by which people negotiate their ways of life, the ways in which they cohere their activity and experience in the world. From this perspective, I argue that the story of the death of the author, for all its charms (and they are considerable), has been misleading; it is not so much wrong as misleading because it's been told in a way that turns agency into the missing link, the subject of forthcoming theories that will fill the conceptual void left when the author died. Theorizing agency, in other words, has turned into a progressive calling for compositionists, warranted by the felt need to rectify modernism's past errors.

For postmodernists, the exigence of updating the faded understandings of modernism seems self-evident, grounded in epochal shifts from Fordist to post-Fordist production, national to globalized societies, manufacturing to knowledge economies, the Cold War to the New

World Order. My purpose here, however, is to suspend for a moment the millennial sense of urgency that seems to drive postmodern theorizing. I want to ask whether we really need—or even can have—a new theory of agency to explain literate acts and literate practices. My skepticism in this matter is based on the suspicion that the death of the author is not so much the starting point of a new understanding of agency as it is a particular type of rumor that calls for investigation. In other words, as this essay's subtitle indicates, I want to make a partial defense of modernism and the author—partial in the sense of limited, unfinished, and partisan.

## The Problem of Theorizing Agency

One of the difficulties of theorizing agency has to do with the multiple and conflicting senses embedded in the term. *Agency* signifies, on one reading, a domain of freedom, autonomy, absence of constraint—an arena of choice and decision. At the same time, another reading suggests that the term means a functioning part of something larger, such as a government agency, an insurance agent, a secret agent, or a double agent. In the first instance, social structures and the workings of ideology appear as forces that qualify an individual's or a group's ability to act authentically by channeling their energies into preexisting grooves. From this perspective, the notion of an author (not to mention the project of keeping one alive) is necessary and useful because it describes a way to resist the forces of conformity that threaten agency. In the second instance, the possibilities of self or group formation—the grounds of agency—seem to be enabled by participation in organizational or institutional goals and practices. By this account, authorship is part of the means of communication and exchange of identities that make up the common social life.

These representations of agency are not difficult to find in composition theory. Agency as lack of constraint plays a key role in expressivist rhetorics and the process movement's figure of the composer, while agency as enabling participation in institutional work is axiomatic in social constructivist and social-epistemic rhetorics. My sense is that this is not a theoretical debate that can be readily resolved. In one sense, the debate is theological, concerning powerful beliefs about free will and predestination (that "always already" effect again). The Elbow-Bartholomae debate, for example, could be transposed to the Reformation and the question of whether acts of faith (Elbow's "believing game") or good works (Bartholomae's "ventriloquy" and "strong readings") will lead to salvation. In secular terms, the Elbow-Bartholomae debate has been absorbed into composition theory as a sign of epochal divide, with authentic selves on one side and textual selves on the other. In this sense, the debate reproduces deeply ingrained habits of mind that polarize the individual and society—then veers back and forth to understand the determinants of writing. Despite recent attempts at synthesis and blurred genres (for example, sociocognition and social-expressivist rhetorics), the taxonomies that guide composition studies simply codify this stalemate.

Agency, as I see it, is the way people live the history of the contemporary, the way they articulate (in the double sense of the term) their desires, needs, and projects, *giving voice* to their lived experience as they *join* their productive labors to the institutions and social structures they live within. As Michel de Certeau (1984) argues, agency is not so much a theory as a matter of strategy and tactics: agency is not about explaining but about maneuvering, not the theory but the *practice* of practice. From this perspective, the question of agency is not why people act as they do; instead, it is a question of what is to be done.

To want to have a theory of agency in the first place—to feel that one is missing—is a desire that grows out of the empty feeling left by the death of the author and the deconstruction of the transcendental subject. This desire for an adequate theory, I argue, seeks to get a grip on a sense of agency that is simply unavailable. In the story of the death of the author, representations of agency are not so much a matter of theory as of assent. We assent to representations of agency not because of their explanatory powers but because of their resonance with our lived experience. Thus, I think it's more useful to think of representations of agency not as theories but as persuasive structures of feeling.

The notion of "structure of feeling" comes, of course, from the work of Raymond Williams, who developed the term in a series of works, including *Preface to Film* (1954), *The Long Revolution* (1961), *Marxism and Literature* (1977), where he treats it in the greatest detail, and *Politics and Letters* (1979), where he develops some important qualifications and refinements. For Williams, structure of feeling refers to a form of practical consciousness that stands in uneasy relation to dominant systems of belief and education. Practical consciousness, as Williams says, is almost always different from official consciousness, not because it signifies a split between the individual and society but because it signifies how the effective presence of personal experience is itself social and resides in the common forms of what is currently being lived. The meanings and values that characterize a structure of feeling supply the motives that bump up against formally held, systematic beliefs. They can be sensed, Williams says, in the elements of "impulse, restraint, and tone" in a speaker's voice or in a writer's work, in the inflection that links a particular use of language to a particular ordering of social affiliation (1977, 132).

Interestingly, Williams links structures of feelings to generations rather than to class. As Williams says, "No generation speaks quite the same language as its predecessors" (1977, 131). Identifying the concept of structure of feeling with generations underscores, in Williams' view, the sense in which structures of feeling signify social consciousness in solution, before it is defined, classified, or codified and yet simultaneously exerts powerful pressures and sets effective limits on experience and action. A structure of feeling is a kind of social experience still in formation and accordingly is often taken to be private and idiosyncratic; yet, it is socially structured at the edge of semantic availability, in the process of precipitating figures of thought.

Following Williams, we may think of agency as a structure of feeling and in so doing insist that agency is not epiphenomenal in the older Marxian sense, but is instead the remainder of lived experience for which there is no necessary external counterpart that compels the shape or allegiances of our experience and action. Agency, then, is a kind of excess that is neither determinately given nor freely enacted but rather flows through people's struggle to make a life in the world. In this sense, the attempt to theorize agency cannot be a "question about causes" capable of explaining why people act as they do. The question rather, as Wittgenstein says, is "How am I able to obey a rule in the way I do?" and agency thereby amounts to a "justification for my following the rule in the way I do" (1953, 85e). In other words, the representations of agency that we make available to ourselves are not the result of determining how to formulate and apply a rule (or a theory) but of our feelings about the possibilities of consequential action and how we recognize and justify what we do.

## Death of the Author: 1968 and 1989

I want to use this sense of agency to revisit the death of the author. I find myself largely in agreement with Terry Eagleton's (1983) remarks on what I'd call the severe textualism of poststructuralist currents that emerged after the failure of the French student-worker alliance to overthrow Gaullism in 1968. From Eagleton's perspective, the death of the author and the primacy of the textual that runs through so much contemporary critical theory can be seen not so much as a moment of theoretical insight as the result of a mood of euphoria and disillusion—euphoria produced by the revolutionary energies and carnival of 1968 and disillusion produced by the betrayals of Stalinized Marxism and the decisive political defeat that reinstituted the Gaullist regime. What happened, as Eagleton describes it, amounts to a kind of compensatory fantasy. He writes, "Unable to break the structures of state power, post-structuralism found it possible instead to subvert the structures of language" and to relocate agency not in the streets but in critical work within the prison house of language (1983, 142).

The death of the author is a key episode in the self-fashioning of the postdiscourses, a decisive move away from the characteristic author figures of modernism—the artistic avant-garde and the revolutionary political vanguard—to a distinctly postmodern topos. Once the author is dead, Ezra Pound's (1935) classic modernist injunction "make it new" no longer makes much sense. Once the author is dead, no one is left to make it new. (And anyone who claims they can is an essentialist and therefore easily dismissed.) In a sense, the author has had to die in order for the postdiscourses to evacuate agency, to represent the world as already written to the saturation point—a world in which pastiche, recombination, recycling, cutting, and splicing are the means of production. The structure of feeling operating here is a deeply felt sense of contingency—of following afterward, belatedly—that marks these discourses as "post," strategically and rhetorically. They can't help but depend on what's just happened; they are reactions, after the fact, to modernism.

In the postdiscourses, the Bolsheviks seem just as depleted as the bohemians. The fall into anarcho-capitalism of the Stalinized worker states in the former Soviet Union and eastern Europe has pretty much put aside the historic commitments of the Marxist left, retired along with the author as a cautionary tale about what happens if you try to make it new. There is a complicated history to the sensibility of left-wing intellectuals who have continued to read and use Marx but have increasingly distanced themselves from Marxist politics since the social, cultural, and political upsurges of 1968. The kind of post-Cold War post-Marxism that thrives on the intellectual left today has been further tempered by the fall of the worker states in 1989, but it is not exactly anticommunist. Its post-ness does not have to do so much with refuting Marxism as expressing incredulity before Marxism's modernist metanarrative. The story of the proletariat and its political vanguard seems like old history now: at best a nostalgic account of the Great Depression and the Spanish Civil War when everyone was young and red, at worst an account of the crimes of Stalin (the purges, liquidations, removal of populations, forced labor camps, and psychiatric prisons).

It would be wrong to say that the postdiscourses have abandoned the great modernist projects to overcome scarcity and emancipate humanity. Rather, they have placed these projects on display, an archive of dated beliefs to fix and sustain the contemporary state of disbelief. Socialism, as Jean Baudrillard has said, is a "summer home" to which the critical spirit can now safely retire. You can hear the embarrassed irony that has become such a widely persuasive structure of feeling when post-Marxists refer to "what we used to call the class struggle." The turn of speech reveals a strategic positioning: it displaces the terms of agency from the political to the textual, where we're left with the shard of an old lexicon instead of a motive for action.

## Enlightenment and Revolution

The question of what you can no longer believe is a complicated one, complicated decisively by the way you represent your former beliefs and where you locate the point things went wrong. For postmodern compositionists, the critique of the author invariably points back to the Enlightenment and the emergence of a Universal Subject. James Berlin, for example, makes the connection between the "unified, coherent, autonomous, self-present subject of the Enlightenment" and authorship: "the subject is a transcendent consciousness . . . acting as a free and rational agent that adjudicates competing claims for action . . . the author of all his or her behavior" (1996, 62). In Berlin's rhetoric—and, of course, more widely in composition theory—much rides on the Enlightenment in the formation of the modern subject. You can see how high the stakes have become when Bruce McComiskey says that the problem with the "Enlightenment conception of the Subject" is that it "leads inevitably to physical and metaphysical violence" (1997, 352).

The idea that the Enlightenment is a source of actual and intellectual terror has become a persistent theme in the postdiscourses. As McComiskey points out, for Derrida the problem is an "identity/difference opposition" characteristic of the "Enlightenment Nation/Subject" that results in xenophobia, racism, anti-Semitism, and national fanaticism (1997, 352). Along similar lines, Lyotard argues against Habermas' defense of the Enlightenment as an "unfinished project." According to Lyotard, the "possible unanimity between rational minds" that Habermas still believes can lead to the enrichment of everyday social life does "violence to the heterogeneity of language games" through a terrorist program of silence or consent (1984, xxiii, xxv).

Linking the Enlightenment to terror accounts for a good deal of the appeal of postmodern theorizing about the subject. Who, after all, wants to defend terror, the suppression of difference, and the implicitly totalitarian claims of the Universal Subject? Given postmodern assumptions, it's hard not to think we need a replacement. What may not be so self-evident, however, is how this connection between the Enlightenment and terror amounts to a rewriting of history. In the wake of failed revolution in 1968, revisionist currents on the Left Bank turned not only on the Enlightenment but also on its progeny, the French Revolution. Breaking with Old Left traditions that hold up the French Revolution as the first stirrings in modernity of popular sovereignty and the people's justice, the "new philosophers" of the post-1968 period as well as renegade former leftists (such as historian François Furet) have, in effect, recapitulated the Thermidorean reaction that overthrew the Jacobins, arguing that collective action to realize the Enlightenment dream of human freedom and a commonwealth based on the general will must inevitably turn into a nightmare—not the Republic of Virtue but the Reign of Terror. The history of struggle that once formed the central revolutionary tradition of the French left—the red thread linking the fall of the Bastille to Toussaint L'Ouverture and the first successful slave uprising in the New World, to the street battles of 1848 and the Paris Commune of 1871, and to proletarian revolution in 1917—became a dystopic tale that leads to the gulag.

In my view, Foucault's argument that one doesn't have to be "for" or "against" the Enlightenment offers a useful starting point to reconsider the relationship between the Enlightenment and the French Revolution. Foucault calls for ending the "blackmail" that "you either accept the Enlightenment and remain within the tradition of its rationalism (this is considered a positive term by some and used by others, on the contrary, as a reproach); or else you criticize the Enlightenment and then try to escape from its principles of rationality (which may be seen once again as good or bad)." In Foucault's view, the task instead is to "proceed with the analysis of ourselves as beings who are historically determined, to a certain extent, by the Enlightenment" (1984, 43).

The "certain extent" of this determination—Foucault's qualifier—depends, I think, on the version of the Enlightenment you want to advance. The question, as Foucault contends, is our orientation toward the "contemporary limits of the necessary" and what we believe to be indispensable in the Enlightenment for the "constitution of ourselves as autonomous subjects" (1984, 43). The figure Foucault wants to emphasize is the Kant of "What Is Enlightenment?": the polemicist who makes "maturity" the task of the modern age. Enlightenment, Kant says, is "man's leaving his self-caused immaturity," growing up and throwing off the yoke of the dependent minor, freeing himself from dependence on his former guardians through the public use of reason (1949, 132).

Foucault's Kant cuts a different silhouette than the figure you find, say, in Richard Rorty's work, where Kant is the founding father of professional philosophy who heroically faces the loss of metaphysical reality only to reground it in epistemology. In Foucault's account, Kant is aligned not so much with this departmentalization of knowledge but with Baudelaire and the modernist urge to test the limits of the present: "a philosophical ethos," Foucault says, "that could be described as a permanent critique of our historical era." From this perspective, there is still something left to be done vis-à-vis the legacy of the Enlightenment, if only we would recognize the thread that connects us and modernity to the Enlightenment. What connects us to the Enlightenment is not "faithfulness to doctrinal elements, but rather the permanent reactivation of an attitude" and a persistent struggle to see the history that we are living as the passage to adult status (1984, 42).

You may have noticed by now that theorists of the modern/postmodern divide like to stage their fight over the Enlightenment on what the historian Robert Darnton refers to as the "summit view of eighteenth-century intellectual history" where people call out the names and recite the ideas of the Age of Reason (1982, 1). I want to extend Foucault's qualified appreciation of the Enlightenment but sidestep for a moment such a "great books" approach in the interest of identifying more worldly threads that might connect us to the Enlightenment. To be fair, Foucault warns that we must see the Enlightenment not only in terms of ideas but as "an event, or a set of events and complex historical processes, that is located at a certain point in the development of European societies" (1984, 43). Nonetheless, Foucault limits himself to a particular "form of philosophical reflection"—namely, the "mode of reflective relation to the present" (44). This is the ethos of the High Enlightenment, the standpoint of the *philosophes* that, Darnton notes, has been "passed on piously from textbook to textbook" (1982, 2).

Darnton, in contrast, proposes to bring the Enlightenment down to earth, with another view of its persistently perplexing connection to the French Revolution. What Darnton has in mind is the "low-life of literature" that flourished under the Old Regime. In the twenty-five years before the Revolution, a literary underground evaded French censors, police, and monopolistic booksellers' guilds to produce and distribute pirated and prohibited books of all sorts. An order from a bookseller in Poitiers to his supplier in Switzerland (a "short list of philosophical books that I want") offers an idea of the kinds of "philosophical" works actually circulating among the French reading public: *Venus in the Cloister or the Nun in a Nightgown, Christianity Unveiled, Memoirs of Mme la Marquise de Pompadour, Inquiry on the Origin of Oriental Despotism, The System of Nature, Theresa the Philosopher, Margot the Campfollower* (quoted in Darnton 1982, 1–2). It's hard to miss how unfamiliar the titles are, suggesting, as Darnton says, "a lot of trash somehow got mixed up in the eighteenth-century idea of philosophy" (2).

Hack writers of the Old Regime produced a constant stream of *libelles*—slanderous, pornographic, and sensationalistic attacks on every aspect of respectable society, from the court, the church, and the aristocracy to the academies, the salons, and the republic of letters. This "gutter Rousseauism" (*Rousseau du ruisseau*), as Darnton says, pilloried aristocratic decadence "with a scurrility that is difficult to imagine today" (1982, 35), greeting the final crisis of the Old Regime with "their greatest barrage of antisocial smut" (29). Although they lacked a coherent ideology and program for the future, the *libellistes*, according to Darnton, "communicated a revolutionary point of view: they showed that social rot was consuming French society, eating its way downward from the top. And their pornographic details got the point across to a public that could not assimilate the *Social Contract*" (35).

In the final years before the Revolution, what had initially seemed so seditious in Voltaire and the Encyclopedists were at least partially assimilated into the Old Regime and institutionalized as the High Enlightenment. In effect, the *philosophes* had professionalized themselves, developing what amounted to a career path and network of contacts, pensions, sinecures, and appointments that enabled them to secure livelihoods that did not depend on the market. Not so for the *libellistes*, who had to make their living through writing. Scorned by Voltaire as *la canaille de la littérature*, the *libellistes* formed a subintelligentsia that seethed with resentment and class hatred for the *grands* and *gens de lettres* who made up *le monde* of French society. As Darnton observes, this literary proletariat "was not merely unintegrated but beyond the pale and . . . wanted not to reform society in some polite, liberal, Voltairean way, but to overturn it" (1982, 36).

The establishment of the High Enlightenment no doubt contributed in important ways to the legitimation crisis of the Old Regime, undermining the elite's faith in tradition and social hierarchy with reason and natural law. Nonetheless, as Darnton argues, the ranks of the *libellistes* were much more likely to spawn revolutionary leadership. The pamphleteers, journalists, and bureaucrats of the Revolution such as Jean Paul Marat, Camille Desmoulins, Jacques-Pierre Brissot, Pierre Louis Manuel, and Jacques Hébert emerged from the literary gutter to turn the cultural and political life of France upside down. They disbanded the academies and salons, canceled the pensions, and in general abolished the privileges and vested interests of the literary mandarins. The result was a startling revolution in the theatre and journalism. After the *Comedie francaise*'s monopoly was revoked, forty-five new theatres opened, and fifteen hundred new plays were staged between 1789 and 1799. Even more striking was the increase in newspapers—from the few dozen that circulated in Paris in the 1780s to the founding of two hundred fifty newspapers in the last six months of 1789 alone. A year later, at least three hundred fifty newspapers circulated.

Habermas (1980) argues that the unfinished business of the Enlightenment is to release science, morality, and art from their esoteric forms and thereby to realign the culture of experts with that of the public. In a sense, this is exactly what the *libellistes* of the Old Regime did as they turned into revolutionaries, though I don't think they are quite the "experts" that Habermas had in mind. Rather, they are the kind of organic intellectuals who speak for the people, *enragées* joining what Darnton calls their "crude, Jacobinical version of Rousseauism" to the revolutionary energies of the *sans-culotterie* (1982, 39). From this perspective, the influence of the Enlightenment on the Revolution runs from the bottom up. We are no longer in the realm of ideas and the Universal Subject; we are in the streets with the partisans.

In my view, this account of popular Enlightenment and the revolutionary forms it assumed provides a much needed corrective to recent theorizing about the politics of modernism. My sense is that what remains valuable about modernist politics is precisely what takes place in the French Revolution—namely, the emergence of the masses as subjects of their own history. Clearly, the revolutionary upsurges of the nineteenth and twentieth centuries have an affinity to Kant's call for "maturity"—to overthrow custodial care and take things into your own hands. At the same time, to the extent we identify with the struggles of the masses, we can loosen the terms *Enlightenment* and *Revolution* from their ritualized use as straw figures in an antimodernist polemic and invest them with pertinence again as we engage in what Foucault calls the "undefined work of freedom," which is the modernist legacy (1984, 46).

In this account of Enlightenment and revolution, moreover, we can see that the fear of the Universal Subject—the grounds of postmodernism's ultimate blackmail—has not only been wildly exaggerated but has also been put, whether or not inadvertently, to questionable political ends. For postmodern theorists, the desire to replace the Universal Subject (due to its potential connections to terror and totalitarianism) with a decentered, fragmented, and nomadic subject amounts to a politics of difference and unassimilated otherness. Now, on the one hand, I see nothing objectionable or especially controversial about this representation of the subject, as long as it is offered as a description of social experience in the era of late capitalism. On the other hand, when this representation becomes normative—when it is offered as a necessary defense against the modernist subject—then I think we enter treacherous political terrain, for such notions of the postmodern subject depend on a structure of feeling that wants to shift the work from the old modernist project of negotiating differences out in the streets to the project of preserving difference as an always uncertain theoretical foundation.

## A Defense of the Author as Producer

The problem as I see it is the extent to which the supposedly new and improved postmodern subject contributes to the psychic Thermidor of the post-1968 and post-1989 period. More specifically, the problem consists in the way this representation of the subject challenges, as unfashionably modernist, the felt sense of presence and agency that individuals and groups experience at those moments of historical crisis when they know what they are doing and join together, with their differences, at the center of their own history, without debilitating irony or doubt. My sense is that you don't need either a Universal Subject or an updated theoretical replacement in order to preserve the possibility of what Susan Jarratt (1991), among others, calls "kairotic discourse"—a discourse through which people cohere their activity in the world and in ways that make them accountable to the moment. Revolutionary sentiment in the modern age, after all, has always been partial, situated, and kairotic, a matter of "us" against "them," where the oppressed and exploited break from their generalized identification with the ruling classes and society in order to act on their own behalf.

Unless we acknowledge this structure of feeling as a living possibility, we risk condemning working people worldwide to an eternal present of globalization, capitalist triumphalism, and the end of history. In my view, what is needed is not a new theory of agency but the old modernist sense of solidarity: the workers against the bosses, the people against the ruling bloc, the oppressed against their oppressors. And just as I want to keep this part of modernism alive, I now want to go back and check the vital signs of the author.

Despite rumors of death, I think there are good reasons to keep at least a version of the author alive and kicking. As it's been told in composition studies, the story of the death of the author has served, paradoxically, as an overcorrection while at the same time not going far enough. The overcorrection consists in identifying the nineteenth-century image of the writer-in-the-garret as the telling figure of the author and in seeking to replace this romantic isolato with a social and collaborative view of writing. This move is due, no doubt, in part to composition's troubled relations with literary studies and a desire to free the study and teaching of writing from high-culture ideologies of authorship and literary value. The problem, however, is that this move gives away too much and offers too little in return. First, an overcorrection mistakes the notoriously bad case of the belletristic author for the category itself, and then proposes that we need to get rid of the author altogether. The proposed gain—to be able to say the writer is "socially constructed"—appears to say more than it actually does by way of explanation and, then, in effect, creates its own difficulties.

Let me put it this way. Compositionists (including myself) habitually claim that writing is a social and collaborative activity. Fair enough. There is no question in my mind that to understand the production, circulation, and use of written texts you need to elaborate complex discursive networks. The difficulty, however, is that dissolving the figure of the author into the relations of writing—the literary circles, publishers, editors, agents, bookstores, critics, and readers—risks at the same time dissolving the class relations that link the author as a producer to precisely those social networks that you want to understand. The notion of writing as collaboration, that is, can lead to idealized representations of the necessarily social work of writing that "forget" the contradictions between labor and capital. There is often a troubling utopian aura around the term *collaboration*, as though it marks a post-capitalist era in which we've transcended market relations and the labor theory of value. But precisely for this reason, we need a notion of the author all the more—as a vital point to organize around, in writers' guilds, unions, congresses, cooperatives, and other associations for self-management. In late capitalist societies, the author still figures as a key site of self-defense within market relations, a self-formed position of struggle to control the conditions and products of work.

The point, as I see it, is not just to rid ourselves of individualistic ideologies of the author and to take up a "social view" of writing. The task, as Walter Benjamin poses it, is to socialize the author as producer. He explains, "What matters is the exemplary character of production, which is able first to induce other producers to produce, and second to put an improved apparatus at their disposal" (1986, 233). Enlightenment and revolution come together in Benjamin's resolutely modernist account of technique—that is, the way writers such as Brecht position their work within the relations of production. In Benjamin's view, Brecht's epic theatre grows out of a struggle over the means of production to turn the capitalist theatrical apparatus—what Brecht calls the "means against the producers"—into its opposite, so that consumers can become producers and spectators can become collaborators (quoted in Benjamin 1986, 233–34). The goal is a "dramatic laboratory" that replaces representation with discovery. In this laboratory, the work is not to reproduce situations (with their climaxes and resolutions) but to dissect the "strictly habitual course" of events. The theatre thereby becomes a socialized (and quasi-scientific) space of tests, experiments, examinations, and truths—a collaboration by which the spectators recognize the conditions in which they live, not with the satisfaction of naturalistic dramaturgy but with revolutionary astonishment.

I admit that I have chosen from Benjamin the most blatantly modernist passages I could find concerning the author, passages in which his language is filled with such seemingly retro terms as *technique*, *apparatus, production, historical tasks,* and *social engineering*. The reason is that this structure of feeling is what I want to preserve as a vital and usable legacy of modernism. The corrosive effects of postmodernism show up most distressingly, I think, in the way theorizing has shaken the old modernist faith in our capacity to socialize the conditions and products of our own labor. Postmodern attacks on planning and productivist ideologies are by now familiar—and, certainly, they have their point. My feeling, though, is that Benjamin's notion of the author as producer remains important precisely because it enables the belief that we can design social futures out of the uneven development and moral ruin of late capitalism, even if we cannot guarantee results with the certainties of an earlier time.

In my view, the persistence of capitalism—not its transformation into a new postmodern epoch but its sheer longevity—presses heavily on us. There is, after all, the long-standing revisionist tendency to explain the defeats of the popular forces and the lulls in class struggle as a matter of objective conditions. At this point in the history of late capitalism, the effort to keep alive the author as a producer figures as part of a larger antirevisionist struggle against an overwhelming sense of contingency and objectivism—of feeling "cast" into the world, in both an existential and a dramatistic sense, without recourse to collective self-defining action. It's not that we can escape the world as the ground of our history. The point is that we don't have to make peace with it.

# PART TWO

# Professionalization of U.S. College Composition

The essays in this section examine three moments in the professionalization of composition—from the late 1940s to the early 1960s, when the field of composition was just beginning to articulate its professional identity and sense of purpose, with the founding of the Conference on College Composition and Communication and its journal *CCC;* the mid-1990s, when the effects of professionalization were starting to register in heady and problematic ways; and the present, when proposals have surfaced to consolidate and amplify professionalization by transforming composition into the discipline of writing studies, with departmental status, a four-year curriculum, and majors and minors. Together, the three essays constitute a sequence of vignettes, not a comprehensive history. Their fragmentary nature gives the essays the character of periodic checkups on the vital signs of U.S. college composition, the style of professional life it has fashioned, and the identities, desires, and interests it makes available.

My abiding concern with the problem of the professionalization of composition is not to decide whether it is a good thing or not, though I am very interested in how others inside and outside the field have made such judgments. But I don't want to be just a bystander, witnessing an irreversible tide of professionalization that makes the current configuration of composition appear to be the inevitable outcome: for it is possible, certainly, to imagine alternative paths composition might have taken over the past fifty years. I don't want to suggest either that professionalization has actually been accomplished, except in partial and uneven ways, once you take into account the exploitative use and poor working conditions of contingent faculty hired to teach the vast majority of writing courses in the United States, and the shutdown or outsourcing at four-year colleges of the basic writing programs that had once been such a vital site of composition's intellectual and political energies. Instead, I want to recognize the constraints and pressures composition has faced and why the logic of professionalization has such an allure as a means of self-organization (and self-defense). And I want to understand how a profession such as composition produces the producers of its services and how the contradictions of professionalism play out in the lived experience of studying and teaching of writing.

Chapter Three, "The 'Communication Battle,' or Whatever Happened to the 4th C?"—which I wrote with Diana George—looks at the early days of the Conference on College Composition and Communication in the late 1940s and early 1950s, the tensions over the nature of the first-year course between teachers of what was then called "Freshman English" and the "communication movement," and how things were resolved in the early 1960s with the withering away of communication courses and the consolidation (or reaffirmation) of written discourse as the focus of the first-year course.

From one angle, the essay challenges the conventional notion that composition formed as a discipline in the 1960s, virtually out of the blue, by doing two things: rejecting current-traditional rhetoric and constituting "composing" as an object of inquiry, in a groundswell to make "invention" and "process not product" the guiding ideas of writing instruction. "The 'Communication Battle'" suggests there is a prehistory to the process movement, in the lines drawn between composition and communication in the main professional association CCCC and in the editorial policy of the main professional journal *CCC*. In this sense, it was not just the "discovery" of composing or the revival of rhetoric that was involved in early discipline formation but also the exclusion of particular theoretical and pedagogical possibilities contained in the communication movement—mass media studies, propaganda analysis, general semantics, linguistics, public speaking, and forms of writing for "social utility."

From another angle, however, "The 'Communication Battle'" argues that the desire to eliminate the 4th C from composition has only resulted in its reincorporation as composition's necessary other, the semiotic practices composition has used to clarify its own purposes. This is evident in Adams Sherman Hill's (1888) tirade against newspapers and pulp fiction in the late nineteenth century, when Harvard instituted the first-year writing requirement, and is apparent residually in Douglas Hesse's recent response to Cindy Selfe's call for multimodal composing, when he wonders if "the curricular space our field inhabits" will leave enough room for "writing extended connective prose"

(2010, 603, 605). What the 4th C continues to signify—in its various identities as popular culture, mass communication, new media, or multiliteracies—is the sheer surplus of signifying practices and resources of representation in the modern age and the difficulties they pose to setting sure disciplinary boundaries around the study and teaching of writing.

Chapter Four, "Writing Instruction and the Politics of Professionalization" picks up where "The 'Communication Battle'" leaves off by examining the mechanisms and results of professionalization, its uneven development and contradictions. It elaborates what is only suggested in "'The Communication Battle'"—namely, that more than a paradigm shift (what Maxine Hairston [1992] called "winds of change") was involved in establishing composition as an academic field. The essay holds that academic disciplines take shape as social formations as well as intellectual undertakings. And, in this regard, the professionalization of writing instruction, as is true of the professions more generally, has relied on an institutional infrastructure, social networks, and mentoring relations to discipline the field and to form the subjectivities of its practitioners by elaborating career paths and criteria about work that counts.

The essay is a frankly cautionary one, meant to counter the easy celebration in the late 1980s and early 1990s of composition's enhanced academic status and legitimacy. Its aim, however, is not to quarrel with what composition had accomplished by 1996, when the essay was published, but to come to terms with the stresses and strains of the field's internal stratification and to consider how composition might deal with the contradictory pressures of professional life and the possibility of redistributing rather than simply consolidating professional expertise.

Since "Writing Instruction and the Politics of Professionalization" appeared, the rhythms of professionalism have accelerated. In the 1990s, many English departments created tenure-track positions for a writing program administrator, a writing across the curriculum coordinator, and a writing center director. More recently, at least until the economic downturn of 2008, recent PhDs in rhetoric and composition with ambitious scholarly agendas could apply for positions where they would be specialists in their field, teaching graduate seminars, advanced undergraduate courses, and perhaps an occasional first-year composition course, with no administrative responsibilities—just faculty, working on their research agendas, like the postcolonial critic or Shakespeare scholar down the hall. In other cases, composition programs managed to bail out of English departments altogether, creating writing and rhetoric departments with a four-year curriculum, majors, and minors.

The final chapter in this section, "Changing the Question: Should Writing Be Studied?" is an attempt to make sense of these recent developments. Originally published in 2003, I have revised it to take into account current proposals to turn composition into writing studies and the first-year course into an introduction to the field, much as chemistry or sociology or art history offers introductory courses. My interest is twofold: first, to examine what it means to invite students not just to produce writing but to study it, to make writing a topic of intellectual inquiry; and second, to identify the impact of these new proposals for writing studies on the sensibilities and professional identities involved in the study and teaching of writing.

## Chapter Three

# The "Communication Battle," or Whatever Happened to the 4th C?

In the December 1962 issue of *CCC,* outgoing CCCC Chair Francis E. Bowman looked back at what the organization had accomplished since its first meeting in 1949, noting that "some of the work CCCC originally set out to do has been completed." One of CCCC's initial objectives, Bowman says, was "to allow the 'communication' approach to prove itself." Apparently, proof had not been forthcoming, for Bowman states rather confidently, with a barely disguised sense of relief, that the "'communication' battle is over" (55). No doubt Bowman was correct, though one might describe the moment he marks in 1962 as the end of a failed alliance as much as the end of a war. After all, the "broad object" of CCCC, as stated in its original Constitution and By-Laws (approved in 1952), was "to *unite* teachers of college composition and communication" ("Constitution and Bylaws" 1952, 19, our italics). In retrospect, the connection between composition and communication, still codified in the title of the leading journal and professional association, looks like a vestige of the late 1940s and 1950s—a brief affair, characterized by mutual attractions and misgivings, that proved unable to imagine a future for itself.

In 1949, the year National Council of Teachers of English (NCTE) established CCCC as a conference group for three years, it might well have been unthinkable that the "communication approach" would ultimately prove unable to demonstrate its viability. In part a practical measure to deal with the massive influx of returning World War II veterans, in part the result of interest in general semantics and mass communication theory, the so-called "communication movement" had spawned courses at over two hundred colleges and universities, almost all integrating instruction in speaking and writing for incoming students and many teaching analysis of propaganda, advertising, and the mass media. As evident at the conference on college communication courses in 1947, cosponsored by the Speech Association of America (SAA) and NCTE and in many respects an anticipation of CCCC's formation two years later, there was a widespread belief in the postwar years that teachers of first-year courses, whether freshman English or the newer communication course, had a good deal in common. And it was precisely this shared interest that produced the fragile alliance between composition and communication in the early days of CCCC, from 1949 to the early 1960s, the watershed date marked symbolically by Bowman's declaration that the war was over.

Early volumes of *CCC*, which devoted an issue each year to the annual meeting of CCCC, provide a glimpse of the nature of this alliance between composition and communication. The reports show that panels and workshops were fairly evenly divided between composition and communication or later merged the two in sessions such as "New Techniques in Teaching Composition/Communication Courses" (1959) or "The Composition/Communication Course in General Education Programs" (1959). Moreover, the journal featured articles such as Sanford Radner's "The Communication Concepts of Harold Innis" (1959) and Howard H. Dean's "The Communication Course: A Ten-Year Perspective" (1959), side by side with articles devoted to teaching composition.

Unifying CCCC teachers, however, posed certain institutional problems. In March 1950, for example, CCCC Secretary George Wykoff reported on a "discussion of the problem of closer unity, cooperation, and coordination between the National Council of Teachers of English and the Speech Association of America, especially in view of the fact that the CCCC (dealing with written composition and communication) is a subsidiary of the NCTE and a similar organization [National Society for the Study of Communication or NSSC] (dealing with oral composition and communication) is a subsidiary of the SAA" (21). The very next year, members of the Executive Committee recommended an alliance between CCCC and NSSC. Consequently, representatives from the two organizations did meet at the 1951 conference.

At first glance, NSSC would seem to have much in common with CCCC. Like CCCC, it was formed in 1949 as an affiliate of a larger organization, SAA. NSSC's stated purpose paralleled that of CCCC with a clear focus on teaching, developing college courses, and engaging in research in communication (Wykoff, 1951, 13). When the two groups met, however, they were sharply divided as CCCC aligned itself with teaching against NSSC's commitment to research. To the suggestion that members of CCCC also become members of NSSC, NCTE Secretary-Treasurer Wilbur Hatfield offered the "terse comment, 'There are already too many organizations'" (14). From the report, it appears that the meeting served only to widen the gap between composition and communication: "The conclusion reached by the panel was there was too much difference between the two organizations to make a merger practical and desirable" (15).

Part of the problem, as can be seen from the report on the 1951 meeting, was that forming an alliance between CCCC and NSSC required not only finding common ground but also undoing a longer history of institutional separation that reached back to 1913 when a small group of public speaking faculty left NCTE to form their own academic departments and professional association. Much of what was left of the nineteenth-century oratorical tradition found a new home in speech communication, institutionally separated from writing instruction. Furthermore, unlike their former colleagues in composition, the founders of speech communication realized that if their departments were to attain academic legitimacy and survive, they needed to articulate a research agenda. The resulting scholarship in mass communication, media studies, rhetorical criticism, and so on in effect consolidated the academic standing of speech communication. But it also produced a professional sensibility that apparently clashed with CCCC's primary investment in teaching and the first-year course.

Further attempts to make clear the connections between CCCC and NSSC did periodically appear in secretaries' reports at least until 1959, but the only real evidence of cooperation was the 1953 appointment of Donald Bird as liaison between the two organizations. In the December 1953 issue, *CCC* instituted an unsigned feature "NSSC News" to parallel a similar column entitled "CCCC News" which was to appear in the *Journal of Communication*. And, though these reports continued to appear at least until 1958, they represented the only tangible connection ever made between the two organizations. Finally, in May 1959, Falk Johnson reports that when Richard Beal of the Committee on Liaison with Other Professional Organizations asked for a clarification of the committee's duties, that committee was abolished with the direction that "future questions of liaison be dealt with by the three chairmen of CCCC" (129).

The history of that failed liaison is the history of the struggles between the "communication movement" and the budding discipline "composition studies." By 1962 the influence of communication studies and courses had diminished significantly at CCCC annual meetings. As Nancy K. Bird notes in her helpful study of CCCC, the 1959 CCCC's "program no longer included separate sessions for 'communication' teachers, and the 1961 program was the last to use the dual term 'composition/communication' in the titles for its sessions" (1977, 101). Increasingly, conference topics emphasized composing processes and the resurgence of interest in rhetoric, as indicated by the 1961 session on "Rhetoric—The Neglected Art?" In 1963, the entire program was devoted to topics concerned with composing and the development of a "new rhetoric," with speakers such as Wayne Booth on the rhetorical stance, Francis Christiansen on generative rhetoric, Edward P. J. Corbett on classical rhetoric, and Josephine Miles on composing.

Much the same was evident in the pages of *CCC*. From the time Ken Macrorie took over as *CCC* editor in 1962, articles on the "communication approach," on mass media, propaganda analysis, and general semantics virtually disappeared from the journal. When William Irmscher replaced Macrorie as *CCC* editor in 1965 and published the first statement of editorial policy to appear in the journal, there was no more than a passing reference to articles "pertaining to the theory, practice, and teaching of composition or communication." By 1967, CCCC Chair Gordon Wilson could write a history of the organization from its founding, making no mention of the communication movement at all. In 1974, when Edward P. J. Corbett became editor, the word *communication* was dropped altogether from his editorial policy statement. Indeed, as Bowman (1962) says, by 1962 the "communication battle" did appear to be over, with the term *communication* dropping out of professional and scholarly use.

How to account for this rapid demise of communication? What did happen to the 4th C, not to mention those 200-plus communication courses? Albert R. Kitzhaber notes in "4C, Freshman English, and the Future" that the "only major respect in which the freshman English scene" in 1963 "differs from that of fifteen years ago is that communication courses, which then were flourishing, now are nearly extinct" (136). According to James A. Berlin, such an extinction, like that of the dinosaurs, "was inevitable." Sometimes housed in a general education program or General College, such as those at Minnesota and Michigan State, other times an informal arrangement of faculty from English, speech, and education, as at the University of Southern California, their "fatal shortcoming," Berlin says, "was the threat they posed to departmental autonomy and academic specialization" (1987, 104). David Russell, in his history of writing in the disciplines, makes a related point: unable either practically or theoretically to connect themselves to writing in the disciplines, communication programs, Russell says, "offered no reason for departments to take an active role in their work" (1991, 261). Without a "recognized disciplinary status or research role, they all sooner or later became marginalized, with few tenure-track faculty and heavy reliance on temporary instructors and graduate assistants" (1991, 260).

Berlin and Russell offer compelling explanations for the disappearance of the communication course from the academic landscape. What they don't explain, however, is what took place within CCCC. The question that interests us concerns the engagement between composition and communication in the formation of CCCC and why eventually the very notion of communication for all practical purposes disappeared. What was the "communication battle" Bowman refers to? Who and what won? What was at stake in the brief flirtation between composition and communication?

It is not enough to say simply that communication courses disappeared and freshman English courses remained. There is, after all, no a priori reason freshman English programs could not have integrated ideas and practices from the communication movement. But the fact of the matter is that the leading forces in CCCC actively rejected the "communication approach" as inimical to what they believed to be the work of CCCC and of the first-year course. The "communication battle," we argue, signals a crucial moment in the formation of a professional identity and a sense of disciplined work for composition teachers and researchers. As we will see, the "communication battle" is in part an argument over what the first-year course should be. At the same time, it also plays out a deep-seated ambivalence on the part of writing teachers toward the means of mass communication that predates the establishment of CCCC and continues after the "communication battle" was over.

## The Communication Battle: Terms of Engagement

The term *the communication movement* makes the communication courses of the late forties and fifties sound more uniform than they actually were. As Howard H. Dean points out in a retrospective review of the communication course published in 1959, the "divergence is perhaps as great among communication courses as it is between communication and composition" (80). Some courses emphasized "life adjustment" skills, personal awareness, and personality development. Others centered around the study of the mass media or the structure of language or general semantics. Many combined elements. Even with this range of topics, Dean says, there is nonetheless a "certain identity" that distinguishes communication from composition courses, an identity that "stems from the inclusion of the four skills in a single course" (81).

Part of the "communication battle," then, was waged over what the first-year course should be, and the inclusion of the four skills—reading, writing, speaking, and listening—offered one of the central justifications for the worth of the communication course compared to the composition course. Gordon W. Couchman's 1952 report on the workshop he chaired on the "Organization and Administration of the Communications Course" presents a representative version of the communication advocates' case. He writes that the communication course, because it addresses so much more than the composition course, was a better preparation for college and for future high school teachers than was composition alone (9–11). Along similar lines, in May 1953, B. E. Fisher argued that "the communication approach is the best to motivate underprepared students" (44).

For Dean and others in the communication movement, the inclusion of the four skills—reading, writing, speaking, and listening—was not simply a quantitative gain over the two-skill composition course. Rather, Dean says, the "fusion of the four skills has led to a central unified objective; and this definitive aim is to see and comprehend the communicative process as a dynamic whole, to create an awareness of the interacting forces that condition it at each turn" (1959, 81). By contrast, George Stout's 1954 workshop on "The Function of Freshman Composition in General Education" provides a typical response to this emphasis on the "communication process as a dynamic whole" and a defense of the composition course: "the consensus of the group was that, in view of the present writing efficiency shown by entering freshmen, English teachers have a need to stress written composition. Beyond this skill function of their course, they need to awaken students to a consciousness of all that is going on around them" (96). Writing skills, in other words, come first, and consciousness-raising (whether of "communication processes" or the more vaguely invoked "all that is going on") comes second. The rationale for the composition course rests, as it has so many times before and since, on students' woeful preparation in writing and the implied warrant of a generalized literacy crisis.

In addition to charging the four-skills approach with neglect of writing in the first-year course, critics of the communication course also argued, as reports from CCCC workshops and *CCC* articles in the 1950s indicate, that the communication course could not adequately cover all of its topics in the time allotted. In 1954, for example, writing of "The Freshman Program at Western Michigan," communication instructor Robert Limpus acknowledged that many in the university considered the communication course, which then competed with a composition course, to be an "interloper: at least, an over-ambitious effort on the part of some restless idealists, at worst an attempt to 'water down' the content of two good courses in order to conform to an educational fad" (6).

In his review of the communication course, Dean (1959) addresses directly the "problem of thoroughness" and the accusation that the course amounts to "spreading ourselves too thin." In doing so, however, Dean "can't resist a little dig" at the "critics who accuse us of thinness for our bit of logic and psychology as applied to communication, and our look at the mass media." According to Dean, these critics ironically "are often the same folk who don't bat an eye at the prospect of introducing students to a chronological survey of poetry, short stories, the drama, the novel, and all forms of essays, along with the other business of the composition course." Dean concludes that "the guilt of thinness, if it is a guilt, is spread rather evenly over the four-C field" (82).

In the early days of CCCC, the "communication battle" often amounted to endorsing one type of course and taking backhanded jibes at the other. Such jockeying for position, however, should not obscure deeper, underlying differences. These come out occasionally, as in the case of Theodore Strandness' narrative in the February 1956 issue of *CCC*, in which he describes the fierce resistance and resentment he felt from older colleagues when he returned from naval duty during World War II to become an assistant professor in the communication program at Michigan State:

> At last year's meeting of the CCCC, I was startled to hear a speaker declare that communication teachers are "adapters" engaged, as he said, in teaching students to "adjust," to regard "mid-western, middle-class culture" as "the culmination of human achievement." Teachers of communication, he said, are "anti-intellectuals," as opposed to men like himself who "belong to the generation of composition rather than the generation of communication." (8)

In part to counter that impression (but no doubt confirming it for some), Strandness goes on to describe recent developments in communication courses:

> Current interest in general semantics, an increased awareness of the role of mass media in our present-day culture, an impatience with the prescriptive approach of the older handbooks, a recognition of group dynamics as concerns man's use of language, sensitivity to propaganda techniques—these are just some of the things that have brought marked changes in many of the courses which have been developed. (10)

The terms of engagement in the "communication battle" are unusually clear here. For the "generation of composition" (with its roots presumably in the liberal culture of embattled humanists and its affiliations to English departments and belles lettres), the "generation of communication" must have seemed to be the heralds of social utility and "life adjustment" skills without the redeeming connection to language and literature sponsored by English studies. By the same token, for the "generation of communication," the old-line compositionists must have seemed stuffy purveyors of what Dean calls "schoolbook English"—"a special variety of language found only in the English classroom and used only by English teachers" (84). If anything, the principle of social utility led communication advocates, as Dean notes, to exclude imaginative literature from the first year course in favor of "more immediately social forms of communication" (84).

There is little question that the communication movement's emphasis on social utility could lead, as Dean says, to "ridiculous" extremes—"teaching students to read the college catalog with understanding, to give directives on how to get from one street to another, to write proper thank-you notes to a week-end hostess" (85). But the notion of social utility also pointed to differences in attitude and orientation toward language and social experience that divided the "generation of communication" not only from English department traditionalists but also from progressive forces in the composition camp.

We get a keen understanding of this clash of sensibilities in two remarkable pieces of writing Ken Macrorie published while the "communication battle" was ongoing—the 1952 *College English* article "World's Best Directions Writer" and the 1960 *CCC* article "Writing's Dying." Both are dialogues between the fictional characters, Ed Zybrowski (the "Best Directions Writer in the World") and George, a beleaguered college teacher of writing. Taken together, the articles form a kind of parable about professional identities, writing assignments, and writing pedagogies. In the first, "World's Best Directions Writer," Macrorie seems determined mainly to satirize the trade writing of Edward Zybrowski and his struggles to reduce the directions on a label from forty-five to twenty-five words; his explanations of how he dispenses with punctuation ("I take care of that by ending one line and starting another" [1952, 278]) and adjectives (in "warmed teapot," "warmed" isn't an adjective, it's "the kind of teapot you've got to use" [277]); his statements of the obvious ("Never say anything like, 'The turn of the cap is accomplished by a twist.' . . . I would say, 'Twist cap to left'" [277]); and his claim to "know more about English usage than 90 percent of the college teachers" (276). Macrorie's thinly disguised parody of functional writing assignments and the social utility emphasis in communication courses ("Givin' directions is really helpin' people, educatin' them" [277]) is meant presumably to leave readers with George the narrator's closing reaction, "shaking our head in wonder" at the direction writer's genial fatuousness and his impoverished sense of writing.

In "Writing's Dying," on the other hand, Macrorie is much more direct and programmatic. The dialogue begins with Ed explaining the real issue is not, as George believes, that students aren't learning to write well but rather that writing itself is dying: "Electronics are taking over. Pictures. Sound. Words in the air" (1960, 206). Macrorie casts Ed Zybrowski, still identified as the "World's Best Directions Writer," as the harbinger of a McLuhan-esque revolution in which writing is not only "outnumbered" by sounds and pictures but "outvolumed by the electronic stream" (207). In turn, George takes on a more active role than he had in the earlier dialogue, arguing for the lasting power of print and defending literacy against the threat of mass communication: "My God! The first line of the war for the mind may be the freshman writing course" (208).

"Writing's Dying," which appeared in *CCC* one issue prior to Macrorie's editorial debut, poses the terms of engagement more sharply than they had been posed in 1952, signaling the decline of the communication course, the growing hegemony of composition, and the emergence of composition studies as a discipline determined to establish its own clear boundaries. When Macrorie has George articulate the dual doctrine of writing as epistemic ("writing not only reflects but generates thought") and as expressive ("You know who you are . . . in a special way from reading your thoughts on paper" [207]), we know we are now on the verge of the process movement and the uncontested identity of CCCC as an organization devoted to composition. From a certain perspective, "Writing's Dying" amounts to one of the closing salvos in the "communication battle"—the coup de grace before Macrorie took over as editor of *CCC* and consolidated the victory of composition over communication.

## Composition Victorious

The division between composition and communication and their clashing sensibilities occurred during CCCC's earliest days in a situation that recalls those unstable historical conjunctures of "dual power," when the authority to govern is temporarily up for grabs and contending forces vie for the allegiance of the masses and control of the state apparatus. In the early 1950s, it might have been hard at any particular moment to say whether composition or communication held greater influence. CCCC was small, with 297 members in 1950 and 339 in 1953. The annual meetings likewise were small and highly participatory.

The workshop was the dominant mode rather than the panel of refereed papers, and CCCC in many respects functioned as an ongoing discussion group as much as a professional association, a forum in which members deliberated and debated the identity and direction of the organization. Things were still fluid, and power was, so to speak, still out in the streets.

By 1957, however, membership had increased to 1,352 and two years later had nearly doubled to 2,604. Given the decline in the number of communication courses, new members tended naturally to come from composition. To many members, the original aim of the organization to unite composition and communication teachers appeared either to be obsolete or lost entirely. For these reasons, in 1959, CCCC Chair Kitzhaber established a Committee on Future Directions, chaired by John C. Gerber, to make recommendations that would resolve the split identity of the organization and consolidate power.

In the February 1960 issue, at the request of the Executive Committee, *CCC* published the "Report of the Committee on Future Directions" (Bailey et al., 1960). Among its recommendations, three are especially noteworthy for our purposes. First, the report presented the Committee's belief that CCCC could be "more effective if its efforts are *focused upon a discipline* rather than upon a course or a particular group of teachers" (3, our italics). Second, the Committee recommended a new statement of purpose for the CCCC Constitution: namely, "to improve college students' understanding and use of the English language, *especially in written discourse*" (3, our italics). Third, the Committee recommended that while CCCC should "give substantially increased attention" to advanced courses in language, composition, and creative writing, "the college freshman course should continue to be the Conference's primary concern" (5).

Clearly, these recommendations were linked. According to the Committee, the study and teaching of writing, seen as an academic discipline, could best provide the organization with a reason for being. Such an emphasis on the disciplinary character of CCCC in effect called for an end to the earlier era of open-ended and ongoing discussion among composition and communication teachers about the first-year course—a discussion in which the course was in many respects an unstable object of attention, fluid and shifting, as much a response to the historical moment and the perceived needs of students as an expression of the faculty's professional identity and an enactment of their expertise. The Committee's recommendations, by way of contrast, sought, at least implicitly, to stabilize the course and to establish some boundaries by submitting it to the disciplinary gaze of composition professionals. And by so doing, the Committee's recommendations in turn redefined why and on what terms teachers would gather under the auspices of CCCC, as disciplined professionals with a shared identity and a common scholarly and pedagogical object, namely the improved understanding and use of written discourse. It's not just that composition won. What may be witnessed in the Report of the Committee on Future Directions is the articulation of composition in the postwar period as a disciplined and professionalized field.

At the same time the Committee on Future Directions was deliberating, another committee—the Committee on Possible Name Change—was circulating a questionnaire among officers and members of the Executive Committee asking for suggestions for a new name for the organization. According to Paul Roberts' report to the Executive Committee in the fall of 1959, the top two contenders were "Council on College Composition" and "Council on College Writing." The Executive Committee, however, decided to delay changing the name until a modified questionnaire could be circulated and what the Secretary's Report calls for the "problem" to be discussed more fully, not only by the Executive Committee but also by members of the organization at the 1960 annual CCCC meeting in Cincinnati (62).

Not everyone in CCCC, of course, accepted the Committee on Future Direction's recommendations or the proposed name change as good ideas. There was extensive and lively discussion of the Report on Future Directions at the 1960 meeting in Cincinnati and the 1960 NCTE convention in Chicago. The February 1961 issue of *CCC* is largely devoted to the report, objections to it, and counterproposals. Eugene F. Grewe, for example, held that the report's emphasis on "written discourse" could "throw strong weight on the possibility that the organization might become linguistics-oriented" (19), thereby turning away many present members. Grewe also worried that the focus on the first-year course posed a problem, for if freshman composition was eliminated, as the University of Michigan was considering at the time, CCCC would lose a chief rationale for its existence. Others were concerned the proposed statement of purpose would "read out of our organization all our members . . . from schools where a communication approach is used," as well as composition teachers with interests in "the beginning literature course, or the literature content of the Freshman course, as taught at some schools" (Gorrell 1961, 5). Communication advocate Harold B. Allen argued that rather than restricting its interest to written discourse, CCCC should increase its emphasis on communication, "our most productive avenue of future development" (quoted in Johnson 1961, 13).

In the end, neither the revised statement of purpose nor the proposal to change the name of the organization was approved. By 1961, the Committee on Future Directions had turned into its successor, the

Committee on Philosophy and Structure, chaired by Robert M. Gorrell, and while the new committee rewrote the Report on Future Directions and continued to sponsor discussion at annual meetings, there was in fact considerable benefit to leaving things unchanged. As Gorrell's report for the Committee on Philosophy and Structure concluded flatly, "There was little agreement about how the purpose of the organization should be described. . . . There was agreement that we should, as quickly as possible, finish worrying about what we are and get on with being it" (1961, 14).

In a sense, there was no real need to approve the proposed changes or to continue the debate, for the Committee on Future Directions had already charted CCCC's future by naming composition a discipline. What triumphed, then, was not a formal vote but an emerging structure of feeling that composition, as a discipline devoted to the study and teaching of written discourse, was at the core of CCCC's identity and its primary reason for existence. In effect, during these years in the early 1960s, CCCC's prehistory ended, and the organization transformed itself from a discussion group of like-minded and loosely affiliated teachers into a professional association. In short, CCCC became the organization we recognize today.

If Ken Macrorie's "Writing's Dying" (1960) offered one of the closing shots in the communication battle, his editorship of *CCC* (1962–1964) in many respects consolidated the victory that CCCC had declined to name, giving the emergent structure of feeling that animated the composition forces an institutional form. Instinctively, Macrorie seemed to have understood what Maureen Daly Goggin describes as the institutional role a journal can play in forming a discipline (1997, 324), transforming *CCC* from a bulletin, whose purpose was chiefly to report conference proceedings, to the authoritative journal in the field.

For one thing, Macrorie discontinued the prevailing practice of publishing reports on all the panels and workshops at the yearly CCCC conference, covering instead only selected sessions. This decision not only reduced the space devoted to the conference from thirty-five pages in 1962 to fifteen pages in 1963. It also recast the relation between the journal and the conference, elevating the article over the panel and workshop as the most important vehicle of professional communication. Second, Macrorie made his long-standing argument with the communication movement about social utility and the mass media into an unstated editorial policy that defined the boundaries of composition. Though he published work inspired by linguistics and the new rhetoric, Macrorie above all promoted a view of "composition as art," an expressive and epistemic activity that resisted the notion of writing as a medium of social communication. Finally, Macrorie did all this with exuberance and flair, for the first time injecting an editor's personality into *CCC*, adopting the graphic artist Arnold N. Fujita's sunburst design as the journal's logo, transforming its visual appearance from what Macrorie called "a parts catalog from an automobile manufacturing company," (quoted in Bird 1977, 106), and proposing unsuccessfully to the Executive Committee that the journal change its title (*Statement, Cadmus, Prometheus, Say,* and *Helios* were suggested titles [Macrorie 1962, 57]). Perhaps the final irony in the communication battle is that Macrorie, himself a former typographer, used the tools of sign-making and graphic design to consolidate the victory of the word over the image.

## Composition and Communication

The victory of composition may appear to be largely a numerical one, the result of simply outlasting the communication course. In part, this is the case, but the communication battle was more than a war of attrition. It was also an argument about the meaning of literacy that is deeply rooted in the history of writing instruction and Freshman English. The question "Whatever happened to the 4th C?" is a complex one that leads beyond the demise of the communication movement in the late 1950s and early 1960s and the subsequent neglect of communication as a topic in composition.

In fact, one might hold that communication is too much with the practitioners of composition, its shadowy and unstated presence never far from their minds. We refer here not just to the communication movement or to scholarly work done in communication studies but to the way the teaching of writing has defined itself historically in opposition to—or at least in suspicion of—the prevailing means of mass communication. The leading institutional histories of the field have largely ignored how the pressures of the mass media have entered into and shaped the mission of Freshman English. In many respects, the first-year course has taken on its identity in the past, and continues to do so in the present, as a means of providing students with a defense against mass communication and the mass media.

In an important rereading of Adams Sherman Hill, Charles Paine (1997, 1999) argues that Hill, the acknowledged architect of the first-year course, cannot be understood, as he is often portrayed, simply as an advocate of mechanical correctness and a current-traditional rhetoric that sought to adjust students to the turn-of-the-century social order of corporate capitalism. Instead, Paine says, Hill allied himself with a group of patrician intellectuals such as E. L. Godkin, editor of the *Nation* and second author of the Harvard reports on composition of the 1890s, who were increasingly frustrated by their loss of public influence to the philistine culture and political power of the plutocrats and what they saw as the growing vulgarity of mass commercialized entertainment and the cheapening of civic discourse.

A former newspaperman himself, who had worked on Horace Greeley's *New York Herald,* Hill responded to the widespread circulation of reading material of all sorts by singling out newspapers and pulp fiction in terms that anticipate Macrorie's laments about the "electronic stream" and the jeremiads heard today about television, the Internet, and video games: "To read nothing but newspapers and second-rate novels tends to weaken the powers of attention and of concentration, to diminish, if not destroy, freshness of thought and individuality of expression, and to relax the mental fibre" (quoted in Paine 1997, 292). The goal of the first-year composition course, therefore, was to provide students with the "moral stamina" to resist the seductions of the sensationalistic products of popular culture and to "arm themselves at all points against the numerous foes that beset pure English on every side, in these days of free speech and free press" (quoted in Paine 1997, 292).

What is so useful about Paine's analysis is his sense that the mission of composition was formed in part as a response to the "communication revolution" of the nineteenth century and the subsequent changes in American reading habits. It is easy enough to see this response, as Paine does, following such American historians of the era as Richard Hofstadter and Alan Trachtenberg, as the dying gasp of an older patrician intellectual leadership in the academy and public affairs. But Hill, Godkin, and others of their circle also sounded a note that recurs in the history of writing instruction and the design of Freshman English. "Mass culture, for Hill," Paine says, "resembled a kind of infection, against which rhetorical training could provide inoculation, a means of resisting mass culture" (1997, 283).

This goal for composition and "rhetorical training" recurs repeatedly in discussions of the first-year course. It is evident, for example, in the *Scrutiny* project F. R. Leavis initiated and the influence Leavis brought to bear on a generation of teachers as well as literary critics. Now admittedly, Leavis is not normally associated with writing instruction or the formation of composition, but his thinking about language and education left its mark on Reuben Brower and Theodore Baird at Amherst and through them Walker Gibson, Roger Sale, and William Coles Jr. (cf. Varnum 1996) in the first generation and David Bartholomae and the Pitt school of composition in the second. Moreover,

Leavisites trained at Cambridge in the 1930s and '40s were instrumental in establishing the National Association of Teachers of English (the British counterpart to NCTE). Many of the British teachers and scholars at the Dartmouth Conference in 1966 were Leavis' students, and, as Joseph Harris notes, his "insistence on the value of lived experience and on the importance of language in bringing order to that experience" contrasted sharply with the subject-based approach of many of the Americans (1997, 7). For the Leavisites, the point of the practical criticism was not so much to develop a technical facility with literary analysis (as textbooks often make the New Criticism out to be) but to use close reading as a means of developing discriminating judgment and a criticism of life.

Leavis collaborated with Denys Thompson (one of the participants at Dartmouth) in 1933 on the textbook *Culture and Environment* to define a curriculum in English. What may come as a surprise is that the textbook consists largely of examples from the mass media and exercises for analysis. There is no literature to speak of. Instead, you will find typically Leavisite laments for the passing of the organic community and warnings about the debilitating effects of mass communication:

> Those who in school are offered (perhaps) the beginnings of education in taste are exposed out of school to the competing exploitation of the cheapest emotional responses; films, newspapers, publicity in all its forms, commercially catered fiction—all offering satisfaction at its lowest level, and inculcate the choosing of the most immediate pleasure, got with the least effort. (Leavis and Thompson 1933, 3)

The polarization in this passage of life in and out of school sets the stage in *Culture and Environment* for Leavis' guarded hope that education could promote the discrimination called for to resist the mass culture encroaching everywhere:

> We cannot, as we might in a healthy state of culture, leave the citizen to be formed unconsciously by his environment; if anything like a worthy idea of satisfactory living is to be saved, he must be trained to discriminate and resist. (5)

The disease metaphor of an unhealthy society is prominent here, and again we find the notion of cultural inoculation at work in Leavis' call for *discrimination*, to raise resistance to the infection of mass culture and the mass media. At the same time, it is worth noting that Leavis and Thompson did put the products of mass communication, such as advertising and journalism, in the curriculum, instituting a tradition of media education in both England and the United States that aimed to teach students to discriminate against the manipulative and homogenizing forces of the mass media.

## Conclusion

Ken Macrorie's parable of the communications/composition battle might well, with few changes, be written today. Macrorie has Ed Zybrowski exclaim over "sound" and "pictures" and "words in the air" as a kind of warning that what we treasure about language is in danger of being lost to more attractive but less intellectually demanding media shows.

But, of course, we don't have to look as far back as Macrorie to encounter similar concerns. In her 1997 CCCC roundtable response to James Berlin's last work, *Rhetorics, Poetics, and Cultures,* Susan Miller worried that "the content of such courses" as the one Berlin describes that stresses a turn toward media analysis, "is not writing—is not persuasion to assume the positions of those whose acts of writing are interventions. Nor is it systematic demonstrations of how to write—not 'well,' but powerfully, to subvert more and less conventional subject positions" (1997, 499). Miller ends her response by urging "more focused meetings of College Composition and Communication, more research reports that offer 'news' about writing practices and processes, more empirical but not positivistic studies of writing development, and more attempts to re-theorize the purposes and results of specific textual conventions in prose discourse" (1997, 500).

We are sympathetic to Miller's concern that media analysis, or more generally what's become known as the "cultural studies approach" to teaching writing, too often winds up being an interpretive activity that emphasizes the reading practices of expert critics instead of the production of writing. But we also want to note that her call for "'news' about writing practices and processes" hearkens back to that 1960 report of the Committee on Future Directions, which insisted that our charge is "to improve college students' understanding and use of the English language, especially in written discourse" (Bailey et al. 1960, 3).

Miller's call is based on the now long-standing counterposition of composition and communication, the history of which is particularly clear in the journal's first decade. In our view, such a polarization is problematical because, for one thing, it obscures the fact that writing itself is a form of visible language and a practice of visual design. Keeping composition and communication separate reproduces deeply engrained logocentric allegiances to the verbal over the visual by holding the intellectual authority of written text over the presumably derivative and immature character of visual communication, thereby making the image subservient to the word. Such a polarization, moreover, abstracts writing from the systems of distribution and exchange through which written texts circulate and acquire precisely the worldly force with which Miller, correctly in our view, is so concerned.

Today, the 4th C continues to prove a sticking point. It may well be the case, as David Bartholomae has argued, that the 4th C "was, and remains, a guarantee that there will always be a missing term, a structural presence to call into question any attempts to unify the field" (1989, 45). Of course, at this point in the history of CCCC, as was true from the late 1940s to the early 1960s, any type of unification, whether in the form of consensus about the goals of writing instruction or a master research program, hardly seems a possibility. At the same time, we believe that the signifier communication is more than a trickster figure, the sign of difference that will keep things unstable and shape-shifting.

"With slightly different timing," Bartholomae notes, "we could have been the Conference on Composition and Linguistics or the Conference on Composition and Semantics. And if these had been our names, we would be a very different organization today" (1989, 45). Yet it is significant that, despite the battle we have detailed here, CCCC has somehow been unable or unwilling to drop the 4th C. This reluctance to abandon the term has been, in our view, a good thing. *Communication* exerts a useful pressure to acknowledge that writing cannot be reduced simply to the mental activity of composing (even if you put composing in a social context). The term is a persistent reminder that to write is to operate a technology that makes visual signs, that encodes messages by inscribing marks on a page or a screen. Communication pulls us toward the worldly, the actual, the material. It makes writing, like other types of composition (musical, graphic, handicraft, engineering design), into an act of labor that quite literally fashions the world.

# Chapter Four

# Writing Instruction and the Politics of Professionalization

One of the issues historians of writing instruction keep returning to is why teaching composition has been held in such low regard by English departments and the academy at large. S. Michael Halloran (1983), Richard Ohmann (1987), James A. Berlin (1996), Sharon Crowley (1998), Susan Miller (1991), Robert J. Connors (1991), and others have pointed to the decline of rhetoric, the emergence of the modern research university, the rise of corporate capitalism, the institutionalization of literary studies, and the feminization of teaching writing as possible causes of the meager status of writing teachers. But if historians have figured causation in various ways, the stories we tell ourselves about the low status of our field seem nonetheless to follow a predictable and unified pattern, a master narrative that recounts the tragic fall of rhetoric from its preeminent position in the oratorical culture of the nineteenth-century college to its current unpretentious position in composition programs as a service function in the multiversity.

As the story goes, in the late nineteenth and early twentieth centuries, with the consolidation of the research model of higher learning and the department system that gives it institutional form, the mission of rhetoric shifted from preparing citizens to participate in public life to training a newly emerging professional-managerial class in written composition—not to go into the public sphere to shape democratic opinion but into corporate America to administer the everyday workings of capitalism and the cultural forms that reproduce capitalist social relations. This is a story I believe to be true in its general outline.

But the fact is stories tend to supply, by the narrativity of telling, their own conclusions, and the master plot of writing instruction is not different: it comes equipped with its own lessons. We understand this master plot to indicate the need to professionalize our activities of studying and teaching writing in both theory and practice. We believe, that is, in the need, revealed to us through our narrative, to transform rhetoric and composition from a service function located at the periphery of academic life into a viable discipline. Various guidelines issued on professional standards, the Wyoming Resolution, the proliferation of scholarly research and publication, the appearance of new journals and book series, the creation of endowed chairs, and the unprecedented growth of graduate programs have all contributed to this climate of opinion. If anything, at this point in our collective history, the field of rhetoric and composition has become a booming enterprise, increasingly self-confident, even feisty, about its standing in the academy and its claims to legitimacy and respectability.

The issue I want to raise addresses something that I fear gets neglected in the way we talk about and enact the growing professionalization of our field. I worry that we are in the thrall of the stories we tell and that our master narrative points to professionalization and discipline formation as the inevitable outcome of the plot. Such an outcome certainly makes for a satisfying ending because it relies on a dramatic reversal of fortune: the lowly and illegitimate have risen up to take their fate into their own hands and to secure the rightful position that was lost but is now within grasp again. It is the sense of closure and narrative satisfaction we derive from Victorian novels that I am referring to here, when the orphaned child, after years of virtuous hard labor and despite the various temptations of the world and the cruel designs of treacherous relatives, finally is restored by happy marriage to his or her legitimate birthright. As comforting as this story must have been to Victorians and for all the charm it still possesses, I want to make this narrative into a cautionary tale. And I think there is good reason to do so, for the processes of professionalization and discipline formation, not unlike the patriarchal bourgeois family in the Victorian novel, are deeply contradictory phenomena. To stretch my analogy, perhaps beyond the breaking point, I want to suggest that before we succumb to the nuptial bliss of middle-class respectability, we ought to consider how the politics of professionalization affects writing teachers, writing programs, and writing scholarship in unequal and contradictory ways.

## Ambivalence About Professionalization

Thus far, we have tended to describe the professionalization of our field and our bid for disciplinary status largely in intellectual terms. There are rhetorics of inquiry that treat composition studies as a discursive formation and unpack the intellectual affiliations, logics, and tropes that constitute the study and teaching of writing. We are becoming more self-conscious about our work as a disciplinary and disciplined project, devoted to questions that matter, and we appeal, therefore, to the volume and quality of research and scholarship produced under the aegis of rhetoric and composition studies to demonstrate how serious we are and how well organized we have become to address the burning issues in our field. Moreover, we have attempted to expand what it means to do scholarship by arguing why and how teaching composition, administering programs, and writing textbooks can and should be counted as scholarly activities, at least when done properly—that is, professionally—as disciplined applications of theory and research.

I do not want to quarrel with these developments, which I consider useful to our self-definition as a field. But I also want to point out that they are the normal moves to establish codes of practice, bodies of knowledge, and general professional standards that disciplines invariably rely on to draw their boundaries, to determine what counts as a contribution, and to regulate members' activities according to the best knowledges available. At the same time, it is fair to say that despite the celebratory tone in many discussions of the heightened visibility of rhetoric and composition as an academic field, there are nonetheless traces of ambivalence that, to my mind, are revealing about the contradictory character of the professions and academic disciplines.

I remember, for example, when Patricia Bizzell and Bruce Herzberg were working on *The Rhetorical Tradition* (2000) and spoke at CCCC about canon formation, and there was considerable resistance to their project. This resistance was based in part on nostalgia for the good old bad days, when writing teachers formed a kind of underground or affinity group of like-minded individuals, circulating mimeographed reading lists and giving each other much needed professional and personal support. And, in part, the resistance was based on the fear that institutionalizing our field as an academic discipline would turn CCCC into another version of the Modern Language Association (MLA), with its typically agonistic style of discourse, its privileging of publishing over teaching, it trendiness, and the self-deception of its academic leftists "striking great blows against capitalism in the realm of theory" (as one well-known critic put it). It was not simply status anxiety or legitimate anger about how literary studies had devalued the study and teaching of writing that was at work in villainizing MLA. In a more telling sense, MLA was taken to represent the occupational hazard of academics' removing the subject of their inquiry—in this case literature—from the world of ordinary readers and making it instead a matter upon which to build individual careers.

This felt sense of the pressure and limits of discipline formation is revealing because it suggests how writing teachers had cast themselves as a kind of religion of the oppressed, small islands of the saved, where the legitimacy of success seemed to threaten their very identities as the humble and unauthorized professors of a truth our literature counterparts cannot bear: namely, that *we* care about students and have invested ourselves, both intellectually and affectively, in their personal growth and well-being instead of in turf warfare over who is qualified to interpret a body of texts. This sentiment, I believe, is a flawed but not altogether unreasonable one. It is flawed because it makes suffering—professional and personal—redemptive. But it is also reasonable in that it points to some very real problems in discipline formation: normalizing of intellectual work, subjugation of counterknowledges, overemphasis on specialization, monopolies of expertise.

These problems have been addressed, though I believe inadequately, in efforts to define rhetoric and composition as a postmodern field that by virtue of its interdisciplinarity transcends the limits of conventional academic fields of study. Andrea Lunsford, Louise Wetherbee Phelps, and others have argued that composition studies emerges on the scene as a postmodern moment in academic life that resists the positivist certainties and foundational accounts that shaped the older disciplines. As a postmodern field, composition studies situates itself in a nondisciplinary or postdisciplinary place where multiple, heterogeneous, and polyvalent discourses, projects, and interests intersect. Composition studies proceeds, that is, in accord with the cultural logic of postmodernism to compose itself as a kind of pastiche, appropriating disparate and incongruous theoretical elements into a unity of differences. As a mobile and decentered intellectual project, composition refuses the emphasis on instrumental control and the proliferation of specialized knowledges that, as Kurt Spellmeyer (1993) puts it, have fragmented reason into many incommensurate ways of knowing and thereby make it exceedingly difficult for laypeople and experts to speak in a common public language.

I share Spellmeyer's concern about the disciplining of knowledge that produces monopolies of expertise, on one hand, and deference to the authority of specialists and public ignorance, on the other. The point I want to make, however, is that the professions and academic disciplines are not simply *intellectual* formations that favor specialization and expertise in ways that inhibit popular participation and democratic discussion. They are also *social* formations. To put it another way, the problem is not specialization per se but the particular forms of social organization that authorize and reproduce specialized expertise. Specialization and expertise are coextensive with the cultural life of the human species. There have always been individuals who have developed personal talents and predispositions in healing, music, art, dance, storytelling, athletics, political leadership, and so on. What distinguishes the professions and academic disciplines is that they are a relatively new kind of social formation that organizes and regulates the specialized work of experts.

## Professional Formations

Let me sketch briefly the history and sociology of these professional formations. According to historian of professionalism Burton J. Bledstein, academic specialization and discipline formation "came into existence to serve and promote professional authority in society" (1976, 290). Public debates about disease, poverty, education, and crime in the late nineteenth and early twentieth centuries offer striking examples of how the culture of professionalism took hold in the United States. These debates, in Bledstein's words, uncovered "abnormality and perversity everywhere" (102). Threats of illness, illiteracy, and violence seemed to call up the services of enlightened, dispassionate, and disinterested civil servants and professionals, independent of both popular prejudices and market forces. After the Civil War, the centralizing impulses of state formation redefined the relation between the state and civil society by creating a layer of bureaucratic institutions devoted to public health, social work, schooling, and corrections that displaced the familial, local, and voluntary associations of an earlier era. As Ohmann suggests, the emergence of the modern corporation and scientific models of management further amplified the movement toward professionalism, and the university increasingly became the "supplier and certifier . . . of professionals and managers" (32). Even popular entertainment, recreation, and sports were becoming professionalized around the turn of the twentieth century.

As industrial capitalism, class struggle, urbanization, and immigration reshaped American society in the late nineteenth century, Americans confronted massive, far-reaching, and bewildering social changes. Without traditional authorities to fall back on, Americans invested faith in science, progress, and professional expertise. As Bledstein suggests, part of the success of the culture of professionalism is that it cast professional values in a peculiarly American idiom, invoking the image of independent and fair-minded individuals whose training and special expertise prepared them to act on behalf of society as a whole—to stand in for the public interest by controlling natural and social forces. In turn, professional expertise defined itself in contrast to the ineptitude of nonprofessionals, who were judged to be incapable of either understanding the skilled practices of professionals or evaluating the results of professional work.

Professionalism, by this account, is all about the cultural authorization of expertise and how the newly emerging social formations organized in professional associations such as the American Bar Association and the American Medical Association and in academic disciplines began to claim, in the name of the public interest, the autonomy of professional work and its self-regulating procedures. Through devices we now take for granted, such as accreditation, certification, peer review, standards of practice, codes of ethics, and so on, the professions and academic disciplines constituted themselves on behalf of the common good, above popular debate and beyond public criticism. And by doing so, the professions and academic disciplines articulated processes of subject formation by which professionals and academics learn to recognize themselves and to enact identities as the agents of disciplined discourses and practices precisely to the extent they assume the rhetorical authority to speak as experts, on behalf of a client population of laypeople who need or want their services.

This portrait of the professions and academic disciplines does not, of course, correspond to their public self-images of rational and efficient bodies of experts responding disinterestedly to pressing social and intellectual needs, as the standard Weberian account might have it. Rather, the professions seek a monopoly of the services they provide by keeping authorized practice independent of other practitioners and other markets while at the same time maintaining themselves as autonomous and self-regulated in relation to their client populations. In this sense, the professions, as Pierre Bourdieu suggests (1977), are social formations that allot recognition and determine who may speak, about what, and on whose behalf. Professionalization, as Bourdieu sees it, deals in the currency of credentials—or symbolic capital—as the primary means of exchange, not simply as personal fame or name recognition but as the power, distributed differentially, to act on the world, to achieve practical results by determining how the world is represented.

## Stratification

Bourdieu's sense of the way professions and academic disciplines allot recognition brings me back to the problem of professionalization in rhetoric and composition. My point, to put it as bluntly as I can, is that production, distribution, exchange, and consumption of symbolic capital in the form of professional credentials follow the same laws that govern the circulation of industrial and finance capital, favoring monopoly and concentration and leading to internal differentiation and a stratified class system, even within the professions and academic disciplines. The formation of professional careers mimics the workings of monopoly capitalism, according to what the sociologist of science Robert K. Merton (1973) calls the "Matthew effect," after the biblical passage "he who hath shall receive," where status and prestige accrue to those who already have it.

The Wyoming Resolution, of course, was an attempt to deal with the problem of equity in the teaching of writing, but it defined the issue largely in terms of the differences between full-time and part-time faculty, between tenured and tenure-track teachers and those on short-term contracts, arguing that part-time and nontenure-stream faculty should have the same conditions, rights, privileges, and prorated pay as full-time tenured and tenure-track faculty. This was a groundbreaking initiative, and the casualization of academic labor has, if anything, taken on even greater significance and urgency since the Wyoming Resolution first appeared. Nonetheless, focusing exclusively on the differences between full- and part-time faculty ignores internal stratification within the full-time faculty and the differences in material conditions that enable and constrain the study and teaching of writing. These differences organize the social and intellectual structure of our field. Let me cite three major differences that we need to know more about to understand the stratification of the field.

### *Differences in the Provision of Writing Instruction Based on Type of Educational Institution*

Here we would need to look at differences in salaries, teaching loads, class size, faculty development, secretarial support, photocopying budgets, computer equipment and frequency of updates for hardware and software, and so on. My sense is that the provision of writing instruction follows the same stratified patterns of class reproduction that Samuel Bowles and Herbert Gintis (1976) identified in American post-secondary education, from community colleges and low-prestige state colleges to high-prestige liberal arts colleges and research universities, with teaching loads and class sizes larger and salaries and institutional support smaller in community and state colleges. The fact that elite colleges and universities often value scholarship over teaching in tenure and promotion decisions should not obscure the fact that the conditions of teaching are better in high-prestige schools. Faculty typically teach few courses (one or two a term instead of three or four) and thereby have more preparation time, even if you figure in the pressures to do research and publish. While some faculty in elite schools are more concerned with released time than with teaching, there is nonetheless a greater investment of resources in teachers and students in high-prestige colleges and universities than in low-prestige ones. I do not mean to suggest that writing teachers at community and state colleges are not providing for their students. My point is a structural, not a personal, one that concerns the unequal distribution of material resources in the political economy of writing instruction.

### *Differences in Access to Opportunities for Research and Professional Development*

Here we would need to take into account differences in availability of travel funds, speakers programs, library resources, expectations about tenure and promotion, released-time policies, and guidelines for research leaves, including pretenure leaves and sabbaticals. I think we would find consequential and stratifying differences in the political economy of research that parallel the political economy of teaching.

But it is not simply that time to do research is unevenly distributed, depending on the type of institution. This uneven distribution of research opportunities also affects the lived experience of writing teachers by determining their nearness to or distance from the social and intellectual networks of the discipline. The relative positioning of individual academics within a field of study typically begins in graduate school and continues in mentoring relationships between senior and junior faculty and in the blurred personal/professional relationships among peers that make up the social networks of a discipline. In the professions, where a good deal of knowledge and skills are not quantifiable or readily communicable in the form of rules, a practitioner's nearness to or distance from the "cutting edge" of a professional field may appear to be mysterious, a matter of personal talents that cannot be taught but rather are enacted through the exercise of individual abilities and efforts. What I want to suggest is that the expression—and recognition—of individual talent is mediated by the material conditions that enable and constrain research and the social relationships and sense of connectedness to the intellectual life of a discipline that sustain the labor required to produce scholarly work.

### *Differences in the Production of Scholarship*

Here the forces in the political economies of writing instruction and research converge, producing marked differences in who publishes, about what, and in what journals. As Theresa Enos (1990) and Sue Ellen Holbrook (1991) have found, there are significant gender differences in publication patterns in rhetoric and composition, with more female authors publishing pedagogical articles in journals devoted to teaching writing while a greater percentage of "theoretical" articles in high-prestige journals were written by men. Though I do not have any hard figures, my guess is that rhetoric and composition resembles other academic fields, in which a fairly small percentage of professionals—10 percent or so—produces around half of the publications. Such stratification is further amplified by the fact that not all publications are equal in influence and prestige. Citation indices that count which articles and books are cited in subsequent publications would reveal, I believe, even greater stratification within the field.

## Insiders and Outsiders

The picture of rhetoric and composition that emerges from these differences prohibits any easy celebration of disciplinary status and professionalization. While the ethos of the profession is certainly more egalitarian and democratic than that of many other academic fields, there is nonetheless a growing felt sense that the field is composed of "insiders" and "outsiders." Two notable documents that appeared in *Rhetoric Review* in 1988 and 1989, "CCCC: Voices in the Parlor, and Responses" (1988) and "The Conversation Continues: Voices in the Parlor" (1989), present a "chorus" charging that CCCC meetings have become characterized by a "star" system of big-name celebrities who sold their idealism for fame and by the grandstanding use of theoretical (and implicitly impenetrable and exclusionary) discourses that seem far removed from the practical realities of teaching. For a field such as rhetoric and composition, which is committed so self-consciously to democratic practices and values, these are troubling charges. On one hand, of course, the "insider/outsider" dichotomy that the "chorus" notes is perhaps a predictable outcome of the meritocratic organization of academic work: the best will rise to the top and a "natural" and justifiable stratification of talents will inevitably occur. On the other hand, however, as I am suggesting, an analysis of the material conditions and social relationships that govern teaching and scholarship challenges such meritocratic premises of equal opportunity and the structural results of stratification within the profession.

The unsigned (but initialed) contributions to "Voices in the Parlor" from two well-known and well-established figures in rhetoric and composition did little to clarify the consequences of professional stratification. Rather, they reproduce some the differences I have already mentioned: the "outsiders" feel excluded, constituted as spectators and someone else's show; while the "insiders" say "Murmuring discontentedly won't cut it," that in fact there is plenty of room on the stage as long as you produce "serious . . . quality work" (RJC 1988, 213)—and besides, as LZB notes, we (the "insiders") "do this work . . . for love, not money" (1989, 408). In other words, both the "insiders" and "outsiders" reproduce the logic of professionalization by assuming that "entering the conversation" depends on personal acts of will, ambition, individual enterprise, and career building.

In one sense, this should not be surprising. As Magali Sarfatti Larson argues, "Most professions produce intangible goods: their product, in other words, . . . is inextricably bound to the person and the personality of the producer" (1977, 14). The relative autonomy of professional work, in which individuals experience their everyday work lives as series of independent decisions and acts of judgment, all too easily disguises the structural constraints within which professionals operate and attributes success and failure to personal effort and talent. What this misses, as Larson goes on to say, is that for a profession to corner the market on a distinct service, it must rely on a fictitious commodity: "the producers themselves have to be produced" (14). From this perspective, the "serious . . . quality work" that RJC invokes may be seen not only as the result of personal effort and talent but also as structurally determined by differences in the production of producers that operate through networks that often begin in graduate school and extend through professional life, shaping the formation of careers. Moreover, to see professional subject formation as a structural phenomenon calls into question the adequacy of self-representations such as LZB's that figure professional work as a vocation or personal call to service, an expression of the individual personality—"work . . . for love, not money"—outside and beyond the market forces and circuits of symbolic capital that organize the political economy of the professions.

## The Contradictions of Professional Life

I have been trying to suggest that professionalization is an uneven and contradictory process. At this point in history, this is true for the legal and medical professions, as well as for academics. Lawyers, who need to generate billable hours, and doctors, who need to see so many patients per day, are finding their work experience defined as much by accountability measures of productivity and cost-efficiency as by the provision of professional services to clients and patients. Increasingly, professional life is characterized by a tension between the desire to perform services well and the material constraints and undemocratic organization of work that have made it more and more difficult to provide services according to even the most minimal professional standard. It would be too doctrinaire and pessimistically deterministic simply to lay the blame on the system, though I certainly believe capitalism deserves it. The contradictions of professional life play themselves out in the experience of actual men and women, lawyers, doctors, teachers, and so on who, despite often debilitating situations, are trying to do the best they can. So the issue, to my way of thinking, is how do we read the contradictory situations within which professionals must operate? How, in other words, can we take into account the contradictions of professionalization without abandoning the hard-won professional expertise accumulated in the study and teaching of writing but without defending the outcomes of composition's meritocracy as the natural selection of the best and brightest?

The contradictory politics of professionalization are enacted not only ritually at CCCC but at the point of production, in the everyday workings of writing programs, and therefore it may be useful to describe how these politics shape the living experience of writing program administrators. By a Foucauldian account of professionalization, writing program administrators (WPAs), precisely because of their professional knowledges, are invariably implicated in acts of surveillance that constitute both staff and students as "docile bodies." Through course design, textbook selection, testing, placement, grading sessions, and classroom observations, WPAs oversee the work of teaching and learning that takes place in writing programs and classrooms. The WPA's professional identity in this regard is inseparable from the micropolitics of discipline—measuring, differentiating, hierarchizing its subjects. In fact, Foucault's description of how discipline works sounds remarkably like a description of a WPA doing course scheduling at the beginning of a term. Discipline, Foucault says, operates "on the principle of elementary location or partitioning. Each individual has his own place; and each place is individual. . . . Disciplinary space tends to be divided into as many sections as there are bodies . . . to be distributed" (1979, 143).

By this account, knowing means mastering, using, and controlling bodies, and the apparently prosaic task of course scheduling reveals that knowledge is invariably a means of discipline and the WPA its human agent. This, I realize, is a rather bleak portrait of the WPA, and one that appears to be without contradictions, a seamless and largely unacknowledged system of power that operates behind the backs of its actors. But Foucault also provides a critical opening into the contradictions in the micropolitics of discipline when he calls for an "insurrection of subjugated knowledges" (1980, 81).

By "subjugated knowledges," Foucault means both the conflicts and struggles suppressed or disguised by the systematization and functional coherence of disciplinary ways of knowing (what I have been referring to as professionalization) and the popular knowledges (*savoir des gens*) of patients, delinquents, students, and so on that have been disqualified as naïve and unscientific from the prevailing cognitive hierarchy. I want to emphasize the connection between these two forms of subjugated knowledge: how, that is, the professionalization and cultural authorization of expertise filter and "purify" the professional subject in such a way that makes it difficult to hear, much less listen to, countervoices and counterknowledges that do not fit readily with existing professional practice. And yet, at the same time, the knowledges subjugated in the formation of the professional subject are not eliminated but rather are driven underground, where they exert a residual tug at the margins of professional experience.

To articulate the knowledges that have been subjugated in the processes of professionalization and the technologies of power that constitute experts and laypeople will require a new look at our discipline and how it has disciplined us. Studies of professionalization, such as Carol Berkenkotter, Thomas N. Huckin, and John Ackerman's (1991) analysis of the socialization of a graduate student in rhetoric and composition too often rely on an expert-novice model that treats alternative forms of knowledge as interference in the acquisition of mastery, white noise that needs to be eliminated or silenced. On the other hand, in a study of women writing in the academy, Gesa Kirsch (1993) gives a much more prominent and problematical place to the desires and knowledges women have had to keep under wraps in their struggles to acquire authority and credibility in their disciplines. One of the striking refrains from Kirsch's informants is the urge to use their professional training to produce not only individual careers but also socially useful knowledge by linking the expertise to social movements and publics outside the academy.

It is not simply that Kirsch's subjects want to write in popular genres, speaking as experts in a language more accessible to laypeople; rather, they want to popularize knowledge by redefining the relationship between professionals and their publics. Nor is it simply a matter of divided loyalties pulling Kirsch's subjects between the need to gain recognition and establish professional identities on one hand and their desire to articulate professional work to forces seeking social change on the other. As Larson (1977) points out, conflicts such as these grow out of a structural contradiction in the political economy of the professions—the contradiction between the exchange value of professional work and the use value of its services. This contradiction, of course, is not peculiar to professionalization. Marx pointed out over a century ago that the contradiction between the social nature of production and the private appropriation of its products haunts capitalism as a mode of production. And for this reason, the contradiction between exchange value and use value is not likely to go away or to be resolved easily in the practice of professional life. But this contradiction does offer a way to understand the everyday struggles of professionals to define themselves and their work.

To return to the WPA, we can see the contradiction between exchange value and use value operating, among other places, in the design and practice of writing across the curriculum (WAC) programs. From one perspective, the goal of any profession is to achieve a perfect monopoly of its services. After all, professional claims to a corner on expertise make little sense if anyone can be an expert or perform a particular service. In fact, one of the key struggles of rhetoric and composition has been to counter the idea that anyone can teach writing, that no particular training or professional knowledge is required. To claim that writing instruction requires professional training based on a standardized body of knowledge and institutional infrastructure of entry into the profession seeks to enhance not only the academic legitimacy of the field but also the exchange value of studying and teaching writing by keeping it distinct from other services, such as teaching Shakespeare or doing research on the eighteenth-century novel. In writing across the curriculum programs, however, the contradiction between the exchange value of writing instruction and its use value arises to the extent that such programs attempt to make professional knowledge about teaching writing more widely accessible in the academy, to popularize it as socially useful knowledge that nonexperts can draw on and put into practice.

While WAC programs appear from one angle as exemplary instances of demonopolizing composition's knowledge of writing and putting it in wider circulation, from another angle, WAC programs reveal persistent dilemmas of professional life and its contradictions. As anyone who has started a WAC program knows, they can be difficult to sustain, for they so often depend on the goodwill of participating faculty who recognize the use value for their teaching of "writing to learn," drafting and revising, and understanding academic writing as various genres and rhetorics of inquiry. There are, to be sure, very real intangible benefits, such as the experience of collegiality and intellectual engagement in WAC workshops and meetings and the professional satisfaction of making sense of student writing and designing better ways to teach it. But the fact is, without sufficient exchange value, in the form of institutional reward and recognition—the symbolic capital that enhances a participating faculty member's credentials through student evaluations, positive annual reviews, merit raises, promotion, and so on—WAC programs can wither away or settle into bureaucratic routines, and, in any case, individual faculty members are faced with the dilemma that their desire to perform professional services well and the extra effort they put into incorporating writing into their courses may be in tension with the exchange values of their institutions. Sometimes they persist, sometimes they drop out, and sometimes they hedge by cutting the number of writing assignments or the amount of time spent talking about writing in their courses.

The problem is that we're always inside the contradictions of professionalism. This does not mean that rearticulations of expertise are impossible. We do not need either to abandon professionalization as an obstacle to socially useful knowledge or to embrace it uncritically as the necessary outcome of our collective history. We need, rather, to develop new ways to read the contradictions of professional life, to grapple daily with the persistent conflicts between building individual careers and popularizing expertise for broader social purposes.

## Chapter Five

# Changing the Question
## Should Writing Be Studied?

Rhetoric and composition, like any academic field, takes shape through debate about its identity, the questions it raises, the work it values, and the practices it endorses. The history of the field can be seen as a matter of what Victor Villanueva (1997) calls "cross-talk in comp theory." Sometimes, such cross-talk takes place live and in person, as in the case of the CCCC sessions in which Patricia Bizzell and Bruce Herzberg debated Lil Brannon and C. H. Knoblauch about academic discourse, or Peter Elbow and David Bartholomae debated writing with or without teachers. More often, though, these exchanges take place in writing. I think of the Ann E. Berthoff–Janice Lauer debate about invention in the early 1970s or the ruckus between Maxine Hairston and composition's cultural left in the 1990s (Trimbur et al., 1993). You can fill in your favorite examples.

A number of years ago, I had resigned myself to the withering away of such discipline-defining debates, as the field becomes more professionalized and internally differentiated. But I was wrong, and another debate is currently brewing. There are early signs of it, for example, in Gary Olson's response (2002) to the late Wendy Bishop's argument that the teaching of writing has fallen victim to the theorists whose convoluted prose has "no clothes, and no heart (no organs at all, no human substance") (1999, 26) and, further, that "self-identified something-like-an-expressivist" writer-teachers such as herself, Peter Elbow, Donald Murray, and Toby Fulwiler are being marginalized by the theory machine—a claim Olson (and I) find suspect on the grounds that Bishop was, after all, elected chair of CCCC. From Olson's perspective, in the provocatively titled "The Death of Composition as an

Intellectual Discipline" (2002), Bishop's complaint represents a backlash against the hard-earned work of composition theorists and researchers to make the field an intellectually respectable discipline.

Now, while my sympathies are largely with Olson in the "theory war" that came and went in the early 2000s, the exchange does point to some of the tremors in composition that accompany the recent trend to establish freestanding writing programs and departments on disciplinary lines, with a four-year writing curriculum, majors, and minors. It is not accidental (and perhaps somewhat ironic) that Olson's "Death of Composition" essay appears in his 2002 collection *Rhetoric and Composition as Intellectual Work,* where back-to-back chapters by Charles Bazerman (2002) and Susan Miller (2002) plainly call for "writing studies," in Bazerman's words, as a "major discipline" and, in Miller's, as an integrative "mode of inquiry." The confidence and vigor of the cases Bazerman and Miller make for writing studies hardly seem to justify Olson's lament. Instead, they—along with many others, including Douglas Downs and Elizabeth Wardle (2007) who propose that the first-year course be transformed into an "Introduction to Writing Studies"—mark what I take to be an important shift in the questions composition asks about the work it does.

I return in a moment to Bishop's reading of the composition scene in the late 1990s, as well as Downs and Wardle and the response to their proposal for making the first-year course an "Introduction to Writing Studies" from Libby Miles et al. (2008) in the University of Rhode Island's Writing and Rhetoric department—to understand what's at stake in claiming a disciplinary identity based on writing studies and asking students to study writing. First, however, to put these matters in perspective, I want to go back to the late 1960s and early 1970s, when advocates of the "new rhetoric" were trying to clarify their theory and practice of writing instruction. Coincidentally, this was just a few years before I started teaching writing, and I remember being both troubled and intrigued by the question that notable people in the field were asking, namely "Can writing be taught?" I found the question troubling because I thought teaching writing was what I had been hired to do, as a part-time instructor of basic writing in an open admissions program. At the same time, since I had no experience teaching writing before nor any training in rhetoric and composition, I was intrigued, as a newcomer, that this field was asking such fundamental questions about its own activity. I could not imagine literature faculty asking whether literature can be taught or such a question arising about American Studies, where I had done my graduate work, or any other academic field for that matter.

What I could not have known at the time, but that now seems clear in retrospect, is how the terms of the question "Can writing be taught?" belong to a particular moment when the new rhetoric was extricating itself from what it called current-traditional rhetoric. Richard Young's "Arts, Crafts, Gifts, and Knacks: Some Disharmonies in the New Rhetoric" (1980) introduced me to the question. Young notes that current-traditional rhetoric, such as John Genung's, divides the activity of composing into an art, which depends on the predispositions of the composer and cannot be taught, on one hand, and, on the other, a craft, which amounts to technical knowledge of conventions and mechanics that teachers can impart to their students. "All the work of origination," Genung says, "must be left to the writer himself" (quoted in Young 1980, 53–54), in one of those statements readers now recognize as the well-known neglect of invention that draws a dividing line between current-traditional and the new rhetorics. For Genung, invention is a rhetorical capacity that exists mysteriously "in the writer himself, in the peculiar bent of his nature" (quoted in Young 1980, 54). Today, of course, we might well remark on the class bias in Genung's thoroughly gendered "bent of *his* nature" and look for the forms of cultural capital, including the rhetorical labor of invention, that Genung both hides and defends by making them unteachable and inaccessible to analysis.

But there is also another division on the question "Can writing be taught?" that Young brings to light. This time, though, it appears within the ranks of the new rhetoric—in what Frank D'Angelo termed the "new romanticism." As Young explains, the new romantics, by putting primary emphasis on the imagination, "maintain that the composing process is, or should be, relatively free of deliberate control" (1980, 55). William E. Coles Jr.'s notion of teaching writing *as writing* provides the terms. Like Genung, Coles sees writing in part as unteachable: "the teaching of writing as writing is the teaching of writing as art. When writing is not taught as art, as more than a craft or skill, it is not writing that is being taught, but something else. . . . On the other hand, art because it is art, cannot be taught." Unlike Genung, however, Coles does not give up on teaching the unteachable. Instead, he poses the paradox that "what is wanted . . . is a way of teaching what cannot be taught, a course to make possible what no other course can do" (quoted in Young 1980, 55).

And this is precisely what the then emergent process movement went on to do. It worked out a way to teach what cannot be taught by reorganizing the social relations in writing classrooms, shifting the role and identity of the teacher from, in Kenneth A. Bruffee's (1972) words, a "donor of knowledge" to someone who sets up the conditions in which students can learn. In a kind of trickster operation, the process movement answered the question "Can writing be taught?" by changing it into the question "How can writing be learned?"

To my mind, this shift is one of the many valuable legacies of the process movement and its workshop model of teaching writing. I do not mean to suggest that no one before the process movement had ever used writing workshops, for that is certainly not the case. Rather, the process movement made the writing workshop—with its repertoire of collaborative learning, drafting and revising, freewriting, peer response, and so on—central to writing pedagogy. For process teachers and theorists, the writing classroom is where students work on writing, and the writing workshop became, in effect, the habitus of writing instruction with an accompanying rhetoric of location and symbolic geography that distinguished the workshop from, say, the lecture hall or seminar room as *our* place, where we turned the rows of traditional instruction into learning circles.

Shifting the question from that of whether writing can be taught to that of how writing teachers can design courses and set up conditions in which students can learn to write brought with it a suspicion of direct instruction, for explicit teaching had already been identified with what current-traditionalists such as Genung thought *could* be taught—namely, conventions and mechanics. In the era of "whole language," process teachers and theorists resisted any suggestion that writing could be divided into a set of skills that could be taught directly to students, such as the three-tiered composition sequences at the community colleges where I was teaching in the 1970s that began with a semester on the sentence, followed by a semester on the paragraph, and finally a third one on the essay. Instead, they imagined an immersion in the process of composing that valued student experience, situated practice, and learning by doing.

Subsequently, of course, there have been any number of doubts raised about the process movement's suspicion of direct instruction, from Lisa Delpit's critique (1988) of the disempowering indirection of process teaching to Joseph M. Williams and Gregory G. Colomb's "The Case for Explicit Teaching: Why What You Don't Know Can't Help You" (1993) to the New London Group's multiliteracy pedagogy (2000) that treats situated practice and overt teaching not as opposites but as complementary moments that lead further to "critical reframing" and "transformed practice." Still, I think it is fair to say that writing teachers' investment in the workshop as vehicle and symbol remains a defining feature of contemporary writing instruction, even in an era we are starting to call "postprocess." In turn, however, this investment in the writing workshop as an answer to the question "How can writing be learned?" has made it difficult to think of writing as a subject of study, to imagine a place in the curriculum for the study of writing as a legitimate field of inquiry.

For this reason, I consider the current trend to think not just of writing courses but of a discipline of writing studies and a curriculum with advanced courses, majors, and minors so interesting and important. Only this time, the question is not "Can writing be taught?" or "How can writing be learned?" but "Should writing be studied?"

Now, I can imagine some readers thinking this is a nonquestion. After all, asking students to study writing is something writing teachers do and have always done. We teach what writing is and how to do it. But I think it is not so simple, for the question "What is writing?" can be asked in more than one way. When we say "writing," do we mean its participial form that refers to writing as an unfolding activity of composing (as in "Don't bother me. I am writing") or do we designate its noun form to refer to the material manifestations and consequences of writing as it circulates in the world (as in "I can't find that piece of writing I was working on yesterday" or "Your writing is making everyone angry")?

I think there is a tension between the participial and noun forms worth exploring, for the terms shape how teachers and students alike encounter the phenomenon of writing. Let me give an example. Reproduced below are pages from "What Is Writing?," the opening chapter of my textbook *The Call to Write* (1999a).

**Writing in Everyday Life***

Writing in everyday life is embedded in our daily routines and private purposes. Much of the writing that takes place in everyday life can be described as self-sponsored because it is up to the individual to decide whether, why and how to write.

The call to write in everyday life emerges from a range of situations. People respond by drawing on various genres to carry out their purposes: they write lists to remember things and organize their daily activities. They write notes for friends or family members to ask for a ride home, to remind someone about a dentist's appointment, to jot down a phone message. People use writing to maintain social relationships—whether by means of a letter of condolence, a thank-you card for a birthday present, or a note passed between friends in class. Some people keep personal diaries to record their experience—and to let off steam, put their feelings in perspective, and cope with the pressures of life. Others write poetry or fiction for similar purposes and for the pleasure of using language to create imaginary worlds.

These purposes have in common a tendency to be personal rather than public. Similarly, intended readers are generally limited to people the writer knows well, intimate acquaintances such as friends and family or even just the writer. Not surprisingly the tone is characteristically informal and familiar. And although these writings are personal, they are, like everyday life itself, tied to the larger social and cultural context.

*From *Call to Write, 3E* by John Trimbur. Copyright © 2005 by Heinle/Arts & Sciences, a part of Cengage Learning, Inc. Reprinted by permission of the publisher.

### Analysis of Writing in Everyday Life: A Shopping List

Nothing could be more ordinary than a shopping list. But this makes a shopping list ideal for our analysis of writing in everyday life. Shopping lists reveal one of the most powerful aspects of writing: writing frees us from having to commit everything to memory. It's easier and more efficient to write items down on paper, to let a list remind us of what we want.

A typical shopping list might look something like this:

| apples | butter | rice |
|---|---|---|
| spaghetti | meat for Sunday dinner | hot dog rolls |
| bananas | milk | cat food |
| eggs | bread | paper towels |
| chicken | two cans of tomatoes | salad stuff |

Notice that only the writer could actually bring home exactly what he or she wants. Someone else wouldn't know, for example, how many apples or what kind of meat to buy. The voice in the writing is imprecise and self-referential, the kind of private code when you want to talk to yourself. If, however, someone else were to do the shopping, the writer would need to be much more specific and make the voice more precise and clear.

With some small changes, the shopping list could be written to be an organizing tool as well as a memory aid. The shopper could compose the list so that it corresponds to the aisles in a grocery store:

| apples | bananas | salad stuff |
|---|---|---|
| chicken | meat for Sunday dinner | |
| two cans of tomatoes | | |
| spaghetti | | |
| paper towels | | |
| butter | milk | eggs |
| bread | hot dog rolls | |
| cat food | | |

This analysis points out how purpose and audience do indeed shape the writing task. Even as simple and straightforward a piece of writing as a shopping list can be written to serve several purposes. From a broader perspective, these lists also express the shopper's relationship to other common cultural activities, such as planning meals, entertaining guests, packing children's lunches, caring for pets, and cleaning and managing a household. The act of writing a shopping list also locates private homes in relationship to social institutions such as the larger economic order of food production and distribution that includes agribusiness, cattle ranches, dairy farms, bakeries, supermarket chains, and the huge corporations that make everything from lasagna to light bulbs.

As you can see, I'm trying to get students to recognize how commonplace writing is to everyday life and what they might learn by analyzing such humble instances of writing. Given my intentions of presenting samples of writing to be studied, I was taken aback when a colleague kindly sent me the responses of a class of honors first-year writing students who had read the chapter. Importantly, he had assigned the chapter without prefacing it and simply asked students in an open-ended assignment to give their reactions. It was the beginning of the term, so students' expectations about the writing course and the textbook were still uncontaminated by instruction. What I found so striking in their responses is that the students felt insulted by such a mundane text as a shopping list. They said they already knew how to write shopping lists, and so they didn't see the point of including one in their textbook. Not to put too fine a point on it, the students thought the textbook author was insipid and that shopping lists did not belong in a college writing curriculum.

My point here has to do with the dominance of the participial form of the word writing. It was precisely because these students expected so thoroughly to be taught how to write, they could not imagine writing in its noun form or the shopping list as an object of inquiry. Because they could not imagine being taught in college how to write shopping lists, they could not imagine any other use for them.

There is a double elimination going on in their responses: first, of writing as a subject of study, and second, of the genre of the shopping list as quotidian and ephemeral, beneath their notice as college students. In other words, the students provide evidence that what Lynn Worsham (1991) calls the "pedagogical imperative" operates from below as well as from above, that students as much as teachers hold an overriding desire to convert anything suggesting the study of writing into classroom lessons in how to write. The students believed the goal of their required first-year writing course was to improve their writing, and for that reason my effort to pose writing as a subject of analysis was misguided at best and at worst impertinent and irrelevant.

Now certainly adherence to the pedagogical imperative on the part of students and teachers alike does make it difficult to imagine writing courses that focus not only on the processes of writing but also on an education in rhetoric and writing studies. Moreover, the shift from the question "How can writing be learned?"—which now has a battery of well-prepared answers in the process movement's workshop practices—to the question "Should writing be studied?" clashes with the sensibilities of many writing teachers, for whom writing is figured not as a field of study that *belongs* in the curriculum but as a practice that *pervades* the curriculum, beginning with the first-year writing course and extending to writing centers and writing across the curriculum and writing in the disciplines programs, where writing specialists urge colleagues to adopt workshop practices.

This shift of questions helps explain what was at stake for Wendy Bishop, when she wrote "Places to Stand: The Reflective Writer-Teacher in Composition" in 1999, casting the "expressivist" writer-teacher (or teacher-writer), whose teaching and identity are grounded in the daily activity of composing, whether alone or in workshops writing with students, as both an endangered species and a construction of social constructionist anxieties about their own professional identities. For Bishop, this "fear of expressivist figures [such as Elbow, Murray, Fulwiler] is one side-effect of the pressure to be professional," brought about by "Current-Market-Forces" (12–13) that demand critical discourse as a means of scholarly certification and thereby purge PhDs in English of their love for the activity of writing and a desire to share it—to coenact it—in writing workshops with their students. In this sense, shifting the question "How can writing be learned?" to "Should writing be studied?" involves a change not only in identity but also in the symbolic geography of the field, away from the all-inclusive writing workshop to the seminar room of discipline-based inquiry.

To put it another way, giving a positive answer to the question "Should writing be studied?" amounts to putting professional expertise at the head of the table, as the directing force of instruction, rather than the activity of composing. Downs and Wardle (2007) make this quite clear in their design of the first-year course as "Introduction to Writing Studies." As they explain, "our concern is not simply to improve writing instruction but also to improve the position of writing studies in the academy"; "change common misconceptions about writing" on the part of students, colleagues, academic administrators, and the public; and "potentially serve as a cornerstone course for writing studies majors beginning to take root across the country" (554). To do this, they reject (correctly, I believe) as a "category mistake" the notion of a generalized "academic writing" or "college writing" course that can be taught by any teacher to all students. Instead, a course devoted to writing studies presents a specialized body of knowledge and, accordingly, requires the instructor to be an "expert reader" of the field, who can guide students in reading the scholarly literature and formulating their own research questions, much in the same way professional credentials are required to teach introduction to psychology or physics or any other field.

There is much to like about the assignments Downs and Wardle describe—the reflective writing, including literacy narratives and autoethnographies; the work on "reading rhetorically and contributively"; the "primary research" projects students conduct; the panels and presentations of that research. In many respects, these are familiar activities to help students see how academic writing *works* as collaborative and conversational inquiry. What makes Downs and Wardle's "Introduction to Writing Studies" so telling, however, is not what they ask students to do but the reasons they give for the course. Their proposal, to be sure, challenges prevailing labor practices in composition that are based on "cultural misconceptions that anyone can teach writing because there is nothing special to know about it" (2007, 575). At the same time, it is important to note that they raise this challenge not on the grounds of social justice, to end exploitative labor relations, but in terms of professional control, to create a perfect monopoly on the provision of services by certified experts. For Downs and Wardle, the problem is how staffing the first-year course reinforces a cascade of misconceptions—"that writing is not a real subject, that writing courses do not require expert instructors, that rhetoric and composition are not genuine research areas or legitimate intellectual pursuits" but instead a "trivial, skill-teaching discipline" (553). One senses the invisible hand of Wendy Bishop's "Current-Market-Forces" at work here, where the aim is not so much redistributing professional expertise, which was more or less the standard model of collegewide writing programs, with writing centers and writing across the curriculum and writing in the disciplines programs, at the turn of the twenty-first century, but the consolidation and legitimation of professional expertise in a course and a discipline.

The response to Downs and Wardle from Libby Miles et al. (2008) in the Writing and Rhetoric Department at the University of Rhode Island makes a number of key points about the question "Should writing be studied?" and about what the future of writing studies might look like. First, they argue that the proposed "Introduction to Writing Studies" course, by focusing almost exclusively on empirical research projects and the scholarly research article, "is simply not rhetorical enough" (504) because it does not provide students with the range of rhetorical situations needed for a proper education in writing and rhetoric. Furthermore, for Miles et al., the proposed course does not represent the range of work that takes place under the auspices of writing studies, including "pure high theory; sometimes provocative exploratory discourse; sometimes historical recovery, or textual criticism, or anthropological micro-ethnographies, or personal memory work, educational philosophy, postmodern geography, environmental studies, critical information technology, even physiological and behavioral" research (510–11).

Second, they see the emphasis in Down and Wardle's proposal on the first-year course as itself a "limiting and limited perspective" for imagining how writing might be studied by undergraduates. For Miles et al., the first-year course has historically been asked to do too much, ending up in a state of what I've called "accumulative disequilibrium," overburdened by the demands of its various stakeholders and its layers of topics and practices. Here is just a partial list: to crack the academic code and manage the literacy tasks of college courses as intellectual conversations; to repair the damage done by high school English teachers; to demystify media and mass culture; to cultivate—and critique—taste; to understand the multimodality of writing and its channels of distribution; to use writing as a means of self-discovery; to negotiate linguistic and cultural differences in a transnational world; to enable students to communicate "effectively" in the workplace, multitask, and work on teams; and to halt the decline of public discourse by making a generation of slackers into responsible citizens (Trimbur 1999b,14). All of these are possible and reasonable learning objectives but, as Miles et al. point out, a vertical curriculum is needed to sequence them over time in a way that develops a deepening understanding of what writing is, how it circulates and takes on worldly force.

If anything, I think it is reasonable to say that it has been precisely the historical and theoretical construction of the first-year course, with all its debates about literacy, rhetoric, culture, and technology, that has laid the groundwork for a vertical curriculum dedicated to the study of writing. This is the result not just of practical teaching experience. Until quite recently, composition as an academic field has been organized in what an outsider might consider a very bizarre arrangement, with full-blown graduate programs turning out specialists on one end, a single required course (or two) for all entering first-year students on the other, and not much in between. But quantity turns into quality, and the years of intellectual investment and programmatic commitment at the graduate level to the first-year course have made a vertical curriculum thinkable precisely to the extent that our knowledges of writing are too much for a single course (or two) to contain. Instead of rehashing stale arguments about whether the first-year course should focus on academic writing, the personal essay, cultural critique, multimodal composing, writing studies, or something else, we might use the space of a vertical curriculum as the setting for a far-reaching discussion of the types of rhetorical situations, genres, and knowledges about writing that we want to teach and how to sequence them.

Third, Miles et al. object to Down and Wardle's suggestion that the first-year course should seek to recruit majors, as introductory courses in all fields have tended to do in the past, as out of step with current thinking about general education that sees the educational role of introductory courses as "teaching transferable procedural knowledge aimed at helping students make connections across disciplines" instead of bodies of knowledge (2008, 507). This is a good reminder that the transformation of first-year composition programs into writing studies departments does not convey the ideal of autonomy that academic disciplines and the professions more broadly like to claim for themselves, to regulate their own workings and pursue their own interests. The low status of composition in the past was linked, to be sure, to its service function in the academy, and, as Sharon Crowley (1998) has argued, this service orientation has weighed heavily on composition's impoverished sense of itself. Still, this does not mean that an increase in status will eliminate the responsibility to serve the institution's general educational mission, and the same is true of all departments, even high-prestige ones.

Finally, in a way that speaks directly to what an affirmative answer to the question "Should writing be studied?" might actually look like in pedagogical practice and program design, Miles et al. note that a four-year vertical curriculum makes it possible not so much to tell "students what Writing Studies is," as they believe Downs and Wardle do (or, as I would put it, to exercise the professional prerogative to correct student misconceptions), but rather "to learn from our students what it might be" (2008, 510). I want to take this comment seriously, to make sure it is not taken as simply a fleeting formulaic gesture on the part of the authors to reassure readers that they are still just as student-centered as anybody ever was at the height of the process movement. To my mind, it's a matter of how professionalism is articulated in initiatives to institutionalize writing studies, whether in the first-year course or a vertical curriculum.

The shift in questions from "How can writing be learned?" to "Should writing be studied?" has released anxieties, as we have seen, that the study of writing will replace the activity of composing and the seminar will replace the workshop as the primary location in the symbolic geography of the field. I think these fears are understandable, as Wendy Bishop (1999) makes us aware, but misplaced. There are good reasons to think the writing workshop and the seminar room devoted to the study of writing are dialectically related instead of counterposed. Joseph Harris (2010), for example, makes a very good case for how this can happen, when he describes how he uses the seminar format to bring in samples of student writing, not to workshop them but so that he, as the teacher and "expert reader," can talk about them, to explain to students, via direct instruction, what he sees as the issues of writing they contain.

For me, the question is why *wouldn't* he (or any other writing teacher) do that? Why wouldn't he tell students what he thinks, as their teacher, based on his professional expertise? Why would he limit his insights, as writing teachers often do, to end comments on student papers or conferences, individualizing and atomizing his knowledge in a way that may be useful to a single student writer but that remains inaccessible to the whole class?

My belief is that these questions point to a self-imposed limit enacted by the process movement's fear of its own authority. No academic field that I know of has been so reticent as composition in bringing its knowledge to students in an explicit way. Of all the fields teaching first-year courses, composition must surely be the most reluctant to name names, identify contributions, chart trends, describe controversies, and otherwise introduce students to the intellectual life of their field of study. Embedding this knowledge in the indirection of workshop practices is not as benign or student-centered as it might seem, for it also obscures the sources of knowledge, keeps them out of student sight, and, dangerously, makes teaching appear to be a personal rather than a professional relationship between instructor and student. No wonder students are always asking writing teachers "What are you looking for?" The issue is not just that response to writing is always a subjective matter. It's that writing teachers don't explain sufficiently the formation of their own subjectivities as "expert readers," to present it as a phenomenon that can be talked about, investigated, and interrogated with students.

This, of course, is in part what Downs and Wardle (2007) are addressing in their proposal to make the first-year course into "Introduction to Writing Studies." But they put the matter of knowledge so thoroughly in terms of correcting student misconceptions and consolidating professional expertise and disciplinary status that they miss what I take to be a critical aim in designing writing studies courses, programs, and majors that Miles et al. point to: namely, how can writing studies make transparent and teachable the social relations and bodies of knowledge that have silently underwritten the first-year course—to organize the study of writing as an intellectual resource for undergraduates and a site of coinvestigation for writing studies faculty and their students?

# PART THREE

# Expert and Lay Knowledges

The three essays in this section examine the relationship between official and popular knowledges. The first two, "Popularizing Science: At the Boundary of Expert and Lay Biomedical Knowledge" (Chapter Six) and "Popular Literacy and the Resources of Print Culture: The South African Committee on Higher Education" (Chapter Seven), are case studies of how expertise was linked to popular aspirations in grassroots health movements in the United States and in the antiapartheid struggles of the 1980s in South Africa. The third, "Composition and the Circulation of Writing" (Chapter Eight), develops a conceptual framework to design writing assignments and writing courses that investigate the cultural authorization of expertise, the contradictions of professional practice, and the possibilities of socially useful knowledge. Taken together, these essays are meant to serve as evidence that the idea of rearticulating professional ways of knowing to the experience and understandings of ordinary people is not just a theoretical horizon but is in fact imaginable and possible as a practical undertaking.

The first two essays were inspired by converging developments within U.S. college composition in the mid- to late-1990s—the turn to public writing, popular literacy, and activist rhetorics, on one hand, and the emergence of writing studies as a mode of inquiry, on the other. In retrospect, it is crucial to note how writing theorists and researchers recast the work of composition studies by examining ordinary writing, grassroots literacies, rhetorics of civil society, and the formation of public forums and counter publics on their own terms, without reference to how they meshed or conflicted with schooled literacy, as had been the case, for example, in such landmark works as Shirley Brice Heath's *Ways with Words* (1983), where the literacy practices of white and African American working-class communities are analyzed in relation to the mainstream literacy practices of the schools, to identify the cultural and sociolinguistic sources of success and failure.

I do not mean to suggest it is not useful to understand how various literacies intersect and interact in and out of school and how they enter into social and cultural judgments about individuals (including students), language practices, and the value of forms of writing. The point, rather, is that by designating schooled literacy as the point of comparison, its cultural dominance and official status create a hierarchy of writing by identifying what the unsanctioned literacies of home and community lack or have been deprived of. In a society and educational system where the representational resources of print culture remain unevenly distributed, this is an important insight. The problem is that the very terms of comparison exert selective pressures on evidence, analysis, and interpretation; the danger is that schooled literacy can come to be seen as not just dominant but *normative*, the unmarked term by which all other literacies are known and the target of pedagogical intervention. Here we may sense the ethos of service in the background, as an instance of how perceptions of need not only shape research design but also activate the social conscience to provide what is lacking.

One of the accomplishments of writing studies in its early phase was to release writing from a comparative framework and to change the question from how home or community literacies enable or constrain students' encounters with schooled literacy to how ordinary people invest the activities of reading and writing with social, cultural, and political meanings. The conceptual turn, as I see it, begins by asking not only how official and popular literacies stand in relation to each other as cultural categories but also how individuals and groups make literacy popular—how they articulate practices of reading and writing to the formation of identities, interests, institutions, and ways of life.

This shift, which is often signified as "postprocess," is now more or less taken for granted, and yet it seems an important and largely neglected development in U.S. college composition's sense of its topics, professional identity, and intellectual projects. For one thing, it signifies a critical break with composition's long-standing dependence on the first-year writing course or schooled writing more generally as its conceptual universe and *raison d'être*. It has been difficult for composition specialists to imagine investigating forms of writing without reference to schooled literacy. Recall, for example, that one of the first studies of writing in the workplace was titled "Writing in a Non-Academic Setting" (Odell and Goswami 1982), which clearly granted academic writing the unmarked status, appearing in 1982, one year before *Ways with Words* (Heath 1983). Even Anne Ruggles Gere's groundbreaking 1993 CCCC Chair's Address "Kitchen Tables and

Rented Rooms: The Extracurriculum of Composition" (1994) still marked popular literacies as "extra" or a surplus to composition's curriculum, while simultaneously making a powerful argument for cultural studies of literacy.

The "pedagogical imperative" that Lynn Worsham (1991) was the first to identify has weighed heavily on U.S. college composition, with its pressures to make research and theory serve the first-year writing curriculum. These pressures remain, at least residually, in writing studies' sense of its work—and they should not be dismissed out of hand. But there can be little question that studies of "nonacademic" writing based on archival sources, ethnographies of grassroots writing, and participant observation in social advocacy now possess a kind of legitimacy that was simply not imaginable when I started teaching writing in the 1970s. The result is that writing studies has enhanced its claim to disciplinary status, at the same time activist rhetoricians have found new prospects to work and to write in solidarity with community organizations, unions, art groups, and political movements.

Chapter Six, "Popularizing Science: At the Boundary of Expert and Lay Biomedical Knowledge," was cowritten with Lundy Braun and draws extensively on her work with breast cancer activists in the National Breast Cancer Coalition's Project LEAD, an educational initiative to train laypeople to participate in scientific knowledge making by sitting on study sections to review grant applications, institutional review boards, data-monitoring committees, and advisory councils. It also taps into our joint interest in how science is popularized by the press, the media, and increasingly by scientists and scientific organizations and how this "public understanding of science" differs from the efforts of grassroots activists in environmental health, breast cancer, and AIDS movements to refashion the available identities of an informed public, a disease constituency, or health consumers into that of lay experts with the scientific knowledge and rhetorical agency to participate in determining what counts as "good science."

Chapter Seven grew out of research I have been doing in South Africa since 2001. "Popular Literacy and the Resources of Print Culture: The South African Committee on Higher Education" examines various educational projects on the part of SACHED during the anti-apartheid struggles of the 1980s and early 1990s. I am particularly interested in how SACHED turned from its early work, which focused on providing access to academic certification and credentials, to projects with trade unions and community organizations and to adult education outside the institutions of formal learning. The issue of how to redistribute expertise was an immediate and practical one for SACHED, as well as for other organizations allied to the liberation movement, and it raised difficult questions about the relation between experts and laypeople and about solidarity or service as the motive of activists. What the essay adds to these recurring themes is a particular attention to the resources of representation available in print culture, including questions about genre awareness and the multimodal possibilities of various forms of writing to develop a sense of rhetorical agency and to imagine a nonracial political future.

The underlying theme of how professionalized expertise can be transformed into socially useful knowledge by popular movements, along with a reprise of the breast cancer and AIDS activism examples, appears in the final chapter, "Composition and the Circulation of Writing." This essay amounts, from one perspective, to my final attempt to come to terms with what a "cultural studies approach to teaching writing" might mean in U.S. college composition, and I rely here on a reading of Karl Marx's *Grundrisse* (1973) to make a case for a materialist framework that represents writing as it circulates through the interlocked and mutually interdependent moments of production, distribution, exchange, and consumption as rhetorical transformations or "passages of form." My ambition in this essay was twofold: first, to go beyond notions of intertextuality and explanations by David R. Russell (1997) and others of how genres constitute "activity systems" to comprehend how the circulation of writing authorizes, distributes, and exchanges expertise within a total system that reproduces not just pockets of intellectual work but capitalist social relations within a dominant mode of production; and second, to devise pedagogical strategies, writing assignments, and writing courses that make the circulation of writing a topic of inquiry in composition's curriculum.

Looking back on this essay, I see an unintentional irony operating, namely that the shift from the pedagogical imperative that linked U.S. college composition's identity to the first-year writing curriculum to a more expansive notion of what it might mean to study writing has, in effect, influenced composition pedagogy in decisive ways. At least, that is what I'm trying to suggest in this essay. In many respects, the question is the same one I started with years ago teaching basic writing, about how lives and writing go together in the racialized and gendered realities of class society. The difference is how the terms and frameworks available to carry out this investigation have changed over the thirty-five years I've been teaching writing.

# Chapter Six

# Popularizing Science

## At the Boundary of Expert and Lay Biomedical Knowledge

It is no mystery to anyone who reads the popular and scientific press that biomedicine is big business. In the United States, scientists argue that large-scale investment in biomedical research will not only improve individual health but also play a central role in the emerging knowledge economy. After the ups and downs of federal funding during the Bush years 2000 to 2008, when the physical sciences were favored at the expense of biomedicine, the Obama administration has demonstrated significant support for the National Institutes of Health (NIH), including a $10.4 billion two-year infusion of stimulus package money in 2009 and a $1 billion or 3.2 percent increase in the 2011 NIH budget. At the press conference announcing the 2011 budget, Department of Health and Human Services Secretary Kathleen Sebelius "highlighted genomics-based studies at NIH and pointed to other plans to initiate 30 new drug trials in 2011 and to double the number of novel compounds in clinical trials by 2016" ("Obama's 'Restrained' 2011 Budget" 2010). In a fiscal year when discretionary nonmilitary spending, such as social programs for the poor, was frozen to rein in the federal deficit, this increase in funding reveals the lure of commercializing biomedical discoveries as well as the broader cultural expectation of conquering disease.

For science policy makers, the sustained flow of tax dollars and labor power needed to realize the potential of "translational" research in gene therapy and drug development depends on an informed public. The citizenry, as voters and workers, must be recruited, in effect, to the research enterprise, persuaded of the public's stake in the ongoing work of science. Accordingly, the leading professional organizations in science have called in recent years for campaigns to increase the public's understanding of science.

Traditionally aloof from public involvement, governed, at least in Robert K. Merton's (1973) classic account, by norms of disinterestedness and humility, bench scientists would hardly seem likely candidates to be public spokespersons, and yet that is exactly what the scientific organizations have been urging them to do since the 1990s—to "go public," to get out of the laboratory and find public forums where they can communicate the promise of biomedical research. If anything, this trend to campaign on behalf of science intensified during the Bush administration, with the politicization of federal science by market and religious fundamentalist appointees.

The public involvement of scientists takes many forms: participation in science education programs in local schools, developing formal and informal lecture series for the public, fostering a collaborative relationship with the popular media, and lobbying Congressional leaders. The National Science Foundation (NSF) has funded "scientifically literate" college students to work in public schools. The National Cancer Institute (NCI) has conducted a series of focus groups to assess scientists' ideas on communicating medical research findings and the public's perception of medical research ("Communicating Science to the Public" 1998). In 2007, the American Association for the Advancement of Science formed a partnership with the National School Boards Association to promote the teaching of science, technology, engineering, and mathematics—and to counter the inroads of creationism, intelligent design, climate change denialism, and abstinence-only campaigns in public schools.

The idea of scientists communicating with a broad public audience is, to be sure, a laudable one, with historical roots in nineteenth-century popular traditions of democratic learning and the diffusion of useful knowledge through mechanics institutes, lecture series, lending libraries, and so on and in the cooperative extension services at land grant universities, established by the Smith-Lever Act of 1914 to bring information about soil science, agriculture, animal husbandry, home economics, and related topics to rural communities. The question remains, though, concerning the nature of the communication and the types of relationships "going public" is meant to establish between scientists and nonexperts. In some cases, such as the 1998 creation at NIH of the Director's Council of Public Representatives, the scientific establishment has sought input from the public, to get advice on policy matters and insight into the public's perception of official science. In the biomedical community, progressive health care workers have developed programs that take advantage of the rich social networks in communities to help improve access and delivery of medical care (cf. Thomas et al. 1998). Nonetheless, the methods scientists use to communicate to laypeople are based, for the most part, on a unidirectional flow of information, from scientific experts to the lay public, often times with the media as go-between. The boundaries between science and nonscience are thought to be clear and unambiguous, and the usually unstated goal of this linear transmission model is to inform the public while maintaining the authority of scientists over knowledge-making practices. According to this model, scientists, not the public, are responsible for determining what research questions are worthy of study, which methodological approaches are relevant, how scientific data are interpreted, and what policy initiatives derive from scientific findings.

Studies of the popularization of scientific knowledge have analyzed how science writers employ various genres to translate the findings of practicing scientists to educated readers (cf. Myers 1990, 141–92). These analyses are useful in what they can tell us about how the popular as well as the scientific press helps maintain the cultural authority of science by reinforcing the boundary between experts and laypeople, producers and consumers of knowledge. What such analyses fail to explore, however, is how laypeople might reimagine their relationship to scientific expertise and become actively engaged in constructing scientific knowledge. By focusing largely on discursive practices, such as genre analysis and rhetoric of inquiry, studies of popular science have, for the most part, overlooked the literate practices that lay activists have devised to popularize science. Beginning in the 1970s with Love Canal, "popular epidemiologists" in grassroots toxic waste movements, as well as AIDS activists and breast cancer organizers who emerged in the 1980s, have struggled to redefine the relationship of laypeople to the biomedical establishment.

In this essay, we explore the relationship between the biomedical research establishment and the public, how this relationship is shaped by popular media accounts of biomedical research, and how popular movements of lay activists are seeking to rearticulate the expert knowledge of official science. As we show, recent efforts by lay activists to popularize science involve not only the acquisition and circulation of scientific knowledge but also a change in the relationship of nonspecialists to the reading and writing practices of scientific experts. For lay activists, popularizing science means participating in its knowledge-making practices.

## Public Understanding of Science

A variety of terms, including *scientific communication, scientific literacy, the rhetoric of science,* and *science education,* are currently used by scholars and scientific organizations to represent the *relationship* of the public to science and its institutions. The terms point to different communication strategies on the part of official science and different areas of research in the academic disciplines (sociology, science studies, communication, rhetoric, education, and public health). This scholarship and the efforts of scientists and laypeople to make science public have been thematized by the term *public understanding of science* (with its unfortunate acronym PUS). What is actually meant by *understanding* in this formulation of the public's relation to the scientific enterprise remains unresolved, a contested terms that refers variously to notions of "appreciation," "acquisition of knowledge," and "ability to use."

In the postwar period, with the military victories of World War II attributed to such scientific and technological advances as penicillin, synthetic rubber, and the atomic bomb, public attitudes toward science were generally enthusiastic, although scientists and policy makers considered the public's knowledge lacking in scientific facts. The launching of Sputnik in 1957 only seemed to confirm the fears of the scientific establishment, which led to major investments in scientific research and in educational initiatives such as the new math and new science curricula designed to introduce students to scientific ways of reasoning.

The success of this investment was assessed in the 1970s and 1980s by a series of quantitative surveys administered to adults to test their scientific literacy (Gregory and Miller 1998, 5). The results shocked scientists and policy makers. Scientific literacy was low in the United States and seemed to be declining, from a high of 14 percent considered scientifically literate in 1979 to a low of 5 percent by 1985. A 1997 NSF survey measuring public attitudes and understanding of science found that many Americans could not define molecules or DNA or even how often the earth revolves around the sun. According to the survey's findings, respondents' interest in science and technology, nearly 70 percent, was at an all-time high, but only one in four Americans understood the nature of scientific investigation well enough to make informed judgments about scientific results reported in the media. In addition, the survey showed that public attitudes toward science and technology were divided, especially over the impact of such technological developments as the use of nuclear power to generate electricity and genetic testing. The upshot for official science, as then NSF director Neal Lane put it, is that "the public has not given science a blank check, and the scientific community needs to communicate its work more clearly and effectively" ("Americans Are Interested in Science" 1998, 1127).

Concern among American scientists about the public understanding of science intensified during the 1990s, largely as a result of sharp cuts in the federal budget for scientific research. These cuts not only jeopardized the careers of a generation of basic scientists, but also threatened efforts to develop new therapies for a wide range of diseases. Since the budget cuts of the 1990s coincided with new research advances on the biological mechanisms of cell growth, there was great fear that the opportunity to translate basic research from molecular biology and biochemistry to the clinical realm would be lost. Accordingly, through their professional associations, many research scientists went public, to persuade ordinary citizens of the biomedical promise of new research findings on the inner workings of the cell and to increase federal funding for basic research, even while draconian cuts, during the Clinton administration, were made in education, welfare, health care, and social services. After basic scientists' intense lobbying of Congress, Harold Varmus, a prominent molecular virologist and Nobel laureate at the University of California at San Francisco (now Director of NCI and cochair of the Council of Advisors on Science and Technology in the Obama administration), made a surprising shift from laboratory to public policy and was appointed Director of the NIH by President Clinton.

It is difficult to assess the effects of this transition from the laboratory to the public forum. *Science and Engineering Indicators: 2010* (National Science Board 2010), reveals widespread support for scientific research, reporting that 84 percent of Americans back federal funding for basic research; that nearly 90 percent believe "because of science and technology, there will be more opportunities for the next generation"; and that Americans express a "great deal" of confidence in scientists and a high degree of interest in science and technology. The data also show that the public's factual knowledge about science has changed little since earlier studies and that television and the Internet are now the primary sources of information.

While the survey results of leading indicators remain mixed, with high levels of support and interest but relatively low levels of knowledge, there is little ambiguity about what scientists believe an understanding of science entitles the public to say and do. These limits became apparent when two important social movements of patient advocates—AIDs and breast cancer activists—demanded and obtained substantial increases in the allocation of funds targeted to AIDS and breast cancer research. In addition, activists demanded direct involvement on committees such as institutional review boards that evaluate the ethics of research on human subjects and study sections that assess the merit of scientific research proposals. For many in the basic research community, the expanded participation of laypeople in the workings of biomedicine amounted to no more than concessions to interest group politics. Instead of picturing the involvement of lay activists as widening the public understanding of science, some in the scientific establishment regarded movements for popular participation in science as a dangerous infringement on basic researchers' freedom to explore the secrets of nature, unfettered by what the scientists thought of as the special interests of consumer advocates and disease constituencies.

In the main, official science has favored education rather than popular participation as the vehicle of extending public understanding of science. The belief in an ongoing scientific literacy crisis, ostensibly demonstrated by the surveys of American adults already mentioned, as well as the declining performances of American elementary and secondary students on international standardized measures, including the 2006 Program for International Student Assessment (National Science Board 2010), has offered a powerful instigation for reform in science education—to recruit the best and brightest students, to overcome the alienation of women and minorities from science, and to prepare the citizenry to understand such issues as nanotechnology, medical marijuana, genetically engineered food, alternative medicine, and physician-assisted suicide. This sense of crisis, however, concerns more than just the public's knowledge of science. For the scientific and biomedical establishment, what is at stake in the public's understanding is the cultural prestige of science and the need to forge and maintain a public consensus on the authority of basic research and mainstream medical practices.

To consolidate such a consensus, mainstream programs for the public understanding of science tend to rely on finished accounts of scientific research, success stories in which knowledge is portrayed as complete, unproblematical, and certain. Mini–medical schools, for example, featuring university medical faculty, started to pop up across the country in the 1990s to explain the latest breakthroughs in research and clinical practice. There are now at least 70 mini–medical programs, including summer camps for high school students and shadow-a-doctor days for adults, and the mini–med schools have spread to Canada, Ireland, and Malta. Sometimes free and other times at costs that keep the programs at least theoretically accessible to a broad audience, the programs now draw thousands of participants and provide scientists and physicians with a public forum to present new discoveries in genetics, genetics testing, and genetics therapy, along with the latest advances in neurosciences, infectious disease, and immunology.

The mini–med school's lecture format, of course, is designed to transmit information rather than engage in exchange with the public. Moreover, by focusing on biomedical success stories, in which scientific knowledge appears to be fully formed, replicable, and accurate, these programs mask the uncertainty and dynamic nature of scientific research. They promote a public understanding of science as a hierarchy of knowledge in which scientific expertise is pictured as "real" and "true," authenticated by laboratory work and clinical studies, where scientific objectivity is immune to the passions of the public forum, above the fragmentary, interested, and incomplete accounts of nonexperts. In turn, the public is cast as passive recipients of a predetermined body of information with little or no attention to what the public thinks they should know, how scientists could most productively share their technical expertise with laypeople, or what the nature of lay knowledges may be.

## Policing the Boundaries Between Scientific and Popular Knowledge

This polarization of expert and lay knowledge has marked the relationship between official science and the public as one of suspicion and frustration. The communication of scientific information in simplified form, stripped of uncertainty and complexity, leaves the public frustrated by locating them outside the realm of knowledge making, marginalized and acutely aware of the asymmetrical distribution of scientific expertise. It should not be surprising, then, that the public's sentiments toward science are frequently ambivalent, ranging from feelings of dependence and vulnerability to eruptions of hostility to the mandates of experts, noncompliance, and passive resistance. By the same token, scientists are frustrated when the information they communicate is not received in a "correct" way, leading to what scientists perceive to be irrational public policy brought about by ignorance and a failure to follow the norms of scientific reasoning. Instead of mutual understanding, we have border skirmishes between experts and laypeople, at the boundary between official and popular science.

The widespread use of alternative medicine by the American public in the face of vehement opposition by the biomedical community offers a good example of such a skirmish about what legitimately counts as health care and who are the rightful bearers of medical knowledge. It is estimated that $34 billion are spent annually on alternative medicine in the United States, or 11 percent of overall out-of-pocket spending on medical care. A 2007 study by the Centers for Disease Control and Prevention found that about 38 percent of American adults use alternative therapies, such as massage, acupuncture, herbal remedies, megavitamins, chiropractors, naturopaths, and so on ("34 Billion"). Even more significant, many do not inform their primary care physician of these practices.

Many scientists and physicians, especially in the United States, view the public's interest in alternative medicine with suspicion and anger, as a "flight-from-reason" that threatens the authority of Western medicine to determine the scientific approach to disease and health. For much of the medical establishment, alternative medicine is just further proof of the public's ignorance of science and, along with creationism, climate change denial, UFOs, feminism, and cultural studies of science, a rejection of reason and objectivity. In a public expression of frustration, Arnold S. Relman, editor-in-chief emeritus of the *New England Journal of Medicine*, argued that there "are not two kinds of medicine. Nor . . . are there two kinds of thinking, or two ways to find out which treatments work and which do not" (1998, 37).

In fact, the public's interest in alternative medicine is not based on a rejection of Western medicine but on a rejection of Relman's argument that there is only one type of medical knowledge worth having. A closer look at the debate over alternative medicine reveals a more complex and ambivalent relationship of the public to medical treatment. The public has certainly not abandoned Western medicine but, at the same time, individuals refuse to exclude the unratified popular knowledge of alternative medicine. Perhaps most frustrating to Relman and other spokespersons for biomedical orthodoxy is that the public's understanding of science recognizes the artificial nature of distinctions between official and popular knowledges. Understandably, the public want to have it both ways.

There is no question that medical treatment should be based on the best-designed studies. Since few alternative therapies have been rigorously tested in clinical trials, the gold standard of mainstream medicine, physicians are legitimately concerned about possible drug interactions in the case of alternative medicines that contain biologically active substances. But more is at stake in the controversy over alternative medicine than potential toxicities, or that alternative treatments may delay the use of more effective ones. Indeed, many mainstream medical treatments have not undergone clinical trials either, and even the most elegant experimental work, whether in laboratory research or clinical trials, may result in uncertainty. The problem with Relman's polarized "kinds of medicine" and "ways of thinking" is that they demand a choice of social allegiances—with us or against us—but offer the public little in the way of handling ambiguity or making sense of differing interpretations, when there is no clear consensus among scientists and physicians.

The debate in the late 1990s over mammography screening guidelines for women aged forty to forty-nine illustrates what can happen when the evidence is ambiguous. After several highly charged meetings of the National Cancer Advisory Board and much politicking behind the scenes, the NCI issued guidelines in 1997 that recommended mammographies every one to two years for women forty years and older. Evidence from randomized controlled clinical trials clearly demonstrated that screening reduces mortality for women over the age of fifty. These studies were not controversial at the time. On the other hand, evidence of benefit for women under fifty was much less certain, and scientists differed in their interpretations of the data. Not surprisingly, these equivocal results turned into a heated controversy.

Some argued that evidence of harm due to false-positives outweighed any protective effect of screening for women under fifty. On the other side, advocates of screening, including the American Cancer Society, radiologists, and manufacturers of mammography machines, claimed that the benefits are overriding. Faced with such differing interpretations of inconclusive evidence, advocacy groups were split. The National Breast Cancer Coalition, the Center for Medical Consumers, and the National Women's Health Network argued that the scientific evidence was not sufficient to recommend screening for women under fifty, while other groups advocated strongly that screening programs include women under fifty on the grounds that screening is one of the few ways they can control the risk of breast cancer.

For others, however, the real problem was neither the evidence nor the interpretations but the controversy itself. According to Jane Wells, writing in the *British Medical Journal*, "the necessity of screening for breast cancer among women in their 40s has assumed an importance out of proportion to its impact on public health" (1998, 1228). While admitting reasonable differences among experts in interpreting the scientific data, Wells went on to question the reasonableness of the public's response. The problem, as she saw it, is that the public found the uncertainty of experimental evidence unacceptable: the "public has been taught to believe in scientific and medical infallibility" and thereby "the expectations of the public and the media contributed to the pressure for definitive guidelines" (1228).

In Wells' account of the mammography controversy, the public is an obstacle to sound clinical practice, in part because of their ignorance of science but also in part because of their unquestioning belief in it. "When trials do not give an unequivocal answer," she says, "when politicians and interest groups become involved, and when professionals responsible for promoting the public's best interest fail to do so, objectivity is likely to suffer" (1228). Rather than acknowledging that the response of the public may be a legitimate way to manage the scientific uncertainty about mammography, the lay public (as well as certain groups of scientists, physicians, and politicians) are blamed for contaminating the establishment of policy informed by scientific principles.

Wells is certainly correct that the public has been taught to believe in the infallibility of science. But she fails to locate the origins of this idea in the institutions of science itself and how they authorize experts as the best interpreters of science for the general public. An alternative way of thinking about the debate over mammography screening would hold that the public did not misunderstand or misinterpret the issues, including the scientific questions, at all. Although guidelines to screen women under fifty may be off the mark, since there is no scientific evidence that such screening increases survival, we would argue that the controversy represents not only a problem in interpreting data but an attempt to renegotiate boundaries, with the nonexpert public taking an active role in defining their relationship with experts. In the absence of a compelling demonstration based on the evidence, the public was simply doing the only thing available, namely, engaging in the deliberative rhetoric of policy making, where the boundary between expert and lay knowledges is a permeable one.

## Boundary Making and the Media

As popularizers of science, positioned between scientists and the public, the media plays a crucial role in regulating the boundary between expert and lay knowledges. For their part, scientists and physicians may feel plagued by what they perceive to be crude and inaccurate representations of their work and exaggerated accounts of cures in the press. At the same time, scientists acknowledge that the media is in a powerful position to influence public opinion and, therefore, is an important mechanism for communicating scientific ideas to the public. Seminars in interacting with the media, for example, have become commonplace at professional scientific meetings and as a component of graduate education.

In *Selling Science*, Dorothy Nelkin (1995) argues that popular accounts of science in the media are characterized by several features, including imagery in the place of content, superficial explanations of research, a focus on the competitive nature of science, and the representation of the scientist as savior (5–7). Promises of cure—for cancer, heart disease, arthritis—carry the most dramatic appeal for the public and often end up on the front page of the news, shaping public views of the "miracles" of biomedicine but also setting up the grounds for subsequent feelings of vulnerability and anxiety when further studies qualify the initial promise of research and new treatments and introduce uncertainty into the picture.

There is no question that science journalism varies greatly in quality. Some accounts are sensationalized, exaggerated, or grossly distorted, whereas others do an excellent job of communicating the best available understanding of biomedical topics in a way that is of value to the public. However, the "difficulty of writing 'popular' articles about science," as Bruno Latour (1987) points out, does not hinge on matters of accuracy or inaccuracy, responsibility or sensationalism. Instead, the difficulty "is a good measure of the accumulation of resources in the hands of a few scientists. . . . It is hard to popularize science because it is designed to force out most people in the first place" (52). Science journalists must struggle daily with an overwhelming amount of highly technical information, trying to balance their own critical judgment of science, the cultural authority of scientific expertise, and the fragility of their networks with practicing scientists.

Nelkin calls particular attention to the relations between journalists and scientists and how they function as "wary collaborators" in the popularization of science (1995, 7). On one hand, both groups share a positivist view of science and the common belief that professional expertise is the final arbiter of what counts as science. In turn, they cast the public variably as passive, duped, dangerous, or irrational consumers of scientific information who are in need of science to make "informed" personal decisions, expected to support rational public policy, but excluded from participation in scientific knowledge-making practices. On the other hand, the norms and values of the two professions differ in their judgment of what is news, what counts as evidence, the distinction between simplification and accuracy, and the relevance of the social and political context to understanding science.

The shifting and ambivalent relationship between scientists and journalists is neither innocent nor disinterested, and official science cannot be understood simply as the external source of knowledge that popular science transmits to the public. Instead, as Nelkin argues, science is a coparticipant with science writers in the construction of popular science. In some instances, scientists seek to use the media to shape public understanding and advance broad agendas for research. For example, following the publication in the *New England Journal of Medicine* of an article that claimed to find no association between exposure to DDT and PCBs and incidence of breast cancer (Hunter et al. 1997), the research group's principal investigator David J. Hunter suggested to a *New York Times* reporter that "perhaps it was time to question the assumption that much breast cancer is caused by unknown environmental agents" (quoted in Kolata 1997, A19)—thereby jumping from the possible elimination of DDT and PCBs in the causation of breast cancer to the elimination of environmental agents altogether, a sweeping and, at least in some scientific circles, highly contested view of the etiology of breast cancer.

Other scientists take on a watchdog role and make it their mission to correct the perceived distortions and misrepresentations of science rampant in the media. This view casts the media as driven by special interest groups, hidden agendas, and an appetite for sensationalism. For example, an article published by a group of investigators in the *American Journal of Public Health* (Frost, Frank, and Maibach 1997) claimed that media reporting of relative risk of mortality is particularly liable to distortion, with serious implications for public health policy. The authors cite as evidence of biased reporting the fact that although homicide ranks eleventh as a cause of death, it received similar press coverage as heart disease, which is the leading cause of death in the United States. What is striking about Frost et al.'s analysis is not only that it ignores there might be legitimate reasons for reporting homicide as opposed to heart disease, given that death from heart disease tends to occur in older age groups and is seen as a natural cause of death compared to the more newsworthy homicide, which is an unnatural and shocking event. The analysis also contends that the real issue is who will control the scientific understanding of a public that is easily misled by biased and inaccurate accounts of risk. "Health professionals," Frost et al. assert, "must focus the attention of the news media and the public on the health issues of greatest concern so that the most prevalent receive appropriate attention" (1999, 844). Notice that the media and public are marked as problematic, with health professionals responsible for determining what health issues warrant the greatest concern.

There is an important sense in which scientists' concerns about the media acknowledge that the popularization of science does not simply transmit information, whether accurately or inaccurately, between experts and laypeople but also shapes the relationship between them. While scientists may seek to use or correct science reporting, accounts of popular science provide readers with information from the laboratory and clinic as well as strategies for managing their relationship to the specialized world of biomedicine and concentration of power and expertise in the hands of health professionals. Media accounts offer readers various ways to compensate for their sense of powerlessness and vulnerability and to recognize themselves in relation to health professionals—for example, as deferential patients, anxious consumers, or do-it-yourself healers.

The dominant strategy—and certainly the preferred and most common one in the establishment press—is that of deference. For example, a 1996 *New York Times* article "Aspirin Proposed for Suspected Heart

Attacks," reports a study that found taking as little as half a regular-strength aspirin at the onset of suspected heart attack significantly reduced the risk of death. The article warns, however, in a dramatic pull quote, that "patients should not act on their own." Certainly there is a reasonable concern, voiced by one of the physicians interviewed for the article, that "patients might try treating themselves without consulting their doctors" (Leary 1996, C9) and then simply wait for the symptoms to subside. What is telling for our purposes, though, is how the article addresses the reader. Typical of science coverage in the establishment press, the article offers readers an accurate and responsibly written account of recent biomedical research and, at the same time, provides them with a reassuring recognition of themselves as patients under a doctor's care.

In other instances, especially in medical advice columns and articles in newspapers and magazines, popular science writing addresses readers not so much as compliant patients but as anxious consumers. Women's magazines in particular mediate consumer anxieties about current medical practices, such as recommended prevention measures, testing and screening, and treatment. In these popular accounts, the boundary between experts and laypeople, so reassuringly in place in the *New York Times* article, is figured as less reliable and perhaps treacherous. The *Glamour* article "How OB-GYNs Fail Women: Read This Before Your Next Checkup" (Laurence 1997) is a typical example, reporting in this case on a survey showing "that doctors are dangerously silent about the most important threat to young women's health," namely sexually transmitted diseases (293). The strategy offered readers here is not one of deference but of distrust. By problematizing the authority of physicians, the article casts the reader back on her own resources and the need for vigilant and informed consumerism. To the extent that a young woman must rely on herself rather than her doctor, the lines between experts and laypeople are blurred as agency shifts from the medical establishment to the individual, although she remains atomized and anxious in the face of a health care system where so much can go wrong. Another *Glamour* article "Your Pap Smear: A Save-Your-Life Guide" acknowledges the pap smear as "one of medicine's success stories" but then goes on to warn women that doctors and cytotechnologists can and do make mistakes. The conclusion is that "you need to do everything you can to reduce the risk of error on your next Pap" (Young 1997, 208).

If the genre of medical advice, with its "eight steps" and "eleven warning signs," offers readers a strategy to manage their relationship to doctors and to compensate for their relative powerlessness by becoming active and informed consumers, a third type of popular science—the do-it-yourself remedies offered by tabloids and alternative health magazines—validates popular knowledges by discounting the authority of official biomedicine altogether. Such remedies range from traditional dietary and herbal folklore, some of which are efficacious, to the magical thinking of crackpot wonder cures, some of which are outright dangerous. The tabloid *Weekly World News*, for example, featured in its 24 October 1995 issue the front-page news "Golden Raisins and Gin Cure Arthritis." The cover story reports the findings of the "noted nutritionist Dr. Lorenzo Abatz" that "for reasons we don't completely understand, the combination of gin and golden raisins acts as a healing lubricant in the human body" (Victoria 1995, 9). In the sensationalized pseudoscience of the tabloids, the mysterious power of gin and golden raisins concocts a kind of magical potion that escapes scientific explanation.

Although it may appear at first glance to be simply a denial of scientific authority, the appeal of such magic is in fact an expression of the powerlessness, disappointment, and desperation when orthodox medical treatments fail to relieve the pain of arthritis sufferers. Unlike the *New York Times* or *Glamour*, the *Weekly World News* is not just offering a way to mediate between experts and laypeople. Its own peculiar directions about how to prepare the gin-soaked raisins are meant to empower readers as self-healers. The relationship of this type of popular science to the medical establishment is made clear in the article's closing passages, where it notes that although the "mainstream medical community has been slow to embrace Dr. Abatz' plan . . . the Boston-based researcher's files are filled with passionate testimonials" (Victoria 1995, 9). In the do-it-yourself world of tabloid science, the personal witnessing of magical cures is really a compensatory gesture, a kind of wishful thinking in the face of the skeptical orthodoxy of the experts.

## Lay Activism and Popularization of Scientific Knowledge

The media's popularization of science negotiates in various ways the exclusion of nonexpert readers from the knowledge-making practices of science. Beginning with Love Canal in the 1970s, however, when residents of Niagara Falls noticed unusual clusters of health problems, which they linked to the dumping of hazardous wastes by local companies, community activists have challenged these formidable barriers between experts and laypeople and, in the process, helped to shape the intellectual content of the emerging fields of environmental epidemiology and environmental health. In addition, AIDS and breast cancer activists have also sought to blur the line between official and popular knowledges. These struggles, to be sure, have been long and difficult ones that highlight profound differences between lay and professional ways of knowing, while at the same time offering telling examples of popular participation in what counts as good science.

Differences in the way scientists and lay activists think about science may be seen in the legal case brought to national attention by the book *A Civil Action* (Harr 1996) and its film version. Residents of Woburn, Massachusetts, charged W. R. Grace Chemical Company and Beatrice Foods that their illegal dumping of trichloroethylene (TCE) had contaminated the drinking water of two wells and caused an unusually high incidence of childhood leukemia. Although Beatrice Foods was found not guilty in the jury trial and W. R. Grace settled out of court for $8 million (a fraction of the anticipated legal award), ultimately the Environmental Protection Agency sued both companies, who were forced to spend millions to clean up the site.

Cancer clusters, as occurred in Woburn, where the etiology of cancer is unknown, pose a particular challenge to interpret, primarily because the numbers of cases are often too small to draw causal inferences with any certainty and may represent nothing more than chance variation in geographic location of a disease. The suffering of the affected population and their desire to know the origin of their disease, however, are real, no matter what difficulties and uncertainties surround the professional study of disease clusters. For this reason, the Woburn activists' sense of urgency often brought them into conflict with legal and scientific experts over standards of causal proof, the significance of anecdotal evidence, and the degree of certainty required for action.

Equally contentious were negotiations over the appropriate roles of laypeople and professionals in the controversy. Community activism is, in many respects, the antithesis of the dominant idea of how science advances through disinterested inquiry, away from the popular passions of the moment (and explains why scientists often approach cases such as toxic waste contamination with trepidation). For the legal and scientific professionals, lay activists can play an important but limited role in providing information and evidence. Nonetheless, as Phil Brown's (1992) study of the Woburn activists argues, their function went beyond that of informants and entered into the actual construction of scientific knowledge, even though their developing scientific expertise was rarely acknowledged by the professionals involved in the case.

Brown shows that the Woburn activists' approach to the scientific problem of the disease cluster—what he calls "popular epidemiology"—is not unlike that pursued by professional epidemiologists. According to Brown, lay involvement in toxic waste cases tends to proceed through a series of methodical steps that resemble conventional scientific inquiry: first, identification of health effects and possible pollutants; second, the formulation of hypotheses to connect pollutants and health effects; third, consensus-building around an hypothesis; fourth, input from scientific experts and government officials; and finally, organization to continue the investigation (1992, 269–71). Although the Woburn activists uncovered the problem in the first place, provided oversight of the activities of the professionals, and recruited outside experts to their cause, they were marginalized once litigation began and never got the opportunity to tell their story in court. Yet, despite the fact that their emerging expertise as popular epidemiologists was silenced by the legal maneuvering of the corporations' lawyer, their questions and investigations made important contributions to the design of future studies and helped construct the field of environmental health.

A further challenge to the validity of the distinction between the supposed rationality of official science and supposed passions of politics occurred when the AIDS epidemic exploded on the national scene in 1981 and profoundly altered the relationship among scientists, physicians, and the lay public. As Steven Epstein (1996) observes, AIDS activists were uniquely positioned to engage the biomedical community for several reasons. AIDS was a deadly disease with a prolonged course that affected young, healthy people who had the physical strength and motivation needed to politicize the disease. Moreover, the first group to be affected in the United States were gay men able to draw on a strong network of gay rights activists, many of whom had prominent positions in government, universities, the arts, and media, for support. Activists thus had the intellectual capital and political connections to challenge the cultural authority of the biomedical establishment with unprecedented vigor.

In his analysis of how AIDS knowledges were constructed during the epidemic, Epstein argues that "knowledge emerges out of credibility struggles" (1996, 10). By exploring the credibility struggles played out in the AIDS epidemic, Epstein shows that scientific evidence is an indispensable factor in establishing credibility but that other equally important factors include the credentials of the claims makers and the plausibility of the claims. The key questions then become who is invested with the proper credentials and how does the credentialing process take place? Are the only credentialed actors in scientific controversy those who have officially sanctioned scientific expertise, or can expertise be developed through interactions between lay activists and the knowledges of science? As a consequence of the organizing efforts of AIDS activists, Epstein argues, there was a "*multiplication of the successful pathways* to the establishment of credibility and *diversification of the personnel* beyond the highly credentialed" (1996, 3). In other words, the polarized conceptualization of layperson and expert was problematized, opening up the process of scientific knowledge making to previously excluded groups. By politicizing AIDS research in such a visible way, AIDS activists positioned themselves to acquire critical credentials to evaluate the scientific evidence and biological plausibility of claims, thereby establishing their own credibility as claims makers. Lay or popular knowledge and expert knowledge thus became inextricably linked and mutually dependent in ways that redefined their relationship to each other.

The transformation of the relationship between the biomedical community and laypeople that AIDS activism started was continued by breast cancer activists. In 1991, a small group of breast cancer survivors founded the National Breast Cancer Coalition (NBCC), a grassroots coalition that has grown to include approximately 400 organizations and 10,000 individual members. Like AIDS activists, breast cancer activists were able to draw on prior organizations and traditions, particularly feminist political action around women's health issues, to launch a social movement that gave breast cancer a position of prominence on the national research agenda.

Several distinctive features of breast cancer, including the lack of any credible knowledge about etiology or means to prevent the disease, as well as the younger age of onset and the relatively long survival period compared to other cancers, combined to make breast cancer the locus of a broad social movement that has also changed how biomedicine is practiced. Breast cancer activists demanded more information about the disease, faster access to experimental drugs, and active participation in allocating funds to shape the direction of breast cancer research. Because the incidence of breast cancer is high in affluent women, breast cancer survivors were able to use the privileges of their social class as cultural capital to gain access to the halls of Congress, the NIH, and scientific meetings.

There are inherent tensions in any social movement centered on disease-related advocacy, and, as Epstein (1996) notes, one important tension that must be negotiated is the simultaneous dependence on science and the need to challenge the authority of the experts to find solutions to problems of disease. Recognizing how little is known about breast cancer after so many years of study, breast cancer activists realized they had to engage with scientists not just at the level of lobbying for more research funding but, more fundamentally, to obtain a voice in what research should be done, how it should be done, and who should do it. Perhaps the most radical demand on the part of breast cancer activists was to participate in the design of experimental studies, an area of research previously the exclusive domain of experts.

The NBCC was successful in getting $407 million allocated to breast cancer research by fiscal year 1993. Because of parliamentary maneuvers, some of the money was funneled through the Department of Defense (DOD). That fact that DOD's procedures for peer review of grant proposals were not highly regarded by scientists enabled NBCC to help shape the composition of the study sections, which were charged with evaluating the scientific merit of proposals for funding, by demanding that at least one "consumer" representative be included on each study section, as well as on the committee at the second level of grant approval. Such lay participation opened up the formerly closed and insular study sections, giving breast cancer activists quite literally a "seat at the table" in the processes of scientific knowledge making.

## Public Understanding of Science in Practice

Many in the biomedical community have now come to accept and to appreciate the participation of laypeople in certain aspects of research, treatment, and prevention of disease. But for laypeople to go beyond accessory roles in biomedical research and to participate actively in what we think of as making science requires engagement with the content as well as the political process. Such participation in the knowledge making practices of science, Epstein (1996) suggests, required not only political clout but a change in identity. AIDS activists turned themselves, in Epstein's words, from a "disease constituency" into an "alternative basis of expertise" by moving beyond the early demands of groups like Act Up for more research, better health care delivery, and faster approval of new drugs (3). By learning science, AIDS activists, in effect, transformed themselves from consumer advocates representing the interests of patients into lay experts capable of participating in knowledge making and, at times, contesting prevailing understandings of what counts as "good science"—in clinical studies at NIH, in the manufacturing of drugs at the pharmaceutical companies, and in the approval of drugs at the Food and Drug Administration.

Education had always been important to breast cancer activists. The support groups for women with breast cancer that proliferated in the late 1970s and 1980s recognized the need to understand the scientific aspects of the disease. Study groups formed, and members pored over the medical literature, realizing in the process that ordinary readers could learn to understand the specialized discourse of science. In the words of one activist, "once you start reading them [medical journal articles], you get the gist of it" (Altman 1996, 303). This desire to popularize science—not to simplify the scientific literature but to make it accessible to lay readers—led NBCC to establish a program for breast cancer activists that developed a strong and systematic foundation in basic principles of biology, molecular biology, and epidemiology.

Entitled Project LEAD (Leadership, Education, and Advocacy Development), the program teaches science to breast cancer activists in order to facilitate their participation in a range of scientific programs. As noted, most models of promoting the public understanding of science involve a top-down, linear approach of transmitting scientific information as fully formed and complete. In contrast, Project LEAD does not act as an intermediary between experts and laypeople or strip scientific knowledge of complexity and uncertainty. Instead, its workshops popularize science by redefining the participants' reading practices and their relationship to the expert knowledge of official science. Through a combination of lectures, interactive small-group sessions, case studies, research seminars, role-playing, and critical appraisals of the literature on breast cancer, participants, together with faculty, grapple with contemporary debates over the causes, prevention, and treatment of breast cancer and how to make sound, though imperfect, policy decisions in the face of inconclusive data and uncertainty.

Project LEAD participants develop an emergent lay expertise based on reading practices that enable them to negotiate their relationship to biomedicine without the debilitating dependence and sense of vulnerability we saw in the situation of the reader as deferential patient or anxious consumer. Drawing on both the rich knowledge of their own lived experience of health and disease and the wide-ranging inquiry into the biology of cancer in the workshop, Project LEAD participants develop an understanding that goes beyond the mere acquisition of information to a critical appraisal of study design and experimental method in basic research and clinical trials. They learn to popularize science by demystifying the scientific literature and submitting it to their own questions—and to use this lay expertise after the workshop in developing research protocols, recruiting clinical trial subjects, participating on study sections to review grant proposals, and serving on institutional review boards, data monitoring committees, and advisory boards.

## Conclusion

The promise that biomedicine will develop solutions to problems of health and disease is enticing, and the business world, scientists, policy makers, and the public all have high expectations. Although their perspectives vary, these groups share the idea that science can deliver "the truth" with certainty. As we have seen, however, the credibility invested in biomedicine and the popular faith in science have created dependence on experts, a desire for scientific certainty, and anxiety and vulnerability when biomedicine does not have the answers. Programs on the part of official science and the biomedical establishment to promote public understanding have not helped laypeople understand the complexities of biology and the dilemmas of policy making in the face of scientific uncertainty. Rather, these initiatives seek to establish a firmer footing for the cultural authority of science. In contrast, movements of toxic waste, AIDS, and breast cancer activists have struggled with the public's dependence on experts by engaging scientific knowledge on their own terms, to set up alternative loci of expertise, and to bring their own questions about what counts as "good science" to deliberations about the direction of research and public policy.

# Chapter Seven

# Popular Literacy and the Resources of Print Culture

## The South African Committee for Higher Education

The South African Committee for Higher Education (SACHED) formed in 1959 as a response to the Extension of University Education Act, which brought the Grand Apartheid scheme of separate and unequal development to higher education. Building on the apartheid policies already established for primary and secondary schools by the Bantu Education Act of 1953, the South African state set up separate universities along racial and ethnic lines, thereby curtailing the ability of students classified as Bantu, Indian, and Coloured to attend white universities.[1] To counter these limitations of educational opportunity, SACHED initiated a program, with financial aid and tutoring, for black South African students to take correspondence courses through the University of London's external degrees division, as an alternative to the "bush colleges" of the apartheid regime.[2]

This initial focus on providing access to a "quality" British education reveals SACHED's roots in the liberal opposition to apartheid education and the tactics it developed to evade the apartheid state by devising alternative routes to formal schooling and tertiary education, with the goal of achieving secondary certificates or university degrees. During the 1960s and 1970s, SACHED established programs such as the Bursary Project, for correspondence courses through the University of South Africa; Turett Correspondence College for distance learning, which developed the Study Centres Programme in townships in

Cape Town, Durban, and Johannesburg; and People's College, a media project that circulated study materials for certificate examinations, as well as general reading materials for postliterate adults, through a twenty-four-page supplement in the *Weekend World.*

The limits of SACHED's initial commitments to alternative education, however, may be seen in the highly problematic Bophuthatswana Teacher Upgrading Project (BTUP), which ran from 1974 to 1977 and, in many respects, appeared to contradict SACHED's goals by contracting with the Bantustan government in Bophuthatswana to set up distance learning study centers for teachers, with the opportunity to prepare for Junior and Senior Certificate examinations. According to Gareth Cornwall (1989), the "most vociferous opposition" to BTUP came from the SACHED center in Cape Town in 1977, when the director Lindy Wilson argued that the project not only failed to see the political implications of collaborating with a homeland government but also equated the improvement of teaching with certification (something that had never been demonstrated) and assumed, moreover, that the capacity to recall subject matter on the teacher's part for examinations somehow led to better instruction. Further, Wilson said, there was no reason that working with teachers required SACHED to cooperate with government (Cornwall 1989, 63).

What is evident in Wilson's remarks is the sense of crisis within SACHED in the late 1970s, following the Durban strike wave of 1973, the Soweto uprising of 1976, and the growing mass mobilizations against the apartheid state, about the meaning of alternative education. The BTUP revealed the danger that simply seeking alternative delivery systems for state-recognized education could, in fact, undermine the wider struggle for equal education by leaving intact and unchallenged the social relations of teaching and learning and the social structures of state-sponsored education in a racialized class society. In other words, as Cornwall says, if SACHED had been attempting "to find education solutions, to what were essentially political problems" (183), this was becoming an increasingly untenable position. With a reorganization of SACHED in 1978, as the major projects that had previously defined the organization ended and a new central leadership took over, the politics of education became more and more a pressing matter.

In its early days, SACHED had been concerned primarily with finding effective (and cost-effective) alternatives for adult learners—defined as anyone fifteen years or older and not in school—largely through distance learning schemes. Accordingly, the subject matter of education remained stable and taken for granted, determined, on the one hand, by the state credentialing system and, on the other, by an agreed upon legacy of the superiority of British-style education. With the emergence of the Black Consciousness movement and the founding of the South African Student Organization (SASO) in 1969, however, questions began to arise about the nature of knowledge imparted by formal education and its relevance to the interests and social locations of students and adult learners entangled in the dynamics of apartheid and the struggle against its forms of domination.

As Neville Alexander points out, "Until 1969, approximately, most people in the liberation movement, most political activists, wanted, and said so in so many words, an education that was equal to the education of Whites. . . . And it didn't strike them until the Black Consciousness Movement came into being that that education was an education for domination, that it was a racist education that prepared people for an oppressive and exploitative position in society" (1992, 106). This shift in understanding the nature of education, as Alexander notes, was part of a radical critique taking place internationally, as manifested in the New Left upsurges of 1968 in France, the United States, Mexico, and elsewhere. For SASO activists, along with their counterparts worldwide, this critique was influenced decisively by Paolo Freire's *Pedagogy of the Oppressed* (1970) and the notion of conscientization as an alternative to education for domination, whether in the form of Bantu education or the older British-style education. Though banned by the apartheid state, 500 or more copies of *Pedagogy of the Oppressed* circulated through the bush colleges, providing inspiration for a number of SASO literacy and educational projects in urban and rural townships (Alexander 1992, 57; Nekhwevha 2002).

This critique of education for domination, moreover, converged in the 1970s and afterward with what was widely perceived among the ruling classes as an education crisis that shook the foundations of governability in South African society, marked initially by the Soweto uprising and its challenge to the legitimacy of Bantu education in 1976 and deepened by the school boycotts of the 1980s, which in 1985 extended to 650,000 black South African students. This growing sense of a crisis in education cannot be understood apart from an economic crisis that emerged from the unprecedented growth and profits of the 1950s and 1960s, based on cheap black labor, as capital increasingly faced a shortage of skilled labor, a restricted domestic market, shrinking foreign investment, and a stagnating economy—all produced to one degree or another by the labor-repressive policies and separate development designs of the apartheid regime, of which Bantu education was a key component. As a result, alternative education became a respectable term within a sector of the ruling class, as multinational corporations and liberal-minded business executives and policy makers at the national level sought moderate ways to modernize education and the economy—and to accommodate or co-opt the radical energies released in the struggle against apartheid.

SACHED was never a homogeneous political formation, and its staff included supporters of the African National Congress (ANC) and the ANC-aligned United Democratic Front (UDF) and National Education Crisis Committee (NECC); leaders and activists in smaller left alternatives to the ANC, such as the Cape Action League and the National Forum; independent Marxists, workerists, and liberals. It should not be surprising, then, that visions of South Africa's political future varied within SACHED. What held SACHED together, rather, was its commitment, as a service organization in the antiapartheid struggle, to transform the social relations of teaching and learning and to redistribute expertise. As a 1987 statement put it, SACHED is "committed to establishing participatory, non-discriminatory and non-authoritarian learning processes. It seeks to transfer skills and resources in such a way that organizations, communities, and individuals are empowered to take charge of their own projects" (quoted in Witz 1988, 370). Just as importantly, while SACHED collaborated with the NECC and other ANC-aligned organizations, it remained politically independent, thereby providing a space for non-ANC leftists, particularly in the Cape Town and Durban centers, to develop educational projects based on nonracialism, socialist politics, and revolutionary internationalism.[3]

In the intensely politicized context of the 1980s, SACHED became the largest and most important nongovernment educational organization in South Africa, responding with remarkable flexibility and imagination to the ongoing crisis in the politics of education. SACHED's growth and increasing relevance in the 1980s can be attributed in part to its heightened emphasis on nonformal education, through publishing initiatives and educational work with community organizations and trade unions, as alternatives to state-authorized education and control of curriculum and certification. But SACHED also found ways to develop innovative programs that were tied to formal schooling, including the establishment of Khanya College in 1986 as a bridge to university enrollment; the Each Working in Education project that provided correspondence courses for detainees held under the 1986 state of emergency in the Eastern Cape; and the African History Project in Cape Town that offered course materials and workshops for teachers who were pressed by students, as well as their own interests, to present an account of African history that countered the distortions and omissions of the official curriculum.

My purpose here is not to provide a comprehensive account of SACHED's work, which would take considerably more space, but rather to examine how SACHED's efforts to popularize literacy was a constant theme in both its formal and nonformal educational projects. By *popularizing literacy*, I do not mean simply teaching the basic skills of reading and writing English to African language speakers, at which SACHED and other educational projects in the 1980s were not particularly successful.[4] Instead, I use the term to refer to the way such SACHED undertakings as People's College Comics, the Labor and Community Resources Project (LACOM), the Publishing Programme, and the African History Project used the resources of print culture to design forms of writing and delivery systems that provided students and postliterate adults with the means to recognize and represent themselves as rhetorical agents, for whom the activities of reading and writing were keys to acquiring the cultural capital denied them by Bantu education and tools of deliberation and social action to participate in building a nonracial political future. What distinguished SACHED from earlier adult education in the South African night school movement was in crucial respects SACHED's experimentation with the multimodal potentialities of print culture and a more or less intuitive understanding that the graphic design of texts not only served as a vehicle for transmitting messages but also could be employed to position readers and writers as accountable and purposeful subjects in the turmoil of intensified social struggle.

There has been surprisingly little written about SACHED, aside from Gareth Cornwall's unpublished thesis on SACHED up to 1987, and an occasional mention in articles on adult education (Aitchison 2003), popular history in the 1980s (Callinicos 1991; Witz 1988), and South African comics (Barnard 2004; Brown 1991; Kruger and Shariff 2001). This seems to me a significant omission in any reasonable understanding of the educational agitations of the period. In U.S. college composition—and more widely in North America—radical education in South Africa during the struggles of the 1980s has been identified for the most part with the themes of "People's Education for People's Power" and "People's English," as articulated by the NECC, which formed in the wake of the Soweto uprising and was linked politically to the UDF and ANC.[5] In contrast, due in part to its political heterogeneity and independence, SACHED developed a forum for popular literacy projects that provided a critical left alternative to the populist nationalism of the ANC and its various supporters that deserves to be more widely known. As I show, SACHED projects offer to those involved in community literacy work, as well as rhetoric and writing studies in general, insights about genre and visual design in the preparation of educational materials, the role of rhetorical deliberation in social movements such as the antiapartheid struggles of the 1980s, and the vexed relationship between experts and the people in popular literacy projects.

My view is that the SACHED projects I examine—People's College Comics, LACOM, the Publishing Programme, and the African History Project—are of great interest because they posed fundamental questions for popular literacy projects that too often go unasked or are taken for granted. Who are the people, after all? Who is included in the popular classes? How are the people represented, in the double sense of being figured as a political force and of being spoken on behalf of? Whose interests are thereby served? The answers that SACHED's popular literacy projects offered to these questions demonstrate, in various ways (some more successfully than others), how the projects depended crucially on an understanding of the people not as the pre-given basis of national unity and liberation but as a political problem of diverse and contradictory interests, identities, and social allegiances that must be negotiated rhetorically in the struggle to form a collective will and to imagine how an alternative political future might emerge from the ruins of apartheid.

## SACHED and the Night School Movement

In the early part of the nineteenth century, missionaries such as William Govan, who was from 1841 to 1870 the first principle at the Lovedale mission school, the largest and most important in South Africa, advocated a classical education, including Latin and Greek, that would enable a native elite to take its place alongside Europeans in the ministry and secular life. This liberal Christian vision of the educability of an African elite was part of an older civilizing mission that was replaced at Lovedale in 1867, when James Stewart received the backing of the Foreign Mission Committee of the Free Church of Scotland to develop a separate curriculum for native students, geared to African "realities" rather than Govan's Enlightenment ideals, substituting English for the classical languages, and emphasizing the industrial education and apprenticeship programs that had already been established, following Sir George Grey's visit to Lovedale in 1855, to train men in masonry, carpentry, wagon making, and blacksmithing and women in laundry work, sewing, and dressmaking. (Later post office and telegraph work were added, and masonry was replaced by printing and bookbinding.)

Lovedale played a key role in establishing not only the principle of white trusteeship and separate development for native students but also an early form of night school, based on the division of mental and manual labor that organized time for Lovedale's vocational students, who pursued their trades during the day, with "their literary as well as their religious education to be carried out, during their apprenticeship, in the evening" (Shepherd 1940, 133). In many respects, this division of the day defined the limited educational opportunities available to all but the very small percentage of black South Africans who attended mission schools and the even smaller percentage of the African elite who were educated beyond the primary level at Lovedale, Fort Hare College, and elsewhere. For the vast majority, with the industrialization and urbanization of South Africa that took place in the first half of the twentieth century and the Native Land Act of 1913 that forced blacks off the land and created an African proletariat to work in gold and diamond mines and in various secondary industries, the slim chance at basic and continuing education was at night, after they had finished their daily labors.

Night schools in South Africa included those set up by the Communist Party in the early 1920s, which emphasized political education and development of professional revolutionaries; adult education established by missionaries and mining companies; the African College and Mayibuye Schools, set up by students from the University of Witwatersrand in the late 1930s, and the Cape Native Education Night Schools Association, set up by students from the University of Cape Town in the 1940s; night classes organized by the municipalities in Durban and Pietermaritzburg (financed by the municipal sale of home-brewed "kaffir beer"); and the various efforts of the country's premier liberal institution, the South African Institute on Race Relations (SAIRR), which viewed its adult education work as a counter to radicalizing influences in other night schools (Bird 1984; Harries 1993; Prinsloo 1995; Wilson 1991).

In its origins and ongoing projects, SACHED may be seen as an outgrowth of the night school movement of adult education. As did many of the night schools, SACHED drew extensively on white students and university-educated volunteers and staff for its various programs. As we will see in a moment, in the case of Peoples Comics, SACHED projects could take on the didactic character of earlier night schools, rooted in the inescapable relations of privilege and dependence that play out when white intellectuals design educational material for black audiences in a historical setting where expertise and access to knowledge have been thoroughly racialized by colonialism, segregation, and apartheid. Nonetheless, what distinguished SACHED from earlier night schools was the recognition from its inception that alternative education in South Africa required alternative means of dissemination. If, as already noted, early SACHED projects relied on a variety of distance learning schemes for adult learners to study for certificates and degrees, this emphasis on the means of delivery took on new and innovative forms as SACHED turned to nonformal education in its popular literacy projects of the 1980s.

## Popular Literacy and the Problem of Simplification

The innovation in SACHED's popular literacy projects in the 1980s can be seen by comparing them to the work in the 1930s and 1940s of Eddie Roux, who is often credited with starting the night school movement in South Africa (Bird 1984, 197). Roux had been a prominent figure in the South African Communist Party, as secretary-general and an outspoken advocate of orienting toward the black proletariat and popular African movements at a time when the party was still concentrated on recruiting white workers. As editor of the party paper *Umsebenzi* (*Worker*) in 1930, Roux added cartoons, published articles in both English and African languages, and nearly doubled circulation, though these gains were reversed rather quickly when the party, still in the sectarian throes of third period Stalinism, insisted on printing "dense theoretical articles" (Drew 2000, 121).

Following his break with the party in 1938, Roux devoted his considerable energies to adult education and especially to developing what he called "Easy English for Africans." Easy English grew out of C. K. Ogden's Basic English (Basic Scientific International Commercial) with a simplified grammar that eliminated most verbs and a vocabulary of 850 words. In the late 1930s, as Roux says, he had "edited a paper in Basic (the *African Defender*) for some years and produced the *Mayibuye Reader* (in Basic)." Unlike Ogden, however, Roux did not view his use of Basic as an attempt to create a new international language so much as a method "to help authors and editors write in English so that they will be understood by the greatest possible amount of African readers who already know a certain amount of English" (Roux 1942a, 262). Eventually, Roux rejected Basic because of its vocabulary's inexact fit with the words "used or understood by rank-and-file Africans who speak English" and the difficulties it posed "for anyone who already has a knowledge of normal English to write or speak it correctly" (1942a, 263). Moreover, Roux believed, there are "certain English constructions which are better than others because they correspond more closely with the forms based in the Bantu languages themselves. This is one reason why I did not adopt the Basic idea of eliminating the verb" (1942b).

As his correspondence with SAIRR in the early 1940s reveals, Roux pushed hard for his scheme of Easy English in publications for African readers. "It is very disappointing," Roux wrote in 1942, "that pamphlets intended for Africans are still being published without any attempt at language simplification. I find it particularly disheartening after all the research I have done on the subject and all the correspondence I have had with the Institute" (1942c). While SAIRR did publish Roux's article "Easy English for Africans" in its journal *African*

*Studies* in 1942 and at least one of the pamphlets Roux produced in Easy English, it is not surprising that SAIRR's guide for adult education and adult literacy became Frank Laubach, the missionary to the Philippines, who visited the Institute in 1948 and whose famous slogan "Each one teach one and win one for Christ" was no doubt more congenial to SAIRR's liberal Christian sensibilities (National Advisory Council for Adult Education 1948).

For his part, Roux importantly acknowledged the suspicion and outright opposition on the part of Africans to language simplification: "When introducing a new book written for Africans, I was asked by students in a night school J.C. [Junior Certificate] class, 'Why does it say on the cover "for Africans?"' . . . Special education for Africans means inferior education, just as all the special things for Africans are inferior things. We want the same books that Europeans have" (Roux 1942a, 261–62). At the same time, Roux held that books written in Easy English "need not be inferior in content" (262), and his writings for adult readers on South African history, such as those gathered in the book *Time Longer Than Rope* (1964), provided an early and important popular history, originally published in 1948.

As Roux makes clear, "Easy English . . . is not primarily a teaching system." Rather, its word list is based "so far as possible on the vocabulary actually used by African adults who buy books in English in order to obtain knowledge or to amuse themselves. It has been designed for the writer (or radio announcer, etc.) who wishes to 'put things across' to Africans through the medium of English" (1945, 164). In this regard, for Roux's publishing ventures in Easy English, English was essentially a technical problem that could be solved through language simplification that matched popular knowledge of English and could thereby serve as a resource and reference point for those writing for black readers. The underlying assumption was that language serves primarily as a means of transmission and, accordingly, that an efficient, simplified English could be devised as a vehicle of communication for postliterate readers eager to find print material.

The problem of language simplification, however, is not so simple as Roux understood it to be. Developing reading material for postliterate South Africans involved, to be sure, attention to appropriate vocabulary and syntax, but the problem of readability goes beyond words and grammatical constructions to include knowledge of genre and how written texts make meaning in terms of their rhetorical situations, textual conventions, and graphic designs. To think clearly about readability in South Africa requires an understanding of the relatively undeveloped state of genre knowledge among postliterate black readers that resulted directly from the educational deprivation and scarcity of print material under apartheid and earlier. For Roux, forms of writing seem to be taken for granted as transparent vessels of Easy English, as though written texts amount simply to the words on the page that readers decode. As SACHED's popular literacy projects in the 1980s make clear, however, the task of publication design is a more complicated matter that called certainly for the simplifications afforded by readability schemes like Easy English but also for a recognition of the limited distribution of reading material in South Africa and the consequent uneven development of familiarity on the part of black South African readers with the range of textual varieties in which writing circulates in print culture.

This relative unfamiliarity with the genres of print culture, for example, became a key issue in LACOM projects that focused on the needs of trade union militants and community activists not just to read but to produce the forms of writing essential to the ongoing activities of organizations in the antiapartheid struggle. In his work on Easy English, Roux identifies black South Africans for the most part as readers but not producers of writing. This latter rhetorical position is reserved for those ("writers, radio announcers") who want to "'put things across' to Africans through the medium of English." In a way that recapitulates the racialized dilemma of white intellectuals writing for black audiences, a monopoly of literate expertise remains in the hands of the "content providers," as a matter of white privilege. In contrast, LACOM, along with other SACHED projects such as *Write Your Own History* (Witz 1988), envisaged a redistribution of the means of producing writing, making it available to organizations, communities, and individuals as a salient resource of representation and persuasion in the struggle for South Africa's political future.

## The Question of Genre: Readers and Writers

The complexities of genre and genre knowledge are apparent in one of the most interesting SACHED publishing projects, the two People's College Comics issued in 1988: *Equiano: The Slave Who Fought to be Free* (based on *The Interesting Narrative of the Life of Olaudah Equiano or Gustavus Vassa, the African, Written by Himself,* the autobiography of the black abolitionist published in 1789) and *Down Second Avenue* (based on Es'kia Mphahlele's autobiography published in 1959). Like SACHED's youth magazine *Upbeat,* the comics were intended for both mass distribution and classroom use, with study guides for teachers. In this sense, like other SACHED popular literacy projects, they blurred the line between formal and nonformal education.

From one perspective, these are remarkable renderings of complex texts into the "simplified" form of the comic strip. As Joshua Brown

**Figure 7–1**
From *Down Second Avenue*

notes, *Equiano* "necessarily simplifies the 'through-line' of Equiano's epic experience, condensing time to create a coherent and direct narrative" that "preserves the integrity of the tale" (1991, 383). At only twelve pages in length, *Down Second Avenue* is considerably more condensed, with each panel presenting a separate incident from Mphahlele's autobiography, giving this comic a more impressionistic and episodic character that calls on readers to integrate the juxtaposed scenes into a meaningful whole (Figure 7–1).

In a SACHED evaluation of the effectiveness of *Equiano* and *Down Second Avenue,* one teacher noted that "visual literacy is learned and so is comic literacy and [neither] should be presumed" (quoted in Brown 1991, 388). Conventions that are taken for granted by Americans and Europeans who grew up reading comic books, such as the difference between dialogue and thought balloons, were "mysterious to many South Africans in a system that [had] successfully isolated accessibility to information and culture" (Brown 1991, 388). Further, some students reported they found the episodic character of *Down Second Avenue,* with its emphasis on decisive moments and lack of narrative resolution, to be confusing. While he considers *Down Second Avenue* to be a "much more nuanced and complex work" as a comic, Brown acknowledges that these "students were more comfortable with *Equiano*'s traditional narrative structure that gave scenes a clear beginning and end (not to mention an explicit lesson or moral)" (1991, 388).

As may be seen, the supposedly simplified form of comics, in fact, has its own complexities, due in part to the resources of representation that the genre draws on. According to the comic theorist Scott McCloud, the genre of comics relies, in design and use, on a relatively standardized repertoire to combine words and pictures in "deliberate sequences," where time and motion are portrayed both within and between panels and a set of recognizable visual symbols are available to represent the invisible world of the senses and emotions. If this multimodality gave the People's College Comics their expressive powers, it also produced difficulties for readers unfamiliar with the difference between dialogue and thought balloons or the kind of closure that comic readers must supply to connect panels and, in McCloud's words, "mentally construct a continuous, unified reality" (1993, 67).

There can be little doubt that the activity on the part of SACHED's artists and writers to simplify and make more broadly accessible literary works like Equiano's *Interesting Narrative* and *Down Second Avenue* took them beyond the monomodality of Eddie Roux's Easy English, with its goal of simplifying the composition of texts at the level of the word and sentence, to look more broadly at the potentialities that reside in the multimodal capacities of print culture. Nonetheless, questions must be raised about People's College Comics that involve the decision to translate literary works into comics and an underlying ambivalence on the part of educated South Africans that cast comics as a simplified and derivative version of an original print text. There are, indeed, traces of what Karen Press (personal communication, email December 12, 2007) calls a "didactic style of choice" in which the simplified comic versions of Equiano's *Interesting Narrative* and *Down Second Avenue* are treated in "a kind of *Pilgrims' Progress* manner" and the visual design is "naturalistic, linear, morally unambiguous in content." In this sense, the absence of "humour, irony, non-literal images" warranted the seriousness of People's College Comics as worthy reading material (once again problematically provided by white intellectuals to black audiences), and, at the same time, show how People's College Comics restricted the forms that comics might take, as exemplified by more experimental currents in African comics,[6] radical alternative educational comics like the Mexican cartoonist Ruis' "For Beginners" series, Japanese manga, American underground comix of the 1960s and 1970s, and the new wave graphic novels of the 1980s. For Press, the self-imposed "limited normality" of People's College Comics short-circuited what could have been a fuller consideration of how to use the resources of representation and visual styles that comics make available in order to mediate black readers' relative unfamiliarity with the genre.

This matter of unfamiliarity with genres of print culture comes up, from another angle, as already noted, in the work of LACOM, a SACHED project that was among the number of service organizations that emerged in the 1980s to provide skills training and educational resources for unions and community groups in the antiapartheid struggle. LACOM was established in Johannesburg in 1982, when the Council of Unions of South Africa (CUSA) and the Federation of South African of South African Unions (FOSATU) asked SACHED to develop administrative and financial training courses. (FOSATU and community-based unions merged with miners from CUSA to form the present Congress of South African Trade Unions—COSATU—in 1985.) LACOM centers quickly spread to Cape Town, East London, Pietermaritzburg, and Durban, offering courses and workshops on bookkeeping, democratic meeting procedures, shop steward training, and labor history, as well as minute-taking, report-writing, and the composition and design of articles, newsletters, press releases, posters, and pamphlets.

Of particular pertinence here is how such humble, ephemeral, and often devalued genres as meeting minutes, reports, and newsletters became the focus of political consideration for shop stewards and community activists—as not just a matter of literacy skills but also of rhetorical force. These "inconspicuous forms" of writing, as Walter Benjamin notes, take on heightened significance in the class struggle:

> Significant literary work can only come into being in a strict alternation between action and writing; it must nurture the inconspicuous forms that better fit its influence in active communities than does the pretentious, universal gesture of the book—in leaflets, brochures, articles, and posters. Only this prompt language shows itself actively equal to the moment. (1986, 61)

In LACOM projects, education in writing occurred in the matrix of organization and struggle, where the "prompt language" that Benjamin names entered consequentially into the determination of outcomes for trade unions and mass organizations: to establish a public presence, to run internal affairs democratically, and to intervene in the struggles of the present. The genres typical of organizations—constitutions and bylaws, minutes, monthly reports, press releases, and so on—are identified not simply in terms of their formal features, as is often the case, say, in business writing courses, but more importantly as forms of rhetorical action, responses to the exigencies that arise in social situations, to enact collective motives "actively equal to the moment."

A LACOM workshop from 1990 on article writing and newsletter layout illustrates how genres of writing embody rhetorical purposes. The workshop began with an overview of the features of a "good article," such as "short and simple sentences" that are "clear and to the point," "don't use big words," and "follow a clear order," as well as the normal journalistic convention of the inverted pyramid that "give[s] as much as possible information in the first paragraph" ("Media Workshop Held at LACOM/SACHED on 09 June 1990" 1990). Following such customary advice, the workshop analyzed two articles by examining the writer's rhetorical stance—conservative, liberal, or radical. In the first article, information about a recent strike was seen in terms of its persuasive purposes. It was noted, for example, that "detail on why workers are striking" was intended not simply to inform readers but to "convince people the strike is the right thing." By the same token, workshop participants found that recounting the success of previous strikes "serves to encourage workers" and that showing "the company is very rich and can afford wages increases" legitimizes the demands of workers as reasonable. In contrast, workshop participants judged that the second article was "written from a very conservative point of view" because, though it provided background information on work conditions, the writer "failed to analyse why we have the problem" and "didn't attempt to find a permanent solution" ("Media Workshop Held at LACOM/SACHED on 09 June 1990" 1990).

The assumption in the two case studies is that the genre of news reporting cannot be understood simply as information transfer where the writer is located outside the fray of class struggle. Rather, informative writing and persuasion are intertwined as the activity of reporting inevitably aligns writers, in one way or another, to the workers and bosses as they confront each other in moments of struggle. These alignments, in Kenneth Burke's terms (1950), are matters of the identifications and divisions that are inherent to rhetorical activity, manifesting themselves in the rhetorical stance that writers and speakers inhabit, whether wittingly or unwittingly, as they draw on such familiar resources of representation as the news article to turn events that are bearing in on them into persuasive accounts of reality. Accordingly, as workshop participants noted in the case of the second article, the lack of analysis and an attempted solution was not just an indication of the writer's ostensible neutrality but further evidence for the recognition that the rhetorical stance of neutrality is itself a "very conservative" position precisely because it fails to discover in the situation being reported either the contradictions between labor and capital that produced the grounds for struggle or the available means of persuasion (or Burkean identification) to promote solidarity and class consciousness among workers.

The aim of the workshop, it is important to note, was not to impose a political line on participants but to use the case studies to clarify the politics of the participants by emphasizing the inescapability of point of view and the accountability entailed in representing fellow workers' experience in a public forum such as a newsletter. This can be seen in the next exercise, where participants rewrote the second article, whether from a conservative, liberal, or radical perspective. Further, as though to underscore the way that writing circulates and takes on worldly force, the workshop a week later was devoted to newsletter layout, using the rewritten article to link the activity of composition and revision to page design and the delivery of writing in its material forms.

## Embedded Narrators

This attention to design and delivery can be seen as well in SACHED's Publishing Programme. Starting in 1982, in a joint venture with Ravan Press, SACHED produced a series of books, some of which—such as guides to reading, writing, and biology were intended primarily for classroom use, while others—*Working Women in South Africa* (Lawson 1985) and *The Right to Learn: The Struggle for Education in South Africa* (Christie 1985), the People's College Comics (1988), and *Write Your Own History* (Witz 1988), written in collaboration with the History Workshop at University of Witwatersrand, were geared to both students and broader audiences. In addition, the LACOM branch in Durban published *Freedom from Below: The Struggle for Freedom* (1989), as well as a series of pamphlets on working-class history.[7] SACHED consulted with a graphic designer from the British Council to refine its approach to book design in 1985 (SACHED 1985), and these books and pamphlets employ many of the visual features that were standard at the time to graphic design—a judicious use of white space, photographs and illustrations, headings, double columns, visual display of information, and attention to typeface—that enhanced the attractiveness and readability of the books.

What distinguish books like *The Right to Learn* and *Freedom from Below,* however, are other features that draw on the multimodal potentialities of book design. For example, in *Freedom from Below,* what we might call an embedded narrator, the cartoon figure Thami, appears, who speaks directly to readers and mediates their reading. As a factory worker in Pinetown, Thami serves as a point of identification for readers and a guide who offers commentary, from a worker's perspective, on the main narrative line. At the beginning of the book, Thami recalls his initial reluctance to join the Durban strike wave in 1973 and his gradual conversion to the cause of the union by 1975. The ethos Thami establishes in the opening pages casts him as someone who has struggled with the decision to join the union and, once he does, still has a number of questions about trade unions in South Africa: "Had there always been trade unions in South Africa? How were these unions organized? What role did African workers play in these unions? I asked myself many questions." Thami reads books and articles written by academics that are recommended to him by his union organizer, only to realize that "this information was being hidden from workers" (9).

The lesson, for Thami, is that workers have to write their own history. Otherwise, "the job of writing will stay with people from the universities. No one will know what really happened in the factory, in the shop stewards' council and in the townships" (10). *Freedom from Below,* accordingly, is presented as an authentic account of workers' struggles in South Africa, uncontaminated by academic specialization and warranted by the hard-won experience of a fellow worker. In this sense, the figure of Thami is meant to enable the rhetorical formation of an audience with its own class interests, a collective "we" in search of knowledge, in a situation where, as Raymond Williams puts it, "the people's questions are not answered by the existing distribution of the educational curriculum" (1989b 160). The knowledge to be gained in *Freedom from Below* depends on whose questions are being asked, and the book is located unequivocally as workers' history (Figure 7–2).

While Thami's initial uncertainty about joining the union and his questions are offered as a matter of credibility, he quickly becomes a rather monological figure, delivering colloquial versions of Durban LACOM's workerist history. Thami is not wrong, for example, when he comments on the Native Land Act of 1913: "Well, this time the growing capitalist farmers did not even need the power of guns and cannons to move African people off their lands. A growing and brutal system of laws began the process of smashing the independent African peasantry" (27). Rather, he simply recapitulates the account in the main text, which says, immediately preceding his comments, that

**Figure 7–2**
From *Freedom from Below*

*Comrades!*

*My name is Thami and I work in a factory in Pinetown near Durban. At Pinetown, we have a lot of factories and the working class is well organised into trade unions. But, this was not always so.*

*I remember the strikes which broke out in Durban in 1973. I didn't go on strike then. I was sure that those workers would lose their jobs.*

*But then in about 1975, some workers in our factory began to talk about organising a union. Again, I said no, that was not for me. All I wanted to do was my job and get my pay at the end of the week.*

*But these workers carried on organising anyway. They formed a shop stewards' steering committee. And after they had signed up many members, they held elections for shop stewards.*

*It was then that I really began to understand what the union was about. Together it would be easier to get our rights from the bosses. Also, if we elected our leaders in our department, then we could control that person. We could make sure that our shop steward represented our position to the bosses clearly.*

*Then I signed up and started thinking about trade unions more carefully. Had there always been trade unions in South Africa? How were these unions organised? What role did African workers play in these unions? I asked myself many questions.*

*Eventually I decided that the only way to find answers was to go and find out for myself.*

*The only way I could do this was to read. I contacted my union organiser who gave me plenty of books and articles about trade unions. But these articles and books were written by people at universities. They were very difficult to understand.*

*For many years I just read. But then I thought that all this information was being hidden from workers. It needed to be written again, so that it is useful for workers who want to understand the history of trade unions.*

"African peasants were squeezed off the land and into wage labour" (27). In this sense, the multimodal potentialities of an embedded narrator are reduced to a tagline that offers no counterpoint or space to think about the history.

In contrast, the embedded narrators in *The Right to Learn*—two unnamed cartoon figures—indicate a more dialogical use of multimodality. In this case, a woman and a man appear throughout the book as "talking heads" who serve, as Thami did, as points of identification and guides. But their interactions also give *The Right to Learn* a more open and questioning aspect, as their conversations consider educational issues from various perspectives. An apt example is the exchange in the opening chapter "What's Education About?" First there appear fourteen quotes ("Different opinions about education") that range from H. F. Verwoerd in 1953 ("When I have control over native education, I will reform it so that natives will be taught from childhood that equality is not for them") to W. L. Rautenbach in 1981 ("We need more technical and vocational education so we can have more skilled workers") to Eric Molobi in 1986 ("The real struggle is to replace an undemocratic, coercive, ineffective and irrelevant education system with a democratic, participatory and relevant alternative"). Then a series of bulleted points characterizes four distinct (if sometimes overlapping) "aims for the education system" that can be drawn from the quotes:

- "training people to work in the economy,"
- "bringing about social change" (including the reformist change sought by mining magnate Harry Oppenheimer and World Bank head Robert McNamara),
- "getting greater social equality and justice" (whether the liberal equal opportunity promoted by SAIRR or total social transformation), and
- "being part of the political process" (whether from the perspective of Verwoerd or Molobi).

All of this serves as a prelude to the appearance of the two cartoon figures, who discuss how "education can be used for different purposes" (Christie 1985, 12–15). As this discussion is represented visually and verbally, the back-and-forth between the two characters can be mapped schematically as introduction of a point (by the woman), questioning (by the man), clarification (by the woman), recognition of the clarification (by the man), and further direction (by the woman). The woman is clearly the more authoritative and knowledgeable figure both here and throughout the book, and her gestures reinforce the power of discourse ascribed to her, to control and direct the conversation, as she points a finger in the air (to introduce a point), puts her hands on her hips (to consolidate a point), and finally folds her arms (as the conversation rests for the moment, in preparation to move on). These figurations, of course, can easily be seen as a part of the nonsexism that was such a powerful current in the antiapartheid struggle (Figure 7–3).

But from another angle, we could also say that these embedded narrators are attempts to "oralicize" the text, to draw on the multimodal resources of representation in print culture in order to make books talk. The design seems addressed to readers such as Phillip,

**Figure 7–3**
From *The Right to Learn*

whose perception of books as "lifeless, passive entities" comes across in the following quote from an unsigned article in *SACHED Journal* in 1990, "A Book Is Not a Book Until It Is Read." Phillip says,

> A piece of paper is dead, it's lifeless. I like an immediate response. Books, they just sit there on the shelf. They don't answer you back. They don't jump out at you. All you can do with them is put them under the leg of a chair. Somebody ought to invent a new kind of book where you could hold a conversation with it. (17)

In a sense, the combination of words, pictures, and gestures in *The Right to Learn* and other SACHED publications is an attempt to invent just such a "new kind of book"—books "that our readers can hold conversations with; books that shout out to readers and prompt them to action" (17).

The idea of such a "talking book," in SACHED's "learner or reader centered" methodology, seeks to "make our books user friendly" by such predictable strategies of design as "using language at a level appropriate to our audience"; "using a friendly often casual tone so we do not alienate the reader"; "not taking readers' knowledge for granted" in regard to diagrams and illustrations; and "facilitating reading through the use of illustrations and photographs and appropriate design strategies" ("A Book Is Not a Book Until It Is Read" 1990, 19). The "new kind of book" that SACHED produced, such as *The Right to Learn* with its embedded narrators, is based on both easy English and a complex use of the potentialities of print culture to redefine the act of reading and to reposition readers in relation to print texts. The rhetorical strategies in *The Right to Learn* cannot be understood merely as simplifications that use such ostensibly subliterate means as speech, pictures, and gestures to convey messages to accommodate a newly literate readership. Rather, there are an ethics and politics of communication that must be taken into account in SACHED's book design.

The represented dialogue of the embedded narrators in *The Right to Learn* makes two important and interrelated rhetorical moves. The first concerns its approach to the question posed in the opening chapter, namely "What's Education About?" The dialogue between the two embedded narrators suggests, at least implicitly, that the question cannot be answered by familiar forms of print culture, such as textbooks or catechisms, that position learners in relation to a monological print authority, where answers depend on memorization and recall by atomized readers. Second, by disrupting such inherited practices of reading, *The Right to Learn,* in turn, establishes the basis for imagining that questions such as "What's education about?" can, in fact, be answered but require an investigation carried out jointly through a dialogue that positions the embedded narrators in relation to other voices (the fourteen quotes distilled into four "aims of education"), as well as in relation to each other. In this sense, the representation of the embedded narrators provides an ethical and political model of rhetorical deliberation, a dialogical practice with the aim of discovering in this particular situation the available means of persuasion to answer the question "What's education about?" The goal is not simply acquiring new knowledge to answer the question but making that knowledge socially useful to formulating policy and a plan of action capable of coalescing a collective will. Through such a deliberative dialogue, the narrators are figured, in

Bakhtin's sense of the term, as *answerable,* both to each other and to the utterances that have, for better or worse, preceded them, not just out of an abstract sense of moral responsibility or the very concrete tactical necessity to recognize other points of view, including those of opponents, but also out of a larger political obligation to respond to the issues of the day, based on the recognition that silence constrains the prospects of justice and social change.[8]

## Popular Literacy and the Problem of Expertise

In a talk to the National Literacy Conference held in Cape Town in 1986, Karl von Holdt posed the question of the relation of literacy and adult education organizations to the liberation struggle. The first task, he said, is "liberation from ignorance. Ignorance is a great weapon in the hands of the ruling class—it prevents the people from seeing clearly and acting clearly" (von Holdt 1986, 68). To say that people need knowledge and understanding, however, as von Holdt goes on to note, only raises further questions: "What is the nature of this knowledge or understanding? Where does it come from? How is it formed?" (69). In order to probe these questions, von Holdt contrasts "two political theories of knowledge/understanding"—those of Freire and of Lenin (or "at least the Lenin pre-1905 [presumably of *What Is To Be Done?*] which is still the most influential Lenin"). As von Holdt sees it, Freire "argued that the intellectual should be a facilitator, helping people discover the knowledge they already have. In their daily lives people already have the means to understand their oppression, and the facilitator's task is to help them become conscious of this through discussion." In contrast, for Lenin, "Party intellectuals had a pure, correct theoretical knowledge which they had to propagate amongst the masses in order to 'raise' their consciousness. It is to all intents and purposes a one way process, from intellectuals to the people." Summing up, von Holdt says, in Lenin's version, "the masses know very little," while in Freire's version, "the masses know everything" (69).

Von Holdt's distinction may be schematic, but it does indicate how radical educators in South Africa and elsewhere have understood and taken up Freire and Lenin, whether or not von Holdt's distinction captures the full measure of their thinking. This distinction, moreover, is a useful one because it highlights the problematical role of intellectuals, artists, and other experts in popular literacy projects. In terms of the role of experts, it is fair to say that many radical South African arts and educational activists tilted toward a version of Freire and the populist position of providing forums for the voiceless to speak, casting their role thereby as facilitators of popular literacy and a kind of conscientization that occurred more or less spontaneously. This may be seen, for example, in the "self-editing" writers' groups and Miriam Tlali's "Soweto Speaking" interviews in the nonelitist literary/cultural journal *Staffrider*, in the worker-poets and over 300 cultural locals in COSATU, and in oral history projects and theatre and dance groups of the antiapartheid struggle in the 1980s, all with their emphasis on performative expression, whereby individuals and groups spoke on behalf of the people.[9] There can be little question about the importance of such public performance, as South Africans formerly denied the status of rhetorical agents articulated realities that had long been suppressed. The role of experts in helping to make this happen, by providing technical assistance and intellectual resources, is likewise an important moment in the development of the antiapartheid struggle.

Still, the role of experts is a vexed one that involves more than just a matter of whether individuals with expertise should facilitate popular expression or propagate "correct" political ideas. To pose the question this way makes it seem to hinge on personal predilection—about how, say, an individual teacher acts toward learners—when the problem of expertise is, in a more fundamental sense, a structural one, rooted in the monopolies of expertise in a racialized class society that served to reproduce ignorance and dependency, on one hand, and privileged access to knowledge and social authority, on the other. Put in these structural terms, we can see how the problem of expertise arose not just in SACHED's popular literacy projects but, more generally, in the relation between the wide range of service organizations that dealt with legal, education, research, and health and safety issues (often with external funding, full-time professional staff, and material resources such as office space, equipment, administrative support, and so on) and mass organizations of trade unionists, students, women, and community groups (often struggling to survive with limited material resources).

The difficulties of these relations can be glimpsed in an exchange in 1987 between Jay Naidoo, then General Secretary of COSATU, and the Durban LACOM-SACHED center. As the discussion indicates, the accountability of service organizations to their funding sources (often European or other foreign donors) raised questions of organizational loyalties to benefactors in relation to consultation with people on the ground in South Africa. In addition, there was the problem of perpetuating expert/nonexpert distinctions and the accompanying tension between developing "future leaders" and the abolition of elitism and dependence on experts (Naidoo 1987; "On the Role of Service Organisations" 1987).

We have already seen how LACOM attempted to deal with the problem of expertise in the writing workshops offered for trade unions and community organizations by seeking to redistribute the resources of print culture, to make them available as means of persuasion on the part of militants and activists. There is a certain balancing act at work that cannot be comprehended as simply Freire-inspired facilitation or Leninist propagandizing but rather has more to do with the recognition of rhetorical motives in literacy practices. The sense is that learning to write a news story on a strike is not just a transfer of expertise but a rearticulation of expertise to popular aspirations, with the understanding that writers are responsible for the way they position themselves in relation to workers and bosses.

## Popular Literacy, Rhetorical Motives, and the Problem of the People

Much the same can be said about the African History Project, designed as an alternative to school textbooks that made apartheid into the culmination of South African history. The question of rhetorical motive figures prominently in Chapter One, "Why Do We Study African History?" The chapter begins by showing that "[e]very person studies the past whether he or she is conscious of doing so or not" (2) and by asking learners to find examples in a family or school situation to illustrate this point and, a few pages later, to tell a "real-life story of how someone's skin colour helped or obstructed his/her advancement in our society" in order to illustrate how "the dominant ideas in our society are the ideas of the dominant classes" (5). The approach of the African History Project, however, is not simply to raise learners' experiences and knowledges to consciousness, in a Freirean sense, but to introduce knowledge from the expert realm of historical studies to mesh with learners' experience and knowledges—by analyzing in the opening chapter the interpretations offered in three accounts of the Xhosa cattle-killing of 1857 and by considering the problem of historical causation and how it positions students of history in relation to past, present, and future.

The aim of the African History Project was to rewrite history from the bottom up, in the interests of those marginalized by the monopoly of historical knowledge in school textbooks, by using the tools and conceptual frameworks of historical analysis for popular ends. This did not mean, however, that such a popular history was seen to be immediately or unproblematically available, as is the case, say, in Luli Callinicos' three-volume *A People's History of South Africa*, a beautifully illustrated large-format series published in 1981, 1987, and 1993 that recounts, in a style indebted to E. P. Thompson, the making of the South African working class. Rather, in the African History Project, the study of history remained a complex and unfinished business, where various interpretations of the past, such as the different theories of imperialism in Africa in Chapter Seven "Responses to Colonial Conquest," have to be weighed and measured in light of what they enabled learners to see and what they constrained in terms of reckoning the present situation and future possibilities. In this sense, the African History Project positioned learners not so much as novices to historical study but as participants in the construction of a new South African history out of contradictory accounts of the past. Further, unlike *A People's History of South Africa*'s single-nation account, the African History Project established an internationalist perspective in the study of history that took the encounter between Africa and European empires as the necessary frame of reference.

The problem of rearticulating the expertise of historical inquiry to popular aspirations, it is important to see, also raised the problem of how popular literacy projects such as the African History Project represent the people. In the versions of Freire and Lenin that von Holdt puts forward, intellectuals encounter the people as a homogeneous mass whose ignorance resides in an inability to articulate their conditions of oppression at the level of consciousness, though the means of raising consciousness differ markedly. The problem of the people, however, cannot be understood simply in terms of how the production of ignorance was institutionalized during the colonial and segregation eras and then refined through the social engineering and repressive underdevelopment of the apartheid years that squandered native intelligence and talent. Ignorance also manifested itself insidiously in the divisions within the people that were based on the divisions of South African racial capitalism—class, race, gender, ethnicity, language, age, social rank, and so on—and the variable responses that followed to the social and political crisis in South Africa during the 1980s.

This understanding of divisions within the people may be seen in a remarkable chapter of the African History Project, "Responses to Colonial Conquest," which considers "how difficult it was (or can be) to decide whether a certain group of people (or leadership) was 'resisting' or 'collaborating'" with European powers in Africa (1). The chapter begins with two "basic problems":

1. Under what circumstances did a people resist conquest by taking up arms? Or, the other side of the question: under what circumstances did a people collaborate with imperialist conquerors? (A vital part of this question is the relationship between the people and their leaders who were mainly chiefs and kings/queens.)
2. Were all resisters "good" and all the collaborators "bad"? (1)

The chapter notes that answers to these questions cannot be derived from nationalist popular histories that mistakenly assume a unity of the people that equates anticolonialism and nationalism as the "deep roots" of modern movements for national liberation. Instead, the chapter suggests that "[l]ittle or no attention is paid to possible and actual divisions within the resisting group or groups of people. In general, a homogeneous social unit is supposed to have existed. But we know now that in very many cases the very opposite was true. There were different interests and many tensions and contradictions within the colonised African communities" (3). In turn, the chapter goes on to examine mini–case studies of armed resistance—the Khoikhoi resistance to the Dutch in seventeenth-century South Africa and the Nyangire rebellion of 1907 in Uganda—as well as the conditions under which collaboration with imperial powers took place and the role of other forms of resistance, such as "tax evasion, lack of cooperation, work slowdowns, destruction of European property, desertion, absenteeism, migration and sporadic attacks on symbols of oppression" (20), and millennial movements inspired by charismatic prophets.

The complexities of African history are readily apparent. "Responses to Colonial Conquest" certainly resisted a monological people's history of heroic struggle and villainous betrayal. But, importantly, it was not meant to present a "balanced" account either. Rather it is an engaged and partisan history that presents divisions and contradictions within the people as problems of political clarification, to study in terms of the insights that might be forthcoming for an active understanding of the struggle against apartheid. Like other SACHED popular literacy projects, such as LACOM's writing workshops and *The Right to Learn* (Christie 1985), the African History Project starts with the premise that learners, as participants in a racialized class society, will necessarily have differing views that must be brought to light and mapped onto the political terrain of the struggle against apartheid.

The issue in all these cases is neither unleashing a spontaneous revolutionary will on the part of the people nor having vanguard cadre correct their false consciousness; instead it is a matter of addressing the crisis of the popular classes precipitated by the wider crisis in South African society. In this view, the people are more like a molecular process of bonding and division than a unified entity. Accordingly, the task for radical educators cannot be understood simply as liberating the people from their ignorance, with all the unfortunate connotations of the intellectual, whether Freirean or Leninist, as a messianic figure. If it is true that only the people can liberate themselves, the unity that is required for liberation cannot be the presumed starting point. The unity of the people, rather, is a political horizon, and rhetorical negotiation provides a means to reach it. This, at least, is what I think the best of the SACHED popular literacy projects recognized and invented strategies to realize.

## Epilogue: The Legacy of SACHED

In seeking to recollect the work of SACHED and to make it available to readers in North America, I have become acutely aware of the allure of the archive and the inclination to romanticize SACHED's role in the struggle for liberation in South Africa. On this account, so that we do not leave SACHED in the now thoroughly mythologized years of the 1980s, I believe it is necessary to offer a final, if tentative, brief description of the demise and complicated legacy of SACHED as a sobering counterpoint. There are two points to be made, one concerning SACHED itself, the other having to do with the political realities of the new South Africa post-1994, during SACHED's final years of operation.

The first point is simply to note the absence of African languages in SACHED's educational materials and popular literacy projects. During the 1980s, English was assumed to be the language of liberation, and the issue remained, as Eddie Roux had posed it nearly a half century before, how to devise an easy English, even factoring in SACHED's ingenious deployment of the resources of print culture. There are, to be sure, explanations for the hegemony of English in the liberation movement, including the association of Afrikaans with Afrikaner nationalism, of African languages with the tribal homelands and the possibilities of ethnolinguistic conflict, and of English with black power in the United States. Nonetheless, SACHED's English-only practices reveal a significant blind spot that became increasingly evident to SACHED activists such as Neville Alexander, who has gone on to extend SACHED's legacy of alternative education by establishing the Project for Alternative Education in South Africa that does research, language planning, and teacher training to promote multilingualism in South African schools and society.

The second point is more dire, for it involves not just SACHED but the host of education, labor, and community organizations that vitalized civil society in South Africa during the 1980s. The telling fact is that most no longer exist. SACHED ended operations by the late 1990s, part of what John Aitchison calls the "decimation of the NGO sector" (2003, 158). There are a number of reasons for this seemingly systematic demobilization of popular energies. For one thing, the negotiated settlement that instituted black majority rule and handed over the state apparatus of racial capitalism to the ANC led a number of foreign donors who had supported important service organizations and grassroots movements in the 1980s to cease funding or to enter directly into agreements with government. This withdrawal of funding fell heavily on nongovernment organizations, including the independent presses, which had played an important role in popular literacy projects, but now, unsubsidized, were forced to close as multinational publishers increasingly took over the South African book market. Second, the trade unions, which had been laboratories for democracy and workers' education in the 1980s, redefined their role as that of a stakeholder, along with government and business, in the new South Africa and an unequal partner, along with the South African Communist Party, in a tripartite political alliance with the ruling ANC. Finally, for its part, the ANC abandoned the populist principles of the Freedom Charter, embraced neoliberalism, and enacted a program of structural adjustment and privatization. As a result, in adult and worker education (as well as in formal schooling), the terms shifted from the consciousness raising of alternative education in the 1980s to capacity building in the neoliberal era of the late 1990s and 2000s, as ANC policy linked education to the development of human capital and the promotion of economic competitiveness in the world market, marginalized nongovernment education organizations, and favored instead private educational providers. As Alexander (1992) puts it, South Africa has become an "ordinary country" in global capitalism, not unlike India or Brazil, run by the logic of the market, with the predictable disparities between rich and poor.[10]

As I mentioned, this is a sobering account but one that provides the needed context to measure the legacy of SACHED. From one angle, SACHED may be seen, in retrospect, as a training ground for future leaders, as many who are now prominent figures in education, government, universities, literature, and arts worked at SACHED, acquiring significant experience, as staff or volunteers, in greater or lesser positions of responsibility. It is perhaps a sign of neoliberal times in South Africa that these trajectories can now be imagined—though only in retrospect—as credential-building career moves by individuals from the thin layer of educated South Africans. From another angle, however, the strengths and weaknesses of SACHED's popular literacy projects, its political independence and what that enabled, and, above all, its commitment to educational alternatives that "empower people to take charge of their own projects" are what need to be reckoned. This legacy, I have tried to show, has its own particular complications, contradictions, and complexities—and for this reason remains highly relevant today, in South Africa, the United States, or wherever radical educators seek to popularize literacy for people who have been deprived of the resources of representation and persuasion.[11]

## Chapter Eight

# Composition and the Circulation of Writing

Aside from newspaper movies such as *Front Page* and *All the President's Men,* where the drama centers around heroic reporters and hard-bitten editors breaking news stories to fight the rich and powerful, it is hard to think of many telling visual representations of the activity of writing. There are, of course, plenty of paintings of writers, such as Manet's portrait of Mallarmé and Picasso's of Gertrude Stein. But, as an activity that unfolds over time, writing does not seem to have much visual value, although Jack Nicholson's performance as a blocked writer in *The Shining* is certainly a chilling exception and a reminder of Stephen King's (and the late Stanley Kubrick's) irrepressible black humor.

At any rate, the apparently uncinematic character of writing makes the opening sequence in the film *My Dinner with André* such a rarity because it represents a writer at work over a period of time, in this case the harried playwright Wallace Shawn. Only he is not writing. Rather he is going about the busy work of a writer, hurrying around Manhattan, getting copies duplicated and a manuscript delivered. This work, director Louis Malle wants us to believe, is mundane and technical, the blue-collar side of writing incidental to the creative moment, and as the film goes on to make clear, this image of the writer as a manual laborer in the bustling metropolis is meant to serve as a foil to the otherworldly cosmopolitan aesthete André, whom Shawn meets for dinner.

This sequence from *My Dinner with André* came to mind at the end of fall term this past year when students, like Wallace Shawn, were hustling to finish and deliver portfolios and senior projects to me when technical difficulties intervened, the computer center closed because of a virus, and no one could print. So I was going to have to accept late work for legitimate reasons. I could not respond to students' pleas of lost files or broken printers as I routinely do as lame excuses for not getting the work done and handy replacements in a cyber-age for the old-fashioned death of relatives or the paper-eating dog. "I don't want to hear it," I usually say. "I just want the paper."

My point here does not have to do with what amounts to a fair policy on late papers but rather with what is contained in my usual response or, better put, what is silenced when I say "I don't want to hear it." For on the other side is precisely that world of the writer at work Malle depicts so tellingly: the material conditions of producing writing and getting it delivered where it needs to go. If my response is a typical one—and I believe it is reasonable to think so—then we might stop to consider what is at stake and the extent to which such pedagogical practices erase the materiality of writing. To say, as I have, "I just want the paper," suggests that the student's words alone are what count and to identify writing with the creative moment of composing, thereby isolating an education in writing from the means of production and delivery.

My purpose is to pose this isolation of writing from the material conditions of production and delivery as a problem. As I will suggest in a moment, the isolation results in part from the pressures and limits of classroom life and the overdetermined social relations between teachers and students. But there is also a conceptual separation of the canons of rhetoric operating in writing instruction that has isolated delivery (and memory, as well) from invention, arrangement, and style. To anticipate the main line of thought in this essay, I argue that neglecting delivery has led writing teachers to equate the activity of composing with writing itself and to miss altogether the complex delivery systems through which writing circulates. By privileging composing as the main site of instruction, the teaching of writing has taken up what Karl Marx calls a "one-sided" view of production and thereby has largely erased the cycle that links the production, distribution, exchange, and consumption of writing. This cycle of interlocked moments is what Marx calls *circulation*. The case I hope to advance holds that the circulation of writing should figure much more prominently in writing instruction.

Rhetoricians will surely notice—and may object to the fact—that I use delivery and the Marxian notion of circulation interchangeably in this chapter. So, before I go on, let me explain my reasons for doing so. My understanding is that delivery was treated rather briefly and unsystematically in classical rhetoric, as a technical aspect of public speaking concerned mainly, Sharon Crowley says, with the "appropriate management of the voice, gestures, and appearance" (1994, 29). As Brenda Gabioud Brown puts it, Aristotle "did not deem [delivery] an elevated subject of inquiry" (1996, 211). Delivery, to be sure, played a central role in oratorical education, especially in the Elocutionary Movement of the eighteenth and nineteenth centuries, with its emphasis on the physicality of speech making (pitch, quality, force, abruptness, and time) and the correct pronunciation of words.

In writing instruction, however, delivery has been an afterthought at best, assigned mainly to technical and professional communication and associated largely with such matters of document design as page layout, typography, visual display of information, and Web design. Delivery, that is, appears for the most part to be a technical issue about physical presentation whether in oral, print, or electronic forms. For the Greeks, this makes a certain amount of sense; after all, the relevant listeners were gathered in public assembly, and the delivery was a live performance. In the modern era, however, this is not the case. Public forums are diffuse, fragmented, and geographically separated. Speech is both literally and metaphorically broadcast through expanded means of communication. To my mind, delivery can no longer be thought of simply as a technical aspect of public discourse. It must be seen also as ethical and political—a democratic aspiration to devise delivery systems that circulate ideas, information, opinions, and knowledge and thereby expand the public forums in which people can deliberate on the issues of the day.

In other words, I want to understand the term *delivery* normatively, not just descriptively, to indicate a critical horizon we imagine the Greeks achieved, at least among the limited citizenry of the polis, in a face-to-face way. My argument is that with the democratic revolutions of the modern age, delivery *must* be seen as inseparable from the circulation of writing and the widening diffusion of socially useful knowledge. Milton's *The Readie and Easie Way to Establish a Free Commonwealth* (1660) sounds an early political and ethical call, taken up by Enlightenment thinkers, radical educators, and social theorists such as Raymond Williams and Jurgen Habermas, to think of democracy as necessarily a communicative process that depends on an extended delivery system. Milton urges his contemporaries to

> spread much more Knowledge and Civility, yea, Religion, through all parts of the Land, by communicating the natural heat of Government and Culture more distributively to all extreme parts, which now lie num and neglected. (quoted in Williams 1983, 88)

Thus, I would summarize the brief I hope to unpack in this essay. In the broadest sense, I want to redefine delivery—and to understand the circulation of writing—in terms of the unfinished work of the democratic revolutions to expand public forums and popular participation in civic life. My argument has a number of parts. First, I suggest that composition has neglected delivery and the circulation of writing by figuring classroom life as a middle-class family drama, in which the teacher, *in loco parentis,* calls directly on students to account for themselves. Second, I examine how neo-Marxist cultural studies approaches to teaching writing have sought, with mixed success, to transcend the domestic space of the writing classroom by linking student work to the circulation of cultural forms and products. Third, I draw on Marx's notebooks from 1857–58, the *Grundrisse* (1973), for what I consider to be a more adequate conceptual model that enables us to see how the circulation of writing materializes contradictory social relations and social processes. Finally, I look at how these contradictions between experts and laypeople, between exchange value and use value, might be taken up in writing classrooms, and I suggest some practical means to link composing and circulation in writing assignments.

## *In Loco Parentis*

Carolyn Steedman says that "children are always episodes in someone else's narratives, not their own people, but rather brought into being for someone else's purposes" (1986, 122). The narrative that "brings into being" the students we teach, I believe, is predominantly a legal and contractual one, in which parents enter their children in a relation of *in loco parentis* with a legally responsible adult, the teacher/surrogate parent, who is in charge of the education of a child or adolescent or young adult. Although she does not use the term *in loco parentis,* Anne Haas-Dyson (1994), in an important reconsideration of the process movement, argues that the child writer has been figured as an active meaning-making pupil in relation to a responsive mother-teacher. In process pedagogies, Haas-Dyson says, the child writer is released into language by the teacher, nurtured, supported, and known through the student's active experience with texts. The controlling metaphors in the process movement that Haas-Dyson points to are familiar ones, calling up organic images of midwifery, of giving birth to natural development, and of promoting growth. But these metaphors, I would add, only point to an attempt to naturalize the historical role of the teacher as a stand-in, *in loco parentis,* to enact the drama of the middle-class family, where inherent capacities must not be squandered by poor parenting—one of the key features that distinguishes the middle-class family from poor and working-class families.

Just as Haas-Dyson reads the story of the process movement and the child writer, one might argue that college writing instruction can also be read as a history of various articulations of *in loco parentis*—different ways of figuring the student writer in relation to the teacher. For example, the notion of *in loco parentis* might offer a new way to look at old debates, such as that between Peter Elbow and David Bartholomae. This debate has conventionally been represented as one concerning personal voice versus academic discourse, authentic versus socially constructed selves, sincerity versus imitation. Instead of relying on these polarities, however, I want to look at the debate as one involving different representations of *in loco parentis*—of writing with or without teachers—two accounts of the presence and authority of the teacher in relation to students.

In the last installment of the debate, published in *CCC* in 1995, the issue comes down to pedagogy: What is the role of the teacher in relation to a student writing a family narrative, to facilitate a rendering of experience or to disrupt the cultural logic of the genre? Clearly the rhetorical (and parental) stance of the teacher differs. On one hand, we have Elbow as the permissive suburban dad, Little League coach, and pal to his kids. On the other, we find the tough love of Bartholomae's demanding yet devoted father, insisting that his children read difficult "quality" material. But despite these stylistic differences, both Elbow and Bartholomae are trying to elicit, by either absence/deference or enhanced presence, writing from the student—to induce, cajole, command, or persuade the student to offer an account and a meaning, whether it concerns the student's personal experience or the student's textual experience in relation to other texts and cultural logics.

To my mind, what has been overlooked in the Elbow-Bartholomae debate is what they have in common. Namely, each relies on a representation of the student writer as an active meaning maker in relation—*in loco parentis*—to a powerful teacher figure. Operating in both Elbow's and Bartholomae's work is a representation of the student writer unlocked by a responsive father-teacher figure, a student released into the activity of interpretation, of discovering and formulating meanings, whether of personal or textual experience. According to this representation, student writers need to have views and give accounts of things, a mastery that evokes the cultural authorization of the professional managerial classes, whose capital resides in their ability to have opinions, make judgments, present views, and offer compelling explanations of their own and other people's experience. It is the kind of performance once learned in the home, at dinnertime, when middle-class fathers called on their sons and sometimes their daughters to give accounts and be held accountable for their views.

I single out the Elbow-Bartholomae debate, in part, to offer a counter-reading that avoids the usual polarized taxonomic categories. But I also want to take the debate as symptomatic in order to call attention to a representation of the meaning-making student in relation to a parental authority, whether permissive or stern, but always asking for an account. For me, the constellated figure of student and teacher *in loco parentis* so thoroughly pervades the study and teaching of writing that it has become commonsensical and unavailable for analysis. From this perspective, the writing classroom turns into a domestic space, not simply because writing instruction has been feminized structurally in its role within the academy (Miller 1991). More immediately, as lived experience, the writing classroom has the intimacy of home, and its language is inflected by the aspirations of middle-class parents seeking to realize their children's potential, to capitalize on their futures. It is no accident that writing teachers frequently contrast the first-year course, in which the teacher knows each student's name and calls on everyone to speak, to the impersonality and anonymity of other courses. If anything, writing teachers like to justify composition courses as places where a kind of domestic intimacy provides some of the comforts of home, a haven in what many students find to be an otherwise alien or hostile environment.

I certainly do not mean to suggest that we can get out of the relations of *in loco parentis* that encompass the work of teaching writing. Instead, I want first to acknowledge that both Elbow and Bartholomae have articulated this relation as a means to democratize liberal culture by enabling students to take on subject positions formerly reserved for the elite. In this sense, the representation of the student writer as an active meaning maker is an outgrowth and an important legacy of the educational reforms of the 1960s and open admissions programs of the early 1970s. Like Head Start, the impulse is to extend good parenting to all students.

At the same time, however, for the purposes of this essay—to explain the relative neglect of delivery and the circulation of writing in composition teaching—I need to point out that by concentrating on the student writer interpreting the world at the point of production, both sides in the debate foreshorten the delivery system, the circuits of production, distribution, exchange, and consumption through which writing circulates as it takes on cultural value and worldly force. Bartholomae and Elbow have, I think, abridged the political economy of written communication by linking production directly to consumption within the intimate space of the classroom/home. Both present the relation between production and consumption as a reciprocal one, joined together by the immediacy of familial life. Elbow links the production of student writing directly to consumption by peer readers, whose readings in turn become productive as they respond to the writer. By contrast, Bartholomae wants to make the consumption of anthologized texts into productive (or "strong") readings, which in turn are consumed as part of the means of production when students write papers.

If you are wondering how it could be otherwise—how Bartholomae or Elbow or any writing teacher for that matter could actually stage the circuits of distribution and exchange through which writing passes—you have a reasonable point. The material constraints of the writing class are very real ones. It is hard to imagine, for example, a textbook publisher willing to reproduce the material forms in which writing actually circulates, everything from the black-and-white newsprint pages of *Nation* to the four-color glossy spreads in *Rolling Stone,* along with accompanying advertisements, letters to the editor, fund-raising appeals, and classified section. Packaged in anthologies and uniform in appearance, written texts take on an equivalent look that belies their actual circulation in the world. By the same token, although student writing does indeed circulate and take on the symbolic exchange value of academic credit, the directions "trade papers with a partner" or "hand in your paper" indicate the limits of the circuit in the intimate space of the classroom in contrast, say, to the broadcasting of messages through the mass media.

Of course, many writing teachers have attempted to deal with the limited circuit of the classroom by seeking to avoid the way *in loco parentis* configures students and teachers in a middle-class family in which good parenting cultivates accountable children. Instead, they have turned to assigning what is sometimes called "real-world" writing, such as letters to the editor, proposals to college administrators or local officials, policy briefings for legislators, newsletters for community organizations, and so on. I endorse the turn to public writing and civic rhetoric that is often invoked in such assignments, but at the same time, I want to resist the notion that student writing is not otherwise part of the real world. While these kinds of assignments do begin to address the problem of circulation in interesting ways, they depend nonetheless on a dichotomy between schooled and "real" writing that rejects the private space of the classroom/home in the name of an unproblematical, immediately available public writing (see Wells 1996). Moreover, counterposing the real world to the classroom draws upon a gendered separation of spheres that fails to see how the public and private merge in the domestic space of the middle-class family. In terms of good parenting, the middle-class family, as Stephanie Coontz (1988) argues, is not so much a refuge from the real world as an idealized space to prepare children for its demands. In this regard, as Bruce Herzberg (1994) has suggested, community service learning in particular does not always come to grips with its own origins in the middle-class project of going into the world to do good works for the less fortunate—a script of benefactors and the needy that has a long history.

And in any case, we are still faced with the issue of how composing can be more fully integrated into the circulation of writing whether or not real-world writing assignments are a practical alternative. The problem remains: how to imagine writing as more than just the moment of production when meaning gets made. How can we see writing as it circulates through linked moments of production, distribution, exchange, and consumption?

## Cultural Studies and the Problem of Circulation

The intellectual and political work at the (now legendary) Centre for Contemporary Cultural Studies in Birmingham has offered some suggestive leads to answer these questions. Richard Johnson's "What Is Cultural Studies Anyway?" (1986–87) and Stuart Hall's "Encoding/Decoding" (1980), for example, have influenced compositionists who are interested in a cultural studies approach to teaching writing by elaborating models of the circulation of cultural forms and products. Johnson and Hall each draw on Marx's analyses in the *Grundrisse* (1973) of the circulation of money, capital, and labor power to argue, homologously, not only that cultural products circulate but also, crucially, that the moments of circulation entail a transformation or "passage of forms." I look at Marx's model of production, distribution, exchange, and consumption in the next section. Here, I want to examine the implications for writing instruction in Johnson's and Hall's neo-Marxist and largely metaphorical appropriation of Marx's notion of circulation as they apply it to processes of communication and cultural production.

In Johnson's version, the circulation of cultural products takes place as a movement from *production* to *textual forms* to *readings* to *lived culture*. For Johnson, each of these moments in the life of a cultural product "depends upon the others and is indispensable to the whole. Each, however, is distinct and involves characteristic changes in form" (1986–87, 46). By Johnson's account, the notion of circulation enables us to see how cultural products pass through a range of meanings and uses as they are taken up at various points in the social formation. The extended example Johnson offers of circulation traces the British Mini-Metro car, widely hailed in the Thatcher era as the salvation of the British automobile industry. According to Johnson, *production* is not the privileged moment of origin, as some Old Left Marxist accounts might have it, but a transformation of a "designer's idea" and "manager's 'concept'" into a cultural product. In turn, such cultural products take on the form of *texts*, from the visual design of the Mini-Metro itself to showroom displays and advertisements to national discourses about foreign competition and the connections between industrial "peace" and economic recovery. In its accumulated meanings, the *text* of the Mini-Metro turns variously into a symbol of Britishness, a response to foreign rivals, and a solution to British Leyland's problems of industrial discipline. In one television ad, for example, a band of Metro-Minis drives foreign imports over the White Cliffs of Dover, combining, Johnson says, "nationalist epic, popular memory of World War II, internal/external threat" (1986–87, 48). At the same time, *readings* of such texts, Johnson notes, will vary considerably, depending on the interests and social location of the reader. The Mini-Metro no doubt elicited quite different readings on the part of Leyland workers who exchanged their labor power to build the car, investors looking for profitable returns, and consumers shopping for a car to drive to work or pick up the kids from school. Incorporated into the everyday experience of *lived culture,* the Mini-Metro could be taken up as a national symbol, a stake in class struggle, a smart investment, a cleverly designed artifact, some combination, or more. And finally, circulation returns to the moment of production—as profits for new investment, of course, but also as market researchers' findings on the "popularity" of the Mini-Metro and management's accumulated experience handling shop floor militancy.

Imagining cultural forms and products circulating through a continuous cycle of relatively autonomous but interlocked moments has some important consequences. For one thing, it enables Johnson to challenge the assumption that the meaning of a message or cultural product can be inferred directly and unproblematically from either its moment of production or its textual manifestation without taking into account the conditions of circulation. In this sense, the notion of cultural circulation breaks decisively with the dominant ideology thesis of Old Left Marxist political economy, which holds that the reigning ideas, cultural products, and social institutions of an era are simply reflections of the mode of production, imposed from above by ruling-class interests. And it also calls into question the tendency inherited from literary studies to constitute cultural forms and products simply as "texts" that can be analyzed, critiqued, and demystified by the expert readings of specialist critics. For Johnson, both the conditions of production and the textual results are important moments for cultural study, analysis, and understanding, but neither, by itself, is sufficient to account for all possible readings and uses.

This sense of the variability and negotiated character of circulation provides an important corrective to some of the work in composition that has taken place under the auspices of a cultural studies approach to teaching writing. In many respects, a left-liberal version of the dominant ideology thesis prevailed in the late 1980s (and continues residually into the present); writing teachers emphasized close readings of cultural texts and ideological critiques with the goal of providing students the interpretive and evaluative tools to be discriminating readers and to resist the dominant culture. For example, when Diana George and I were working on the first edition of *Reading Culture* (1992), arguably the first cultural studies reader, we joked that our aim was to prevent students from being the victims of semiosis, and in retrospect the comment is a revealing one. While we and others working in the cultural studies vein were aware of the danger of representing students as cultural dupes, with no defenses against interpellation into an Althusserian ideological state apparatus, the tendency nonetheless was to identify students as readers, consumers, viewers, and spectators in need of training to resist the onslaughts of mass culture.

It should not be surprising, given their backgrounds in English departments and the influence of literary theory on composition, that writing teachers looking to cultural studies in the late 1980s and early 1990s constituted the forms, products, and practices of cultural life as "texts" that could be read and written about. In the simplest sense, to focus on issues of representation gave us something with which we were familiar and that appeared to be immediately teachable. The typical writing assignment, therefore, was the interpretive essay, often modeled on Roland Barthes' (1972) essays in denaturalizing mass culture and everyday life in *Mythologies*. One of the results of such assignments was that they threatened to make cultural studies into just a new set of materials for the writing classroom—a new set of "texts," although imagined in the broadest terms to include not only familiar written forms but also forms of the media, popular culture, leisure, everyday life, schooling, and work.

In other words, in the hope of fortifying student resistance to the dominant culture, such assignments unwittingly smuggled in and restored the close text-based readings of the specialist critic as the privileged practice of the writing classroom—the old story of explaining and having views. And this old story, as always, revealed the uneven distribution of cultural capital among students. If anything, interpretive attention to signifying practices and consumer culture came "naturally" to some students, especially to the middle-class students on a trajectory to enter what Scott Lash and John Urry, invoking Pierre Bourdieu, call the "habitus" of a new class fraction, "the postmodern petite bourgeoisie" in the information and service sectors, in advertising, the media, social services, human relations, consulting, and design (1987, 292–96). These were typically the students who wrote the papers with style, irreverence, and edge—their "structure of feeling" already attuned to the knowing and often ironic consumption of cultural products.

Close reading and interpretation are, of course, useful and inevitable practices of cultural analysis. My point is that by fixating at one moment in the circulation of cultural forms—by imagining culture to be a "text" capable of being read—cultural studies writing assignments and classroom practices once again (and *in loco parentis*) called on the active meaning-making student to give an interpretive account. Such a pedagogy not only plays into the predisposition of the professional classes to explain their own and everybody else's signifying practices. It also neglects the other moments in the circulation of cultural forms and products. "Processes," Johnson says, "disappear in results" (1986–87, 46), which was very much the case, I believe, for the tendency to make ideological critique and the interpretive essay into the main vehicles of cultural studies in the writing classroom. While a sector of students learned to do sophisticated readings of a wide variety of cultural texts, the circulation of cultural products receded from view and became unavailable for analysis.

I do not want to suggest that writing teachers who aligned themselves with cultural studies were unaware of the pressures and limits of the interpretive essay and its deeply rooted project of the meaning-making student writer giving an account to a responsive teacher. In fact, there emerged rather rapidly what I would call a "second-generation" cultural studies writing assignment—the microethnography—in which the emphasis shifted from the student writer who took on the demystifying role of the expert critic to the student as a participant-observer investigating how ordinary people produced their own "readings" of cultural texts and incorporated them into "lived culture" (cf. Faigley 1992). To my mind, this shift of attention has been valuable because it locates critical work for students within the circuits through which cultural meanings are produced, circulated, and used. And yet, at the same time, by focusing on moments of cultural consumption, microethnographies of reading and lived experience raise important questions about the adequacy of the prevailing model of communication in cultural studies to comprehend the full scope of the delivery system and its multiple transformations.

This issue arises quite clearly with the turn in cultural studies away from linear models of communication, where messages pass unproblematically from a sender to a receiver, to the "active audience," where the meanings of cultural products are determined as much by the user, the viewer, the spectator, or the fan as by the producer, and consumption itself becomes productive of multiple and sometimes indeterminate appropriations. Audience research, to be sure, has a long history in communication (of effects, uses, and gratification), but we can trace the present interest in the "active audience" to subcultural and media studies, whether ethnographic (Willis 1977; Morley 1980; McRobbie 1983; Radway 1984) or semiotic (Hebdige 1979), that replace the expert reader's text-based analyses with analysis of how ordinary readers make sense of and use texts and other cultural products. Recently, though, this line of inquiry has been taken to problematical lengths in the work of John Fiske and others, for whom ordinary people are persistently resisting and evading the dominant culture and an oppressive social order by making their own personally liberating meanings through their use of the mall, video arcades, the beach, television game shows, and Madonna. For Fiske, popular culture—or better, what he calls "popular discrimination," inverting F. R. Leavis in a way that would horrify him—is always insubordinate, for it is "formed always in reaction to, and never as part of, the forces of domination" (1989, 43).

In one sense, Fiske's work—and more generally what Philip Schlesinger (1991) characterizes as the "new revisionism" in cultural and media studies—are perhaps an inevitable response not only to the limits of the Old Left dominant ideology thesis, with its emphasis on the false consciousness of the mass audience, but also to the "moral panic" about the media, young people, and popular culture generated periodically by conservative forces in England and the United States. The term *moral panic* was coined by Stanley Cohen (1973) in his classic study of how the "deviance" of 1960s mods and rockers in the United Kingdom was amplified by "the control culture," but it has been a recurrent theme in the sensational press and cultural commentary since at least the hooligans of the 1890s. We can see it operating recently, for example, in William Bennett's attacks on gangsta rap and daytime talk television, the formation of Tipper Gore's Parents Music Resource Group and its call for labeling records (and now television programs), and President Clinton's proposals for curfews and school uniforms. Predictably, the high school shootings at Littleton, Colorado, set off a new round of moral panic about ultraviolent video games, black trench coats, heavy metal music, Goths, and geek subcultures.

In a critical examination of how the press covered "Popular TV and Schoolchildren," a report issued in 1983 by the Department of Education and Science in the United Kingdom, media educationalist David Lusted notes three themes in moral panics over children's television viewing that can be generalized more widely to audiences of all sorts: (1) a "copycat" thesis, generated by middle-class anxieties that popular culture products can actually activate antisocial behavior, lead people to emulate characters on television, or engage in mindless hedonism; (2) an "anaesthetic" thesis, generated by middle-class anxieties that television will pacify their children (thereby squandering their potential) and desensitize viewers at large; and (3) the "sex and violence" thesis, which encapsulates elements of the first two in a puritanical framework that believes viewers will both imitate and be desensitized to the sex and violence they see on television.

So, if it is understandable that Fiske and others want to counterpose to the moral panic a viewer who is not the passive zombie or behaviorist pawn responding automatically to media stimuli, their antimoralistic and antijudgmental stance amounts to an overcorrection that holds, in Dorothy Hobson's words on soap opera viewers, that the "audience is always in control" and "the viewer *always knows* best" (quoted in McGuigan 1992, 144, emphasis in original). By assigning *all* the agency to the audience, the "new revisionists" have made it virtually impossible to mount any kind of critique of the media—to ask, for instance, how the "active audience" itself is packaged and sold as a commodity (the "market share" of viewers) to advertisers. The problem is not just that the "new revisionists" have overemphasized the agency of the audience and popular practices of consumption. In effect, by doing so, they have severed the relation between production and consumption altogether, viewing the use of cultural forms and products in isolation from the social conditions that formed them. By fixating on moments of "reading" and "lived culture" in Johnson's circuit, the "new revisionists" have dematerialized precisely those cultural products whose consumption they seek to analyze by stripping their production of any determinate role in structuring ordinary people's interactions with the media and popular culture. And, as Jim McGuigan points out, the cultural populism espoused in the name of pleasure and audience empowerment is constantly at risk of sliding into an "abjectly uncritical complicity with prevailing 'free market' ideology and its hidden powers" (1992, 75).

No doubt the classic attempt to grant agency to viewers, readers, spectators, and fans and yet to avoid slippage into separating production and consumption altogether is Hall's "encoding/decoding" (1980). In his formulation, the "active audience" is not always "right" or "in control." Instead, for Hall, viewers' responses are open but not indeterminate, bounded by the pressures and limits of messages encoded at the point of production according to the prevailing "knowledge-in-use concerning the routines of production, historically defined technical skills, professional ideologies, institutional knowledge, definitions and assumptions, assumptions about the audience and so on" (1980, 129). Hall hypothesizes three by now familiar positions viewers take as they respond to encoded messages: a *dominant-hegemonic position* from which the viewer "is operating inside the dominant code" (136); a *negotiated position* from which decoding "contains a mixture of adaptive and oppositional elements" (137); and finally an *oppositional position* from which decoding "detotalizes the message in the preferred code in order to retotalize the message within some alternative framework of reference" (138). To make Hall's encoding/decoding model more concrete, think, for example, of the possible responses of viewers to a popular television show such as *Ally McBeal*. Some will take up the dominant-hegemonic position and identify with Ally's weekly dilemmas as a "you go, girl" single professional woman. Others, though, from a negotiated position, may worry Ally is just too ditzy, while at the same time investing credibility in the dilemmas scripted for her. Still others will hold, from an oppositional position, that Ally cannot be understood apart from postfeminist cultural currents that have trivialized the struggles of the women's movement.

One of the striking features of Hall's encoding/decoding model is how it seeks to represent the receiver as an active agent without giving up on the effectivity of ideology in the process of communication. To put it another way, for Hall, there *is* a dominant ideology, but he has reconceptualized it in terms of the negotiation of "preferred readings." In many respects, this balancing act is characteristic of Hall's version of cultural studies, and we can read his "Encoding/Decoding" essay as a remarkably compressed rendition of Hall's neo-Gramscian synthesis and his effort to balance the dominant ideology thesis against lived experience by way of the notion of hegemony as negotiated consent. By figuring the relation between production and consumption—what Hall refers to as the "so-called 'unity' of a discourse"—as "the articulation of different, distinct elements which can be rearticulated in different ways because they have no necessary 'belonginess'" (1986, 53), Hall represents the signifying practices of the mass media, on one hand, and viewers' experience at the point of reception, on the other, as a contested circuit that operates within determinate boundaries but is always open to change. It is a typical gesture in Hall's strategy of handling what he calls the two paradigms in cultural studies, the structuralist and the culturalist, Althusser's ideological state apparatus and Raymond Williams' notion of culture as a way of life.

In composition, James Berlin (1996), in particular, has made fruitful use of Hall's encoding/decoding model and the neo-Gramscian synthesis that underwrites it. The assignments he designed to help students understand the performative rules that code the production of media messages (such as privileged dichotomies, denotation and connotation, underlying narrative, and preferred meanings) as well as the variable positions (dominant, negotiated, and oppositional) available in decoding at the point of consumption are an important legacy Berlin has left composition. Nonetheless, while Berlin, like Stuart Hall, struggled to represent the relation between production and consumption as open and contested, I think it is accurate to say that neither fully captures how the circulation of messages—including the circuits of distribution and exchange—enters into and influences production and consumption. I do not mean that Berlin and Hall are unaware of these circuits. As Hall notes, the moment of production itself is shaped "via a number of skewed and structured 'feedbacks,'" as circulation and reception are "reincorporated" into the production process (1980, 130). But, for Hall, as well as Berlin, the literary legacy of cultural studies and its residual textualism continue to weigh heavily on their work, and the acts of encoding and decoding, writing and reading, production and consumption remain the privileged moments of analysis without adequate attention to the systems through which cultural products and media messages circulate or the transformations they thereby undergo.

There are, it seems to me, consequential differences for understanding media messages that hinge on the particular means of distribution and exchange in use. Take, for example, *The Honeymooners* (or any popular 1950s sitcom, for that matter). What Hall correctly calls its "specific modality and conditions of existence" (1980, 129) cannot be understood apart from its circulation (and the underlying political economy). That is, the encoding and decoding of a television show depend in important respects on whether it was broadcast on prime time in the 1950s, appears on *Nick at Nite* as a syndicated rerun, turns up as a clip in a documentary on the "Golden Age of Television," or is discussed in a scholarly article on representations of the family in the postwar period. Moreover, "guerrilla" redistributions, which evade the prevailing exchange relations, also need to be taken into account. When Warner Bros. television network responded to attacks on media sex and violence following the Columbine school shooting by not airing in the United States the final episode of the cult favorite *Buffy the Vampire Slayer* (which featured a high school bloodbath in the style of Brian De Palma's *Carrie*), a Canadian *Buffy* fan copied the entire program from Canadian television, where the episode was shown, and put it up on his website, to be downloaded in turn by *Buffy* fans everywhere. My point is that the epistemological and discursive status of a television show such as *The Honeymooners* or *Buffy the Vampire Slayer*—how, in other words, it can be known in its various transformations or "passages of form"—depends on how it circulates and, in effect, how it is exchanged and capitalized. To see how we might develop such a model of circulation, I need at this point to turn to Marx himself.

## Marx's *Grundrisse*

As mentioned earlier, both Richard Johnson (1986–87) and Stuart Hall (1980) acknowledge their intellectual debt to the notion of circulation that Marx develops in the *Grundrisse* (literally "basic outline" or "foundation"), the series of seven notebooks drafted over the winter of 1857–58, for the model it offers to describe and analyze the circulation of cultural products and media messages. Lost for many years, the manuscript of the *Grundrisse* was published originally in a two-volume limited edition by Foreign Language Publishers in Moscow in 1939 and 1941 but only became widely available in English with the 1973 translation by Martin Nicolau. Written, as Nicolau notes, "midway between the *Manifesto of the Communist Party* (1848) and the publication of the first volume of *Capital* in 1867" (8), the *Grundrisse* occupies a pivotal position in Marx's thinking. Following the defeat of the revolutionary upsurges in 1848–50, Marx withdrew from political life for over a decade to work out his ideas on dialectics, the historical development of capitalism, and the theoretical foundations of communism, only to reemerge as an activist with the founding of the International Workingmen's Association in 1864. The *Grundrisse* is a massive work—nearly 900 pages of what must surely be one of the most sustained "writing-to-learn" projects in existence. Depending on whose reading of the *Grundrisse* you find persuasive, the notebooks either divide or link Marx's early work as a left-Hegelian, such as the *Economic and Philosophical Manuscripts of 1844* and the *German Ideology* and what orthodox Marxists consider the "mature," "scientific" political economy of the later Marx in *Capital.*

I will leave aside these Marxological controversies. For my purposes, the key point in Marx's developing notion of circulation is contained in the introduction to the *Grundrisse* (which confusingly and for reasons not fully understood was added as an afterword in some editions of the *Contribution to the Critique of Political Economy* [1859]). In the introduction, Marx takes to task the classical political economists such as Say and Ricardo for their model of production, distribution, exchange, and consumption. According to Marx, the problem with the model is that it is a linear one, in which the moments are autonomous and sequential. As Marx puts it, this is the "obvious, trite notion":

> in production the members of society appropriate (create, shape) the products of nature in accord with human needs; distribution determines the proportion in which the individual shares in the product; exchange delivers the particular products into which the individual desires to convert the portion which distribution has assigned to him; and finally, in consumption, the products become objects of gratification, of individual appropriation. (1973, 88–89)

For the classical political economists, this linear circuit forms what Marx calls a "regular syllogism" (89), which guarantees, in effect, that everyone gets what he or she deserves, according to the equivalence of exchange in a market economy, where workers are "free" to trade their labor for wages that enable them to buy what they choose.

You do not have to be a political economist—and I am certainly not one—to recognize some familiar themes and problems in this linear model of circulation. For one thing, by separating distribution from production, it anticipates liberal policies of social justice that tinker with the economy by redistributing goods and services, through taxation and entitlement programs, in a way that leaves the actual relations of production for profit untouched. Next, the classical model represents exchange as an individual act of personal preference, undertaken in autonomy from relations of production and distribution, a key figure in the ideology of "personal choice" that has become indispensable to free-market deregulators such as Thatcher and Reagan, Bush, and Clinton, as well as the promoters of consumer culture hedonism, including the postmodern "politics of pleasure" crowd. Finally, by isolating consumption from the other moments of circulation, the classical model fails to register how consumption itself is reproductive of the relations of production, including the labor power of individual workers.

For cultural theorists such as Johnson and Hall, the attraction and usefulness of Marx's critique of the linear model of circulation in classical political economy must have been compelling for at least two reasons. First, unlike the classical economists who believed they had discovered universal laws of political economy, Marx insisted that the problem of analyzing circulation was always a historically specific one, a matter of explaining the circulation of a particular, historically determined system of production characterized by capitalist exchange relations. (For Marx, the "universal" feature of this mode of production is its tendency to define social relations in terms of their "universally" equivalent exchange values.) Second, and perhaps more important, Marx wanted to explain the various moments in the circulation of commodities—the cycle of production, distribution, exchange, and consumption—not as a series of separate events taking place in a predetermined order over time but dialectically, as mediations in mutual and coterminous relations that constitute the capitalist mode of production as a total system.

In other words, as we've already seen, representing circulation as a historically contingent process of interdependent moments fit quite readily into and—if anything, amplified—the cultural studies agenda of developing a nonreductionist, nonlinear model to understand cultural production and communication in all their complexity. In this sense, the "discovery" of the *Grundrisse* in the early 1970s marks a key point in cultural studies' New Left appropriation of Marxist theory. Still, there is something crucial missing or underpredicated in this appropriation that I must now call attention to and that led me earlier to characterize Johnson's and Hall's readings and applications of the *Grundrisse* as largely metaphorical ones. The issue here concerns *what* it *is* exactly that circulates through the system of production, distribution, exchange, and consumption.

For Johnson, it is cultural forms and products. For Hall, media messages. Fair enough. At this point, it may well sound obvious and redundant to say as much, and I wouldn't blame readers for thinking I am simply naming once again Johnson's and Halls' objects of inquiry. But there is a further point. Namely, from Marx's perspective, the circulation of cultural products or media messages takes place at the phenomenal (or empirical) level of sense perception. Underlying this, in Marx's materialist version of Hegelian dialectics, is the conceptual or "real" level at which we may grasp not only the momentary forms that the product or message takes on but also its inner workings and the process of its movement.

Marx's great clarification in the *Grundrisse* occurs, significantly, at the end of the final notebook, marked with the annotation "This section to be brought forward" (881), revealing how Marx, through an extended process of exploratory writing, thought himself through to the telling point. Here he designates the *commodity* as the "first category in which bourgeois wealth presents itself" (881) and, in effect, provides a name for what circulates through the circuit of production, distribution, exchange, and consumption as well as the theoretical starting point for *Capital.* The term *category* is crucial here, for what Marx means by the *commodity* is not simply a thing (whether a product, message, good, or service) but the materialization of an underlying and contradictory social process. Unlike the classical political economists, who assumed commonsensically that commodities are the naturally occurring results of human labor (which, as Nicolau points out, "is only another way of saying that nature decreed the bourgeois mode of production" [45]), Marx held that the commodity form must be understood dialectically as the "unity of two aspects—use value and exchange value" (881). Use value, Marx says, refers to the "material basis in which a specific economic relation presents itself" (881) in terms of satisfying human needs. As Marx explains, use value does not depend on a given mode of production: "Wheat, e.g., possesses the same use value, whether cultivated by slaves, serfs, or free labourers. It would not lose its use value if it fell from the sky like snow" (881). What transforms use value into a commodity—the determination by which the commodity form appears historically—is its realization as exchange value (881). As Marx puts it, "the commodity only becomes a commodity . . . in so far as its owner does not relate to it as use value" (881) but instead as a means of extracting exchange value from the labor process in the form of profits and the accumulation of capital.

In this sense, the commodity (including labor power, the only commodity workers have to exchange) cannot pass transparently and unproblematically through the cycle of production, distribution, exchange, and consumption, as it does for the classical economists, because it is always fatally divided, its exchange value and use value always in an asymmetrical relationship. According to Marx, the unity of opposites in the commodity—use value (production for human needs) and exchange value (production for profit)—points out the fundamental contradiction in the capitalist mode of production: The human productive activity (the labor power) "congealed" in the commodity form not only produces worldly goods but also reproduces the prevailing and contradictory social and economic relations of capitalism, where socialized production, with its promise of overcoming material scarcity, is at odds with the goal of private profit.

To my mind, Marx's notion of the commodity, with its divided inner workings, is the key figure missing from many present-day cultural studies' accounts of the circulation of cultural products and media messages. We can see, for example, how Marx's notion of the commodity provides a necessary corrective to the "new revisionists" who ignore the internal contradiction of the commodity by separating the use value of cultural products (what, say, viewers do with media messages) from their exchange value (and the reproduction of a capitalist mode of production and social relations). In contrast, for neo-Marxists, such as Richard Johnson and Stuart Hall, although they certainly offer a fuller and more complex sense of circulation, there is nonetheless a peculiar reluctance to talk about cultural products and media messages as commodities. This reluctance may well be due to residual New Leftish fears of being labeled "economist" or "orthodox" in the Old Left style of political economy. But it is unfortunate, too, for this retreat from historical materialism submerges what I take to be the lesson of Marx's theorizing about the commodity form, namely, that it enabled him to imagine how the contradictory workings of capitalist production establish the groundwork for a new way of life in which the circulation of products can be devoted to use value and the satisfaction of human needs.

## An Ending: What Is Socially Useful Knowledge?

Karl Marx, as everyone knows, was a revolutionary communist, and his interest in the circulation of commodities went far beyond settling theoretical issues in political economy: He wanted to chart a strategy for the working class to overthrow capitalism and reorganize production to meet social needs. While this still seems like a good idea to me, my goal here must necessarily be a more modest one. (It would be fatuous, of course, to call for socialism in one classroom.) My task now is to explain what the primer I've offered on Marxian political economy has to do with the study and teaching of writing. What, that is, does the circulation of commodities Marx develops in the *Grundrisse* hold for the problem of the circulation of writing I've been trying to discuss? As I see it, two interrelated points can be made.

The first concerns the distribution of written texts. Let's ask, for example, what determines the distribution of familiar periodicals such as the *Wall Street Journal* and the *National Enquirer.* The answer at first glance appears no doubt to be self-evident: They are distributed to the places where their readers can find them. Both, of course, are delivered to subscribers' homes, but beyond this, they take quite different routes—the *Wall Street Journal* to corporate offices, academic institutions, policy centers, and so on, while the *National Enquirer* is more likely to appear at the checkout stand in supermarkets and the news rack in convenience stores.

What are we to make of these differences? For classical political economists, there's not much to say that would interest writing teachers. Once produced (in response presumably to perceived needs and an anticipated share in the periodical market), the two commodities are roughly equivalent in terms of their exchange value, and, according to the laws of supply and demand, some people choose to read the *Wall Street Journal,* while others prefer the *National Enquirer.* In a capitalist market, after all, where commodities supposedly circulate freely, producers and consumers appear to be joined together seamlessly as a single figure by distribution and exchange.

According to Marx, however, distribution does not just issue forth from the moment of production, and the question to begin with is not so much where the commodity goes as what it carries in its internal workings as it circulates. Also according to Marx, the distribution of commodities cannot be understood apart from the distribution of the means of production and of the members of society in the various forms of production. To put it another way, the distribution of the *Wall Street Journal* and the distribution of the *National Enquirer* no longer figure simply as equivalent moments in the circulation of commodities, guided by the law of supply and demand. Instead, what gets distributed by these quite different types of reading matter is the productive means to name the world, to give it shape and coherent meaning. The activities and abilities of publishers, editors, writers, photographers, graphic designers, production crews, and so on are themselves exchanged and, in effect, consumed in the process of production, and the commodity form will necessarily carry traces of this productive activity.

For this reason, it doesn't make much sense to decry the sleaziness of the tabloids in comparison to the responsibility of the establishment press, as has become a common theme these days among liberals and conservatives alike. Such hand-wringing (and subsequent proposals to curb the sleaze or elevate readers' taste) misses the point: The process of production determines—and distributes—a hierarchy of knowledge and information that is tied to the cultural authorization of expertise, professionalism, and respectability. You can see how this works in the recent television ad for the *Wall Street Journal* showing twin brothers, separated at birth, one of whom reads the *Wall Street Journal* and ends up rich and successful, while the other reads fishing magazines and lives at home with his parents.

By saying all this, I don't mean to foreclose the possibility of rhetorical analysis (in Johnson's terms "text-based" studies), such as William Covino's (1991) wonderful work on tabloids and magical thinking or the variety of possible readings and uses people make of the periodical press (e.g., untargeted audiences such as radical economists and trade unionists reading the *Wall Street Journal* or intellectuals creating camp pleasures from the *National Enquirer*). My point is simply that we cannot understand what is entailed when people encounter written texts without taking into account how the labor power embodied in the commodity form articulates a mode of production and its prevailing social relations.

And this leads to my second point, namely, that the unity of opposites in the commodity form—exchange value and use value—enables not only tangential and impertinent readings. Its unity is a contradictory one. Now, when the contradictory character of the commodity form surfaces—when, say, a product fails to find consumers—classical economists are once again likely to cite the laws of supply and demand and the stern judgment of the market that eliminates those goods and services that cannot turn a profit: No perceived use value leads to no exchange value. In a negative sense, use value and exchange value remain united in a relation of identity. But once again, there is little here to interest writing teachers and not much to say beyond the obvious—writers can't always get published, some books don't sell, and periodicals go out of business. Everybody knows it's a tough world out there in commercial publishing and academic and professional writing, and you can no doubt think of your own examples of published works and periodicals whose use value was not "recognized" by the market's need for profit. From a Marxist perspective, however, the point is not simply to describe the competition of the capitalist market, with its disciplinary force and underlying assumption that the fittest will survive and prosper—that, in effect, exchange value verifies use value. To do as much simply justifies the status quo as inevitable. Marx enables us to see, rather, that exchange value and use value are united dialectically, not in a relation of identity but one of contradiction.

It may seem easy enough to identify this contradiction when writing that appears altogether worthwhile in terms of its use value is not "rewarded" by the exchange value of the market. But the contradiction, importantly, works the other way, too. Bibliometric citation counts, for example, demonstrate how the exchange value of scholarly articles and the symbolic capital they accumulate as peer-reviewed credentials on an individual's CV may or may not take on use value in the ongoing intellectual life of an academic field, depending on whether anyone cites them. A more worldly example comes from the annals of public health. As it happened, there had traditionally been a high incidence of scrotum cancer among chimney sweeps in early modern Western Europe. In the late eighteenth century, however, an investigator found that if chimney sweeps bathed, the incidence of the disease could be dramatically reduced. This information got to the chimney sweeps guild in Denmark rather quickly. The guild mandated that their members bathe, and the results were as predicted—scrotum cancer virtually disappeared. For reasons that are not clear, however, British chimney sweeps began bathing regularly only in the late 1800s—leaving a rather appalling gap of a century between the finding, which presumably brought the researcher some measure of credit, and its transformation into socially useful knowledge (Butlin 1892).

In its utter simplicity, the case of the chimney sweeps offers a paradigmatic instance of the point I have been building toward: The contradiction between exchange value and use value weighs heavily on the circulation of professional and academic writing of all types. We can see signs of this contradiction, for example, in the growing sentiment that scholarship, especially on the part of the academic left, is arcane and exclusionary, a matter of career building, the accumulation of capital within a restricted coterie of cothinkers, and a limited social usefulness for wider audiences. There seems, that is, to be a radical disconnect between the desire of academic leftists to make their work relevant to ordinary people and the way it actually circulates through normal academic channels.

There is a difficult point here. For, on one hand, as Peter Mortensen argues, not all academics can—or even should—write in a popular vein (1998, 195), and I certainly do not mean to suggest that there is no social good that comes from the higher learning, advanced research, and the specialized practices and vocabularies of the disciplines. At the same time, the matter is not so simple, as some on the academic left seem to believe, that by changing one's prose style (to write the kind of "plain American," as Marianne Moore put it so mordantly, that "cats and dogs can read" [1982, 46]), one can thereby take on a new identity as a "public intellectual." If anything, this wish for such a transformation, although surely understandable and well intentioned, amounts nevertheless to what I've already mentioned as the "one-sided" view of production that Marx critiques—the fallacy that by changing the manner of writing, one can somehow solve the problem of circulation. Instead, as Marx points out, to understand and, potentially, to change the way knowledge circulates requires thinking about how the means of production are distributed in the first place.

It is no easy task to imagine how writing, media messages, or signifying practices of any sort can be turned into socially useful knowledge. But, given the present social circumstances, if we cannot resolve the contradiction between exchange value and use value in capitalist production, we can at least call attention to the problematical nature of expertise in the circulation of academic and professional writing. This, at any rate, is what I've been trying to do in an advanced writing course, "Writing About Disease and Public Health." I want to present two assignments I have been experimenting with, not as fully developed models but as works in progress, that seek to embody the notion of circulation and to raise questions about the contradictory nature of professional writing.

The initial assignment may appear at first glance to be a traditional genre exercise, well known in science writing classes, that asks students to turn a journal article into a news report that might appear in the Science Times section of the Tuesday *New York Times*. And in many respects that is exactly what it is. The students' task is to write a news story that reports on an article in *JAMA: Journal of the American Medical Association*, presenting a study of the willingness of high-risk members of families with hereditary breast and/or ovarian cancer to undergo genetic testing for the BRCAl gene; the mutation of this gene is tied to these cancers (Lerman et al. 1996). I must admit that on one level I do want my students to be able to translate highly specialized information from biomedicine to general readers. But I also have another agenda: I want students to understand how that act of translation necessarily participates in and shapes the circulation of biomedical discourse in ways that go beyond simple information transfer and the attendant problem of accuracy/inaccuracy that so often frames such assignments. To do this, we need to reconstruct the systems of distribution and exchange through which messages about breast cancer circulate; to identify how the means of production (laboratories, equipment, scientific expertise) are distributed, materialized, and reproduced; and to consider how moments of consumption are articulated within this circuit.

In other words, I want to assemble a set of cultural products that can demonstrate the rhetorical transformations that occur as a "passage of forms"—from the article in *Science* where Mark Skolnick and his coworkers announced the discovery of the BRCAl gene (Miki et al. 1994), to news reports at the moment (Angier 1994a, 1994b), to medical advice columns (Brody 1997), to the patent and screening test that materialized and capitalized Skolnick's finding, to pending legislation concerning genetic discrimination. While it may appear that this circuit privileges the moment of scientific discovery as the origin of production, my goal is to show students how the rhetorical transformations that take place between the various specimens of writing make up a total system of production. More precisely, I want students to see that the shift in register and genre between a journal article and a news report amounts to a shift in modality—the relative credibility and authoritativeness invested in written statements—that marks journal articles as "original" contributions and news reports as secondary and derivative. My experience is that students can recognize rather quickly not only how experimental articles and news reports differ in genre but also how they are joined together in the distribution and authorization of expertise. They see, that is, that science writing in the establishment press does more than simply translate experimental findings to educated readers. The rhetorical transformation that turns the highly technical prose of a scientific article into a news report also figures the work of science as a heroic and agonistic struggle, with modest winners and gracious losers in the race for priority. Students recognize, too, how the symbolic capital of scientific articles and news stories is exchanged in the competition for grant funding and public recognition and materialized as actual capital in the form of highly profitable screening tests. And they recognize finally how news reports silence the voices of cancer patients and reinforce dependence on experts and "magic bullets": a theme that medical advice columns treat routinely as they situate women as consumers, in alternating dependence on and suspicion of biomedical practice.

What I am trying to do is amplify the students' sense of what constitutes the production of writing by tracing its circulation in order to raise questions about how professional expertise is articulated to the social formation, how it undergoes rhetorical transformations (or "passages of form"), and how it might produce not only individual careers but also socially useful knowledge. I take this issue up in the final assignment in the "Writing About Disease and Public Health" class when I ask students to work in groups to produce in any medium they choose (e.g., brochures, pamphlets, flyers, posters, videos, radio announcements, skits, websites, T-shirts) public health publicity on teen or college-age sexuality. To prepare for this project, we do considerable reading and critical analysis of journalistic versions of the "moral panic" over teenage sex and pregnancy, an ethnographic study of a failed public health education project in a working-class neighborhood in Philadelphia (Balshem 1993), a history of sexually transmitted diseases in the United States (Brandt 1987), samples of publicity put out by Planned Parenthood and other organizations, and critiques of sex education in schools and AIDS education campaigns (Fine 1988; Green 1996; Odets 1995). The critical reading and writing that students do are not intended as an end in themselves that might result, say, in an interpretive essay on some aspect of the topic. Instead, this critical work is crucial but subordinate to the production of socially useful knowledge. In this sense, the assignment tries to get away from positioning the student writer as an active meaning maker, having views and giving accounts. But at the same time, it is not meant to be real-world writing either, where the student writer uses expertise to intervene directly in the world. Rather, its intention is to problematize that expertise, not from outside but from within the process of production and the circulation of public health messages.

There is a great need, in my view, to problematize expertise, to find ways to rearticulate it within the circulation of knowledge. There are great obstacles as well. The growing corporatization of health care is perhaps the starkest recent example of how exchange value and use value clash in the performance of professional work—changing within a breathtakingly short period of time an entire system of production, distribution, exchange, and consumption. Marx would marvel, perhaps, at how the financiers, insurance companies, and health care corporations got away with it but not be surprised by capitalism's insatiable urge to revolutionize the means of production and extract more profit. And at the level of lived experience, health care providers daily confront the contradiction between their desire to perform professional services well (use value) and the pressure from HMOs to see more patients, cut down on hospital stays, and limit tests and treatment (exchange value).

At the same time, there are hopeful developments in biomedicine. One example is the National Breast Cancer Coalition (NBCC), which has trained lay breast cancer activists to sit on study sections that rank grant proposals at the federal and local levels and on institutional review boards in hospitals and universities that oversee research on human subjects. There is more involved here than just adding the perspective of breast cancer survivors to deliberations about the direction of scientific research. As these women learn about the biology of cancer and the design of epidemiological studies, there is also a redistribution of expertise taking place that has changed the production and circulation of scientific knowledge. The same is true of AIDS activists who turned themselves, in the words of Steven Epstein (1996), from a "disease constituency" into an "alternative basis of expertise" by moving beyond the early demands of groups such as Act Up for more research and faster approval of new drugs to contest what the FDA and the biomedical establishment count as "good science." By learning science, AIDS activists, in effect, have transformed themselves from patients and consumers protesting the delivery of health services to lay experts capable of intervening in the process of production and changing the way science gets done—in the clinical trials at the National Institutes of Health, in the manufacturing of drugs at the pharmaceutical companies, and in the approval of drugs at the FDA.

NBCC and AIDS activists challenge the dominant notion that the production of knowledge—scientific or otherwise—is a neutral activity, the results of which may be used for good or ill purposes. Instead, their interventions suggest that systems of distribution, exchange, and consumption enter into and determine consequentially how the means of production operate. In many respects, both groups have sidestepped the Old Left call to replace private ownership of the means of production with a public monopoly to act in terms of the common good. The issue is not to substitute one group of experts for another but to redistribute the means of production in order to increase public participation in the conduct of scientific work. Interestingly, the strategies of NBCC and AIDS activists recall Raymond Williams' model of democratic communication, which sought to "detach the idea of public service" from "the idea of public monopoly" (1962, 134) by imagining a circulation of information and access to the means of communication independent of either state control or the commercialized market.

The struggles of the NBCC and AIDS activists to redistribute expertise, to create new public forums, and to increase popular participation in knowledge and decision making raise old questions that, Richard Johnson shows, were central to nineteenth-century working-class traditions of radical education. The notion of "really useful knowledge" was often invoked in the 1800s to distinguish popular education from the work of the Society for the Diffusion of Useful Knowledge, a paternalistic philanthropic organization formed to provide education to the working class, the aims of which according to a Chartist circular, were "to stifle inquiry respecting the great principles which question their right to larger shares of the national produce than those which the physical producers of the wealth themselves enjoy" (quoted in Johnson 1979, 78). Although varied in educational practice, radicals nonetheless repeatedly called for an end to the monopoly of knowledge held by the privileged classes. Really useful knowledge, by contrast, would be widely available, circulating throughout the land. In one of the more colorful and earthy explanations of the need for the circulation of knowledge, the *Poor Man's Guardian* wrote the following:

> If manure be suffered to lie in idle heaps, it breeds stink and vermin. If properly diffused, it unifies and fertilizes. The same is true of capital and knowledge. A monopoly of either breeds filth and abomina-

> tion. A proper diffusion of them fills a country with joy and abundance. (quoted in Johnson 1979, 85)

The crux of really useful knowledge, radical educators agreed, depends in large part on whose questions are taken up. The aim of education should be practical but not in the service of capitalist utility. It should be wide-ranging but not self-improving in the middle-class sense. Perhaps it is best put by another line from the *Poor Man's Guardian:* "What we want to be informed about is—*how to get out of our present troubles*" (quoted in Johnson 1979, 84). The emphasis is in the original but remains true to our situation today. Our "present troubles" in writing instruction, at least as I understand them, have to do with whose questions we take up—students, laypersons, and experts in the disciplines and professions. I do not think there is an easy answer. And I am aware that every answer leads in its own way to further "troubles." The argument I have been pressing here holds that answers to how we might "get out of our present troubles" involve thinking not only about the production of writing at the point of composing but also about the circulation of writing and its relation to the unfinished business of democratic communication.

## Afterword

# The Crisis of Expertise

The two health education projects that I'll present in a moment illustrate how strategic differences in rhetorical motives take active form in professional practice. I want to use the two projects to return, in this closing essay, to the keywords in the title of this collection, *solidarity* and *service*, for three reasons: first, to revisit and update some of the pedagogical themes that appear in earlier essays; second, to raise an issue that has only been hinted at so far, namely that the authority of professional knowledge is in a current state of crisis, or delegitimization, in which expertise is just as needed as in the past but the persuasiveness of its claims have been called into question without identifying an alternative basis of credibility; and third, to ask what is reasonable to expect from U.S. college composition, given these unsettled circumstances, in terms of its ambitions and the courses and programs it seeks to develop.

The first health education project comes from the 1980s, when Fox Chase Cancer Center in Philadelphia set up a cancer-prevention initiative, Project CAN-DO, funded by the National Cancer Institute, to respond to the unusually high incidence of cancer in a working-class neighborhood in the city. The predominantly Polish-American residents were well aware of the cancer rate in their community, known in the popular press as a "cancer ward" and epidemiological "hot spot," and had their own ideas about what was causing disease, including the presence in the neighborhood of chemical factories that spewed out toxic pollutants. Project CAN-DO educators fixated nonetheless on lifestyle issues, such as smoking, drinking, illicit drug use, morbid obesity, poor prenatal care, and teenage pregnancy, in effect casting the prevalence of cancer as self-induced by bad health choices on the part of neighborhood residents.

To add to this picture of working-class depravity, Project CAN-DO surveyed local residents' knowledge about cancer, identifying seven "misconceptions" or "myths" that, to the researchers' professional eyes, revealed the community's lack of knowledge about disease causation and prevention:

1. There is nothing you can do to prevent cancer.
2. There is cancer hidden in everybody. It is a matter of time until it becomes activated.
3. Cancer can be triggered by a bruise or blow to the body (often, but not exclusively said about breast cancer).
4. Cancer is inherited. You can be born with it in your body.
5. Surgery can cause cancer to spread.
6. Cancer treatment is worse than the disease itself.
7. Cancer is a death sentence. (Balshem 1993, 64)

Martha Balshem, an anthropologist who worked for Project CAN-DO and ended up writing a highly critical study of the project, *Cancer in the Community: Class and Medical Authority,* makes the telling point: what the surveys reveal are not so much the ignorance of the community as the limits of Project CAN-DO's professional understanding. In fact, the community beliefs about cancer are neither misconceptions nor myths at all but rather intelligent ways of thinking that can, with a little effort, be translated into the terms of scientific debate and the available biomedical findings about the etiology and treatment of cancer. What Project CAN-DO interpreted as working-class "fatalism" can be seen, for example, as the sober recognition that there is little known about how to prevent many cancers or that the risk of certain cancers are transmitted from generation to generation. However, instead of recognizing the community's attempts to come to terms with cancer risk, genetic predisposition, survival rates, and the rigors of treatment, Project CAN-DO researchers diagnosed the community's knowledge base as faulty and in need of correction, thereby confirming the timeliness of the cancer-prevention project and the authority of professional health educators.

For people in the neighborhood, who were living next to chemical factories pumping out known carcinogenic pollutants, Project CAN-DO's predictable public health advice about a better diet, exercise, and regular screenings was not a very convincing account of how to prevent cancer. The issue, however, is hardly a matter of working-class fatalism, as Project CAN-DO wanted to pose the community's resistance to its health messages. Instead, there is something profoundly out of touch about how Project CAN-DO ignored the environmental causation of cancer altogether, retreating behind the uncertainties of government-sponsored studies and the declared need for more research. Of course, it is easier to blame working-class lifestyles than confront chemical companies. But by denying both the possibility of environmental causation and the legitimacy of popular understandings of cancer, the Fox Chase cancer-prevention team utterly undermined its professional credibility in the community by recommending that the working-class residents convert to middle-class norms, go to the gym, stop smoking, and eat better.

To see another side of things, compare the mismatch between experts and laypeople in Project CAN-DO to the article "Doin' It Well" by Robert Butler (2001) in the street-smart zine *Spill,* put out by Health Initiatives for Youth (HIFY) in San Francisco, that features writing by teens, with an occasional piece from HIFY staff. Butler was a seventeen-year old Diversity Works Intern when this was published in a 2001 issue of *Spill* on safety and vulnerability:

> Drugs . . . you either use them or you don't. The main thing is, if you're gonna do drugs, you might as well do it safe. It doesn't matter if the drug is weed, crack, or even cigarettes or "drank" (alcohol). If you're doing a drug of any sort here are a few suggestions:
>
> 1. Don't smoke with anybody that you don't know.
> 2. If you gotta roll it (weed, crack, etc.) watch to make sure it ain't being laced.
> 3. If it's drank make sure they didn't mix it with nothing else, unless you know what it was mixed with and you not trippin'.
> 4. If you use needles of any sort you need to clean them yourself, and make sure that you don't try to take more than you can handle.
>
> These are just some suggestions for safer drug use. If you use drugs on a regular basis, try not to overdose on anything, and if you feel that you're gonna take a lot of drugs at one time make sure you're with someone you trust in case anything happens. (40)

"Doin' It Well" rejects the zero-tolerance, "just-say-no" style of health advice from professionals and employs instead a popular knowledge of drug use that draws on the language and lived experience of young street people. This is what we might call "health messages from below." There is none of the social distance so evident in the relations between Project CAN-DO educators and the community. Instead, the *Spill* article begins with the sense that we are all in this together ("make sure you're with someone you trust") and need to find a way to come to grips with the reality we are facing ("try not to overdose on anything").

The rhetorical stances and terms of address in the two examples differ dramatically. Based on its view of the authority of professional knowledge, Project CAN-DO presented its work as a service to instruct the uninformed. This is a prime instance of what the sociologist C. Wright Mills (1958) called "crackpot realism," where professionals are so encapsulated in their own knowledge and institutions that they cannot begin to register the intellectual or practical value of alternative ways of knowing. In contrast, the articles in *Spill,* including ones on cutting, rape, carrying guns, and testifying in court, as well as advice about what to do when stopped by the police (from ACLU) and interviews with teens on violence in the media and on a recent sexual abstinence campaign, approached its readers in a spirit of solidarity, recognizing popular knowledge as a valuable resource that can be mobilized along socially useful lines. In this case, health educators and street people are working together, as the practical advice in "Doin' It Well" grants its readers considerable agency in managing the risks of taking drugs. The overall approach of *Spill* is to help young people, who are often living in dangerous situations they cannot fully control, with the ever-present threats of disease, violence, gangs, and the state hovering over them, develop a social consciousness, as then program director Jessica Meyer puts it, to "sort out these contradictions for yourself" (2001, 4).

* * * * *

I mention these two examples of health education projects in part because they became a pedagogical touchstone in the professional writing program I directed for nearly twenty years at Worcester Polytechnic Institute (WPI). I was lucky to work with three great colleagues, Chrysanthe Demetry, Lorraine Higgins, and Ruth Smith, who shared my interest in developing a noncorporate professional writing major with internships and senior projects in health communication, biomedical rhetoric, public relations, information and visual design, social advocacy, and digital media at various nonprofits, government agencies, medical institutions, and community organizations. What became evident early on is that the majors (or, more often, double majors) were drawn to the professional writing program because they wanted to use their emerging rhetorical and technical expertise in socially useful ways, as they would put it, to "give back to the community," "solve problems," and "make a difference." At the same time, they identified very strongly with the ethos of professionalism and its ostensibly disinterested commitment to serving the public good, with little sense of the complexity and contradictions in the relationships between experts and laypeople. They were very bright students and very decent human beings, and the question, I suppose, is how could they have believed otherwise? They had been educated—and self-selected—according to a view of the world that is amenable to the intervention of problem-solving experts in the name of science, rationality, and progress. For example, in the class I taught on "Writing About Disease and Public Health," when students were asked to turn a biomedical article on genetic testing for risk of breast cancer (Lerman et al. 1996) into a newspaper report, many couldn't help but describe the findings as "another step forward in the war against cancer," even though the experimental results were tentative, ambiguous, and indecisive in their implications for disease prevention, clinical practice, patient rights, or public policy.

So, the case studies of the two health education projects became useful in posing questions about the role of professionals and their relationships to ordinary people when the course "Writing About Disease and Public Health" moved to an assignment that called on students to design health communication messages about teen and young adult sexuality. The language available in mainstream sources to query expertise, about, say, "stakeholders," "cultural sensitivity," and "building coalitions," seemed to me inadequate and beside the point because it pictured the expert outside or above what was actually happening, in a position of managing things. In turn, the critique of expertise in Balshem's *Cancer in the Community* and the counterexample of *Spill* seemed what was called for as a critical preparation for students to produce their own health messages.

Still, there is a difficult pedagogical point involved concerning student identification with professionalism. It was clear enough to me, as just indicated in my presentation of the two examples, that Project CAN-DO stood for what Raymond Williams (1989a) called in British adult education "the missionary sense, the sense of going out to remedy a deficit" by "taking *understanding* to people." To this, he contrasted the "taking of tools of understanding" to adult learners as part of "a process which would then be an interaction with what was often very solid experience in areas in which the learned were in fact ignorant." Williams has a certain qualified respect for those who act out of social conscience, to serve the common good, but he is also quite pointed when he says "that in a society in which learning is unequal certain distinctive kinds of ignorance accumulate in the very heartland of learning" (1989a, 160).

Understandably, WPI students found this idea troubling. At first, they couldn't figure out what was wrong with Project CAN-DO promoting healthy lifestyles, even if the advice offered, though sensible in the most general terms, was often based on little evidence of efficacy in actually preventing cancer. By seeing such an intervention as better than none at all, they couldn't identify how ignorance operates structurally in the formation of professional authority and professional consciousness. They couldn't imagine what Williams called "a social order which really does not know in what crucial respects it is ignorant, in what crucial respects it is incompletely conscious" (1989a, 166). They had been led to believe that professional expertise could clear it all up.

By the same token, some of the students were taken aback initially by "Doin' It Well" as a public health message. Despite the fact that they were "doin' it well" (or not so well) in terms of their own drug, not to mention alcohol, use, the "just-say-no" initiatives of the 1980s and 1990s weighed heavily on them, and they wondered whether *Spill*'s kind of health advice wasn't simply encouraging a social problem that should be stamped out, though they had no intention of doing so in their own lives. If anything, at least on a first reading, many students found "Doin' It Well" a bit unseemly, out of step with the "wellness campaigns" and condom use initiatives they were familiar with, where the health message is clear, crisp, and authoritative.

Their perspectives started to shift when the question turned from "Is this good or bad, accurate or inaccurate advice?" to "How are experts and laypeople—and the relationship between them—represented in the health advice?" I think what happened is that students began to mobilize social knowledges and identifications that had been inaccessible when the issues were posed, as they often are in health communication, about "incentives" to "modify behavior" or "preferred channels and formats." Without abandoning their own professional allegiances (they were majors in a professional writing program after all), a good number of students came to see the blind spots in Project CAN-DO and the agency to manage risk ascribed to street kids in "Doin' It Well" by drawing on their own experience in the eastern cities and ethnic-class cultures of New England neighborhoods where most of them grew up, along with their considerable knowledge of contemporary youth cultures. Moreover, at least a handful began to grasp the idea that the radical potential of health education isn't really about problem solving in its narrow sense but, again in Raymond Williams' (1989a) words, about the "building of social consciousness" or "real understanding of the world," in which health risks are distributed unequally and thereby require not so much more and better "social marketing" to prevent disease but a redefinition of disease as the biological expression of social relations and a reinvigoration of the very idea of public health.

I do not mean to turn this into one of those pedagogical success stories that plague the study and teaching of writing. There is little question in my mind that posing the most basic rhetorical issues—about who is speaking, on what grounds, to whom, on what occasion, and for what reason—made it possible to open professionalized expertise to critical inquiry and for students to draw critical lessons about the design of public health messages. That's important to note but hardly

**Figure A–1**
This hand-drawn sketch for a campaign to encourage young women to insist their male sexual partners wear condoms shows how a group of African American students from Brooklyn handled rhetorical questions of representation by employing girlfriend talk to destigmatize condom use and, at the same time, picture young women in control of their own sexuality.

news about what students can accomplish when they link their own knowledge and experience to the tools of rhetorical understanding (Figure A–1).

Nonetheless, I did learn something in a very immediate sense from teaching the health message assignment that I thought I knew before on conceptual grounds: namely, that the shaping of professional identities tends to screen out the knowledges and lived experience of ordinary people (including the knowledge and experience of professionals in training) and that the outcome, accordingly, is not only the particular types of expertise that define the professions but also the systematically produced ignorance of professionals. Furthermore, I became convinced that a kind of critical vocationalism was possible as an informing principle in course and curriculum design, to make questions of professional consciousness and the relations of experts and laypeople subjects of interrogation, not so much to promote critical inquiry as a pedagogical end in itself but rather as a means to clarify the rhetorical and political grounds of students' emerging expertise and the possibilities of future professional practice.

* * * * *

On another level, the resistance of local residents to Project CAN-DO raises the problem of professional credibility and the fault lines in the cultural authorization of expertise. A number of the earlier chapters, for example, Chapter Four ("Writing Instruction and the Politics of Professionalization") and Chapter Eight ("Composition and the Circulation of Writing"), emphasize the internal contradictions of the professional-managerial class, in particular between use-value and exchange-value. To be sure, this played a role in Project CAN-DO, as Martha Balshem (1993) points out, in the concerns of the health education team to establish their own professional standing in relation to physicians and the wider biomedical establishment. Credentials, status, and authority were, indeed, at stake, as the usual symbolic capital available to professionals whose only exchangeable commodity is their own expertise. Project CAN-DO's failure, however, cannot be explained simply as the health educators looking over their shoulders to make sure their messages conformed to biomedical orthodoxy. It is also emblematic of a larger systemic crisis in the credibility of experts.

In *Risk Society: Towards a New Modernity*, Ulrich Beck (1992) says that "primary scientization" is a basic feature of industrial capitalism that "gains its dynamism from the contrast of tradition and modernity, lay people and experts." The emergent technoeconomic order of the late eighteenth and nineteenth centuries claimed to represent an emancipatory rationality with the mission of sweeping away the superstitions of traditional authority, unfettering the productive forces, and overcoming the intellectual and material impoverishment of earlier times. As Beck points out, this spirit of the modern age was based on "*skepticism* in the internal relations of science" (and, I would add, other forms of expertise that derive their authority from scientific rationality), while simultaneously the "application of scientific results is advanced in an *authoritarian* fashion in external relations." This results in the familiar configuration of experts, whose authority rests on their success and the "promises of liberation from constraints not yet understood" (155), on one hand, and laypeople, whose dependence and deference underwrite the regime of expertise, on the other.

This situation, however, could not last. As Chapter Six, "Popularizing Science: At the Boundary of Expert and Lay Biomedical Knowledge," notes, the dependence of laypeople and their belief in experts can turn into a sense of frustration, feelings of vulnerability, and suspicion of professionals when the promises of biomedicine to conquer disease and keep people healthy are unmet. In effect, laypeople are faced with the uncertainty produced by the very skepticism at the heart of the biomedical sciences and the experimental method of scientific rationality more generally: the ambiguous findings, shifting guidelines, treatments promoted then shelved, miracle drugs revealed to have devastating side effects. Science, as Beck (1992) puts it, comes to be seen as not only a solution to problems "but also a *cause of problems.*" And this perception is not limited to laypeople. The critical scrutiny that science applies to its methods and results has led to an intensified awareness of the risks that technoscience has produced (e.g., climate change, environmental pollution, occupational disease and unsafe workplaces, degradation of food sources, and extinction of species) and of its own fallibilism. "Demystification," Beck says, "spreads to the demystifier and in so doing changes the conditions of demystification" (156). It is not simply patients, clients, or health consumers—laypeople who might be dismissed otherwise as noncompliant or antiscience—but the technoscientific establishment itself that has, perhaps unwittingly but in keeping with the norms of disinterested skepticism, shaken its own foundations.

For Beck, this crisis of expertise is part of a recognition that in "advanced modernity the social production of *wealth* is accompanied by the social production of *risks*" (1992, 19). In one sense, his book *Risk Society* amounts to a rewriting of Lyotard's (1983) "postmodern condition" and its "incredulity toward metanarratives." Both are concerned with shifts in sensibility, notions of legitimacy, diminished expectations, and heightened insecurities in advanced societies since the mid-twentieth century. Both offer sweeping accounts of epochal change—and that always gets my guard up, since I believe we're still living under capitalism, where the bosses extract surplus value from a now globalized work force, in a very late, senescent, and highly destructive moment. In any case, while Lyotard's postmodernity seems fatally accented by the disappointment and political fatigue in sectors of the French left that followed the failures of the worker-student alliance to overthrow Gaullism in May 1968, I think Beck's notion of "reflexive modernity" is more adequate in explaining how the practices of scientific (and more broadly professional) knowledge production have led, dialectically, to their undermining—to delegitimization and incredulity.

According to Beck, the reflexivity of advanced modernity has generated a "momentous *demonopolization of scientific knowledge claims*": as "science becomes more and more *necessary*" to identifying the risks it has produced, it is also "*less and less sufficient* for the socially binding definition of truth" (1992, 156). The "scientization" so deeply rooted in industrial capitalism and now in the so-called knowledge economies of postindustrial society has resulted in uncertainties that have turned "the target groups and appliers of scientific results in politics, business, and the public into *active coproducers* in the social process of knowledge definition." Importantly, as Beck notes, this is a contradictory development in the way it opens new possibilities for public participation. It includes, on one hand, the "opportunity to emancipate social practice *from* science *through* science," as is true in the cases of how "popular epidemiologists" and AIDS and breast cancer activists developed a lay expertise to participate consequentially in defining what counts as "good science." But it also, in Beck's words, "throws the door open to a feudalization of scientific knowledge practices through economic and political interests and 'new dogmas'" (157) that range from the influence of pharmaceutical companies and health care corporations to the infiltration of religious and free-market fundamentalists into the making of science and health policy during the last Bush administration.

*Risk Society* was originally published in Germany in 1986 but still provides, I think, a potent account of where the crisis of expertise stands twenty-five years later, one decade into the twenty-first century. I've been concerned in this collection, for the most part, with the progressive possibilities of popular participation in knowledge making. But, I must say, Beck's characterization of the "feudalization of scientific knowledge practices" is a trend that has to be reckoned with. Let's hold for a moment on the corporatization side, for it's wrongheaded to think that "economic and political interests" are suddenly intruding on the production of scientific knowledge: any proper materialist history of science will show that these interests have always been a codetermining presence, though they may be more unabashedly and publicly mobilized at the present time. Rather, I'm concerned with what Beck calls the "new dogmas" as forms of popular consciousness and how they constitute not so much knowledge as antiknowledges that are skewed, obscurantist, racist, sexist, and xenophobic.

To put it more directly, there is at present a right-wing populist backlash against experts of all sorts—in science, government, media, and academia—the "regulators" or "liberal elites" who think they know what is best for ordinary people or, as it's often put these days, want to "take away our freedom." This is the world of talk radio, Fox News, Sarah Palin, and the Tea Party movement, where truly alternative (in the sense of unhinged) accounts and explanations of reality circulate.

From one perspective, this populist backlash is the logical outgrowth of neoliberalism and the free-market fundamentalism that started with Reagan and has continued in subsequent administrations. In this sense, today's right-wing populism is an extreme manifestation of what can happen when the "personal choice" and niche marketing of postmodern consumption meet "personal responsibility" and the neoliberal rigors of a "pay as you go" society. Privatization takes hold at the level of individual consciousness as the impact of the free market and the decline of the social state register in disorienting and distorted ways, and individuals redefine themselves not so much as citizens but as taxpayers and home owners, private subjects beleaguered by "big government."

On one hand, there are, understandably enough in a "winner-take-all" society, heightened feelings of economic and personal vulnerability. Individuals experience their life situations as increasingly atomized, without reliable social bonds or institutions to face what seem to be random and free-floating threats of being identified as redundant, at the risk not just of being unemployed in the globalized world of fast capitalism but of being unneeded and, in Zygmunt Bauman's words, "consigned to 'human waste' because of individual inadequacies or misfortunes" (2004, 89), expelled from the middle class and the American dream by a blind fate. At the same time, as individuals seek to give a name to the source of their anxieties, economic insecurities converge with (and are rethematized in terms of) another set of anxieties and insecurities: the war on terror, the porousness of national borders, the constant state of security alerts, the perceived (if not always real) dangers of everyday life and threats to personal safety in a world of increasing social, cultural, and linguistic differences. This is where the slogan "Take back America" comes from, to reestablish the existential security of towns and neighborhoods imagined to have once been homogeneous and safe.

As Beck notes, this reaction against big government and experts, with its repudiation of the existence of society and the idea of a public good, results in important respects from the regime of expertise itself, from the perceptions of risk, feelings of insecurity, and profound sense that nobody is doing anything about it. These are the preconditions, brought about by the growing identification of risks on the part of experts, for what Beck calls "denial from fear" and scapegoating:

> Precisely as the dangers increase along with political inaction, the risk society contains an inherent tendency to become a scapegoat society: suddenly it is not the hazards, but those who point them out that provoke the general uneasiness. . . . Is not the whole thing an *intellectual fantasy*, a canard from the desks of intellectual nervous nellies and risk promoters? Is it not spies, communists, Jews, Turks, or asylum

> seekers from the Third World who are ultimately behind it? The very intangibility of the threat and people's helplessness as it grows promote *radical and fanatical reactions and political tendencies* that make social stereotypes and the groups afflicted by them into "lightning rods" for the invisible threats which are inaccessible to direct action. (1992, 75)

Beck's characterization of a "scapegoat society" is helpful in distinguishing between types of popular consciousness and their clashes with professional expertise. In some cases, these clashes arise from systemically produced "misunderstandings" that occur when expert and lay knowledges collide and no means of negotiation are available, as the difficulties of Project CAN-DO reveal. Perhaps an even more pointed example is Brian Wynne's fieldwork (1996), which investigated the differences between Cumbrian sheep farmers and government scientists over the causes of radiation contamination in the uplands of the Lake District following the 1986 Chernobyl accident.

When levels of radioactive caesium persisted in the upland pastures beyond the scientists' predictions, farmers had the choice either of selling lambs at ruinously low prices or maintaining them at the risk of disease or starvation by buying expensive commercial feed. Given the circumstances—the maze of shifting bureaucratic regulation, admittedly flawed studies, and scaled-back conclusions on the part of the scientists, the denial that the sheep farmers' long-standing familiarity with the land or their expertise in animal husbandry had anything to add to the government's environmental studies or animal testing, and the absence of any meaningful consultation—the sheep farmers began to ask if the excess in predicted radiation levels was due to emissions from the nearby Sellafield nuclear plant, which in 1957 experienced the worst nuclear reactor accident before Chernobyl and had been identified in 1984 as the cause of child leukemia. Unsurprisingly, they began to suspect a government cover-up had started years before, and they used government data in quite forceful ways to make the case it was Sellafield and not fallout from Chernobyl that accounted for the unpredicted persistence of radiation.

Like the case of Project CAN-DO, this was a perfect storm of misunderstanding and mistrust. As Wynne makes clear, the colliding storm fronts were two different and incompatible systems of knowledge: the "artificial standardisation of variations in local physical environment, farming conditions, and practices (hence farmers)" and the "ethos of prediction and control, which engendered an exaggerated sense of certainty" on the part of the scientists; and the "long-established individualism, informality, and flexibility of farm-management decision-making" and an "ethos of adaptation and acceptance of intrinsic lack of control" on the part of the farmers (1996, 37). In a sense, the sheep farmers, who were not uniformly opposed to the Sellafield nuclear plant, as environmental activists were, but ambivalent about it, since many friends and relatives worked there, were better equipped than the scientists and government officials for the uncertainties of Beck's risk society. One might even imagine, in a different scenario, that another outcome was possible, by activating the knowledge and experience of the sheep farmers to develop, in concert with experts, a social consciousness of how to manage, if not eliminate, risk in a more democratic and socially useful manner.

The same cannot be said, however, of the "new dogmas" of right-wing populism. At first glance, it may appear there are similarities to the grievances the sheep farmers held against the government scientists and officials as being arrogant, overbearing, and rigidly bureaucratic. The crucial difference, however, as Wynne's fieldwork makes clear, is that while two systems of knowledge collided in the case of the sheep farmers and government, the lack of credible solutions and the political stalemates in risk society not only can lead to conflicts with experts but also, as Beck says, can "*cause* a lack of consciousness" (1992, 75), producing, in effect, antiknowledges or "new dogmas" that displace risks and social anxieties onto ill-defined yet highly threatening imaginary phantoms such as intellectuals, immigrants, minorities, terrorists, experts, big government, and so on. The Cumbrian sheep farmers produced socially useful knowledge about the sources of contamination because they continued to observe and learn, as they always had, about the environment they lived and worked in. The "new dogmas," on the other hand, are forms of popular consciousness that have immunized themselves against learning by retreating into a state of "agnosis" or "not wanting to know." This is the condition that James Moffett describes in *Storm in the Mountains* (1988), his study of the infamous 1974 campaign to ban textbooks in Kanawha County, West Virginia, an event that prefigures in many ways the rejection of self-consciousness and reflexivity in the current right-wing populist upsurge.

* * * * *

The leading terms to locate contemporary social and intellectual life in a historical framework—*postmodernism, postindustrialism, nonfoundationalism, post-Marxism, postcolonialism, transnationalism, reflexive modernity*—all, to one degree or another, identify the present situation as an in-between place, a kind of interregnum, where the past has been used up but the shape of the future has not quite come into view. There's a sense of suspension, not so much of the intellect (which, if anything, is hyperactive) but of the will. It's not that the kind of people who worry about these things—leftist intellectuals, writers, academics, and professionals of various sorts—have given up their ideals of social justice. The difficulty rather is knowing what to do when the very notion of expertise is in crisis and the task of rearticulating professional knowledges is in its formative stages—when the dilemma of professional practice, in Beck's refrain, is that it is "*more and more necessary*, but at the same time *less and less sufficient*" (1992, 167).

There are signs that the professions and academic disciplines are starting to deal with this demonopolization of expertise in active ways—for example, through increased community involvement and lay participation in public health initiatives, environmental studies, social work, urban design, education, architecture, biomedical research, and other fields. Sociologists and anthropologists are now more likely to think of their subjects as collaborators in the production of knowledge, not simply informants. Across the professions, the idea of engaging the public as more than atomized clients is beginning to dissolve some of the boundaries between professionals and laypeople or, at least, to make the divisions between experts and nonspecialists more transparent and negotiable. Similarly, many of the professions and academic disciplines have initiated discussions about the lines that once demarcated them so sharply from each other—lines that are at once epistemological, institutional, and practical—and the potential value of blurring these boundaries and making them more permeable in knowledge production, social and cultural work, and public policy.

In U.S. college composition, though it has always defined the field as interdisciplinary and student-centered, there are certain obstacles to thinking clearly about the crisis of expertise and the dilemmas of professionalism, as well as promising developments. One of the obstacles, as I suggested in Chapter Five, "Changing the Question: Should Writing Be Studied?" is that composition in the era of the process movement was actually quite reticent about bringing its professional knowledge into the classroom, as tools of analysis and understanding that might be examined in light of other knowledges students bring to the classroom. Instead, it defined the teacher's relationship to students as personal and quasi-familial rather than professional, thereby in effect both hiding and defending its own expertise through the indirection of process pedagogy. To my mind, this is why proposals such as Douglas Downs and Elizabeth Wardle's (2007) to make the first-year course into an "Introduction to Writing Studies" are appealing, though I would want to stress the goal of making the disciplinary knowledge of writing studies more transparent to students and more negotiable with teachers—as both an intellectual resource and a topic for critical investigation—instead of emphasizing as much as Downs and Wardle do the goal of legitimizing composition as a specialized academic field, another monopoly of expertise clearly set off from other disciplines.

Genre-based writing instruction raises another possibility of examining the lines that divide disciplines and designing curriculum that brings professional knowledge into the classroom in productive and critical ways. There is already a well-established genealogy of genre theory in U.S. college composition that starts with Lloyd Bitzer's (1968) notion of the rhetorical situation, then moves ahead through Carolyn R. Miller's "Genre as Social Action" (1984), the genre debates in Australia (cf. Kress 2003, 89–92), David R. Russell on genre and activity fields (1997), and the work of Charles Bazerman (1994), John Swales (1990), Amy Devitt (2004), Anis Bawarshi (2003), and others. Since this has become, more or less, the official history, with an important developing pedagogy, I want to turn to two unacknowledged sources that have also been instrumental in the reception and development of genre theory and genre-based writing courses.

One is the attention to literary nonfiction and the essay, memoir, profile, natural history, travel writing, and so on as potential objects of inquiry. I say "potential" because, as I noted in the Introduction, too often the essay, as well as other genres of literary nonfiction, are posed against the specialized discourses of the professions with their canons of exemplary figures (e.g., George Orwell and James Baldwin as essayists, Mary Karr as memoirist, John McPhee on natural history, Paul Theroux as travel writer) and are talked about in terms of writerly craft without mentioning the historicity of the genres, the subject positions they make available, or the way they circulate in literate culture. Even so, simply naming the essay and other forms of writing as *genres* breaks the spell of their identification with "good writing" and makes it at least theoretically possible to teach them in new ways, as a particular type of expert practice that has its own codes and conventions, social networks, professional associations (e.g., Associated Writing Programs), and career pathways, as is readily evident in the professionalization of "creative writing" or "literary arts" in undergraduate and Masters of Fine Arts programs, where nonfiction genres now have a solid place alongside poetry, the short story, and the novel. It does little good to dismiss these domains of writing by raising the specter of expressivism from the now thoroughly depleted taxonomy wars—or, perhaps more typically, just saying that "creative writers" are "different"—especially when the institutional presence of "creative writing" has established potentially productive grounds for interchange with composition and writing studies about professional identities, ways of knowing, and the terms of valuing writing (cf. Mayers 2005).

The second source of unacknowledged genre awareness in U.S. college composition is the turn toward community literacy projects, civic engagement, and writing for social advocacy. This has brought into view devalued and neglected genres, such as flyers, fact sheets, posters, press kits, visual displays of information, public service announcements, and so on, that had formerly been associated with professional communication, public relations, and advertising. In an important respect, this now widespread development has promoted the shift, as Diana George (2002) puts it, from the analysis to the design of texts as the subject and productive art of composition, as well as dovetailing with recent attention to new media and the multimodality of writing.

The turn to civic literacy and writing for the public is hardly a uniform one. In some cases, it amounts to simply more of the uncritical community service, such as working in food pantries, homeless shelters, day care or senior centers, and after-school, English as a second language, and adult education programs, that high school students accumulate to bulk up their college applications and, as Bruce Herzberg (1994) and Paula Mathieu (2005) have pointed out, may actually increase social distance between students, cast in the role of benefactors, and community people, cast as needy. In other cases, however, depending on the project and the writing assignments, the study and design of social advocacy campaigns, for instance, can lead to the critical investigation of how rhetorical situations are constructed, how rhetorical agency is distributed, and how various genres can coalesce counterpublics. Further, as the case study of Project CAN-DO and *Spill* shows, health education and other types of writing for targeted audiences provide opportunities to examine how genres of writing mediate the relations between experts and laypeople and to problematize professional knowledges, their circulation, and their relation to popular knowledges.

If this collection of essays has an underlying thesis, it is the argument that U.S. college composition should not only pay attention to its own professionalization, about which it is nearly obsessed, but also make more central to the design of its writing assignments, courses, curriculum, and programs the dilemmas, contradictions, and crises of professional work in the early twenty-first century. As Min-Zhan Lu and Bruce Horner (2009) note, composition has been split in the past between *instrumentalist* or *pragmatic* pedagogies to help students advance their careers and *critical* pedagogies that believe the point of writing courses is to persuade and enable students to change the world. For leftist teachers, theorists, and program administrators (and I include myself in these ranks), it was comforting to define our ostensibly politically conscious work against the accommodationists, whether that was Maxine Hairston, Richard Fulkerson, or Russel K. Durst.

For Lu and Horner, however, this is no longer a tenable position (and maybe never was) but rather one side of a false dichotomy that counterposes "teachers' and student's concerns with financial security and career" and "their concerns with making the world a better place for all" (2009, 114). They go on to show how key terms such as "mobility, career, and marketable skills" (120) that shape expectations about work have been destabilized, at a time of uncertainty when both Fordist and fast capitalist regimes beckon to professionals and to students as aspiring professionals. On one hand, there is the image if only the limited and quickly disappearing possibility of security in pursuing a career and a settled heteronormative life as a "company man," getting married, having a family, becoming established in the local community, and rising through the ranks on the escalator model of professional advancement (which, of course, is the model of advancement for tenure-track faculty in academia). On the other hand is the recognition of the inevitability of flexible specialization (which amounts to a lack of long-term commitment by employers, managerial prerogative to make and remake the division of labor in the workplace, and increased demand for productivity) and the idealized portrait of the "extra-territorially mobile portfolio man" (or woman) who relies on his wits and entrepreneurial will, constantly retooling his skill set as he glides across the globe from one exciting project to another.

Lu and Horner provide a vivid picture of professional work lives in the interregnum I referred to earlier, the state of suspense and uncertainty characteristic of the present moment, when for most people mobility consists at best of what Richard Sennett calls "ambiguously lateral moves" (quoted in Lu and Horner 2009, 123) and the threat of layoffs and prolonged unemployment, the redefinition of professional positions as short-term consulting contracts, and the unwelcome prospects of a "career transition" to part-time work in low-paying retail and service jobs are always near at hand. These material conditions are a necessary part of any proper understanding of the lived experience of professional work and the formation of professional identities and desires. It helps us see that the professions are not monolithic entities or actors in their own right but rather internally stratified social formations where life chances are fashioned and refashioned in highly volatile and insecure circumstances.

Furthermore, given these insecure conditions, both professionals and students contemplating their futures as professionals feel thrust back on their own resources, under the pressure to make themselves visible and to get marketplace credit for their accomplishments and credentials through social networking, LinkedIn (where "relationships matter"), websites, blogs, Twitter, Facebook, YouTube, and so on. What is involved is not just the reach of Generation 2.0 digital media but also a kind of informal demystification of professional credibility and the power of its knowledges to solve social problems, a chilling, if accurate, acknowledgment that all you've got to sell is yourself as a credentialed commodity—whether online, in professional development workshops, or at alumni cocktail parties. I have no question these networks, both virtual and real, lead to new jobs, new start-up companies, and other new career opportunities. The point to emphasize is that thinking of yourself as a CV and the owner and operator of a particular set of credentials is part of larger pressures to privatize consciousness, even though any given individual may well take part in community service, serve on arts and culture boards, or work on political, social, or environmental advocacy campaigns.

I don't mean to suggest that it's possible to determine if people's motives are pure or that it even matters. My argument rather is that colleges and universities (and sometimes writing programs) are aiding and abetting the privatization of consciousness by encouraging students to think of themselves as marketable commodities, enriched and enhanced by study abroad and high levels of involvement in college and community activities. The electronic portfolios many colleges and universities are encouraging students to set up or are using as part of outcomes assessment to show parents, prospective employers, and the public at large the "value added" in four years of education are just one example of this self-marketing.

Nonetheless, while the boundaries between personal, professional, and public spheres seem to be collapsing, with civic engagement turning into résumé building, the privatization of consciousness all of this appears to herald must be seen as a conjunctural feature of the current interregnum and not a *fait accompli*. The tensions in professional work between building a career and working for the good of society have been amplified but not eliminated by the insecurities and uncertainties that mark the present moment. There is, if anything, as Beck (1992) says, even greater dependence on professional expertise, given the stakes in a risk society, while, at the same time, government, business, and the public are more independent of its findings and judgments. For these reasons, it makes a good deal of sense, as Lu and Horner (2009) suggest, to investigate with students how notions of mobility, careers, and marketable skills shape their hopes and expectations about professional work in an era suspended between Fordism and fast capitalism and to consider, as well, how professional knowledges might be brought into a more active relation to the experience and knowledges of ordinary people in order to develop a social consciousness capable of influencing public policy and imagining alternative social futures.

* * * * *

As everyone knows, Stanley Fish has been on the case lately, warning that composition (and other disciplines) should drop any hint of politicizing the classroom and just teach their subject matter, though that might include political material as long as it's taught professionally, from a disciplinary perspective. I appreciate Fish's concern in *Save The World on Your Own Time* (2008) about preempting outside interference in the affairs of academia, particularly given the fact that "new dogmas" in the culture wars—like David Horowitz's Freedom Center and the David Project—are taking names, keeping files, and harassing faculty and administrators, sometimes successfully, as a "weak link in the war against terrorism."

And I don't disagree with Fish's argument that the primary responsibility of academics is to teach their fields, which is a backhanded way of conceding the obvious but still implying that Fish is missing something. For one thing, as Donald Lazere (2009) and Patricia Bizzell (2009) have noted, there are good reasons to think that Fish doesn't really understand the field of composition. The point I want to make is related but somewhat different. Whether you want to save the world (as in Fish's self-consciously hyperbolic characterization of leftist faculty), improve it (as Bizzell says is a more realistic prospect), or teach what it's really like and how to get ahead in it (as the accommodationists mentioned earlier supposedly want to do), you've first got to constitute *a world* as the grounds of inquiry and action. Fish might agree with this, as a normal nonfoundationalist observation about how intellectual practices work.

As I've tried to show earlier, however, by drawing on Beck, the world as we know it—the world that we live in, the world where writing circulates and takes on force and value—has become less and less legible to professionals and academic specialists, less and less receptive to interventions with predictable results, and more and more resistant to credible knowledge claims. Accordingly, as Lu and Horner (2009) suggest, it's hard to know *where we are* in the global/local maelstrom, to find a standpoint to chart life paths and career trajectories. To my mind, these are practical intellectual problems that belong as much to the ancient canon of rhetorical invention as to technoscience or social theory or any other field—proper and realistic topoi of writing instruction and its professional responsibility to examine how the productive arts of composing represent the world and the pressures and limits of rhetorical activity. If there is a politics involved, it has to do in the first instance with the relationship between teachers and students and the interactions between professional and popular knowledges in carrying out investigations of a runaway world, its uncertain future, and what rhetorical agency might mean and be able to do.

# Notes

1. Separate ethnic universities were established in 1959 for Coloured, Indian, Zulu, and Sotho-Tswana students, while Fort Hare College, which was founded in 1916 and had drawn students from across southern Africa, was designated for Xhosas. With the Bantu Homelands Constitution Act of 1971, the supposedly independent tribal homelands in Bophuthatswana, Transkei, Venda, and Qwa Qwa also set up their own universities (Davenport and Saunders 2000, 398, 680). For background on Bantu education, see Hartshorne 1992; Hyslop 1999; and Kallaway's two edited collections *Apartheid and Education: The Education of Black South Africans* (1984) and *The History of Education under Apartheid: The Doors of Learning and Culture Shall Be Opened* (2002).
2. I use the term *black* in accordance with its common usage in the liberation struggle and afterward, to refer to South Africans formerly designated by apartheid as Bantu, Indian, and Coloured.
3. Neville Alexander (personal communication, July 12, 2006) recounts an episode when he and John Samuel were discussing funding for SACHED with a potential European donor. The donor said the SACHED project must be vetted by the ANC. Alexander and Samuel refused these terms. While the project was funded, this instance shows the power of the ANC in exile to control events on the ground in South Africa and the uncompromising political independence of Alexander and Samuel as SACHED leaders.
4. *LACOM News* articles that discuss difficulties of adult literacy projects include "Literacy Teaching for Workers" and "The Role of the English Literacy Project." Neville Alexander and Kathleen Heugh give a brief analysis of the "failure of ESL programmes in South Africa," including the National Language Project, with which they were associated (2001, 24–27), in "Language Policy in the New South Africa."
5. There was a good deal of overlap in the late 1980s and early 1990s between the notions of people's education and alternative education, and the terms were sometimes used interchangeably. Nonetheless, there were political differences, such as those noted by George Mashamba (1990), who drew a distinction between People's Education, which he considered the "most important development" in alternative education, as opposed to the "alternative socialist educational programme" promoted by the National Forum, which was especially influential in the Cape Town

SACHED local (48). From the SACHED side, the Durban LACOM noted that though the People's Education Secretariat envisioned the establishment of "people's authority alongside the state authority" in a situation of dual power, it did not see a "specific role" for workers' organizations ("People's Education for All" 1986, 8). A good overview of People's Education can be found in Motala and Vally (2002). See also the articles assembled in *People's Education: A Collection of Articles* (Mashamba 1990). On People's English, see Gardiner (1987); Peirce (1989). Pippa Moll's unpublished paper "An Examination of the Concept of 'People's English'" provides a valuable critical analysis of the term.

6. As Okwui Enwezor notes, by the mid-1970s, there had appeared in the *Lagos Weekend*, the satirical comic *Wakaabout*, in Nigerian pidgin, by Chinaka Fynen, about "a combination *flaneur* and urban detective, a phantom floating through the murky depths of the city and the corridors of governmental power" (2006, 18). For more on African comics, see essays in *Africa Comics*.
7. LACOM pamphlets included ones on the French Revolution, the Luddites, Chartism, the Paris Commune, and the Spanish Civil War, and were meant to promote an internationalist working-class solidarity.
8. For more extended discussions of Bakhtin's notion of answerability, see Clark (1990) and Ewald (1993).
9. *Ten Years of Staffrider 1978–1988*, edited by Oliphant and Vladislavic (1988), offers a representative selection of writing and graphics from that era. See also Qabala, Hlatshwayo, and Malange, *Black Mamba Rising: South African Worker Poets in Struggle* (1986).
10. Accounts of what happened to adult, worker, and alternative education under the ANC in the late 1990s can be found in Aitchison (2003), Cooper et al. (2002), and Vally (2004). For analyses of ANC's shift to neoliberalism, see Alexander, *An Ordinary Country* (2002); Bond (2000); and Marais (1998).
11. I want to thank David W. Johnson, Rochelle Kapp, and Karen Press for reading and commenting on an earlier version of this essay. Their suggestions were altogether helpful. Also thanks to Neville Alexander, for conversations about SACHED. My debt to Gunther Kress for the notion of multimodality in print culture should be evident.

# Works Cited

"34 Billion Spent Yearly on Alternative Medicine." MSNBC. 30 July 2009. www.msnbc.msn.com/id/32219873/ns/health-alternative_medicine/. Accessed August 17, 2010.

Abbott, Andrew. 1988. *The System of Professions: An Essay on the Division of Expert Labor*. Chicago: University of Chicago Press.

African History Project. n.d. Chapter One: "Why Do We Study History?" Chapter Seven: "Responses to Colonial Conquest." Stenciled print.

Aitchison, John. 2003. "Struggle and Compromise: A History of South African Adult Education from 1960 to 2001." *Journal of Education* 29 (1): 125–77.

Alexander, Neville. 1992. *Education and the Struggle for National Liberation in South Africa*. Trenton, NJ: Africa World Press.

———. 2002. *An Ordinary Country: Issues in the Transition from Apartheid to Democracy in South Africa*. Pietermaritzburg: University of Natal Press.

——— and Kathleen Heugh. 2001. "Language Policy in the New South Africa." *Culture in the New South Africa. After Apartheid*. Vol. 2. Edited by Robert Krieger and Abebe Zegeye, 15–39. Cape Town: Kwela Books.

Altman, Roberta. 1996. *Waking Up, Fighting Back: The Politics of Breast Cancer*. Boston: Little, Brown.

"Americans Are Interested in Science; Lack Understanding of the Basics." 1998. *Journal of the National Cancer Institute* 90: 1127–28.

Angier, Natalie. 1994a. "Fierce Competition Marked Fervid Race for Cancer Gene." *New York Times*. Sept. 20: C1, C3.

———. 1994b. "Scientists Identify a Mutant Gene Tied to Hereditary Breast Cancer." *New York Times*. Sept. 15: Al, A16.

Bailey, Dudley, et al. 1960. "Report of the Committee on Future Directions." *College Composition and Communication* 11 (1): 3–7.

Ball, Carolyn C. 1992. "The Politics of Citation." Presented at CCCC Convention, Cincinnati, Ohio, March 19.

Balshem, Martha. 1993. *Cancer in the Community: Class and Medical Authority*. Washington, DC: Smithsonian Institution.

Barnard, Rita. 2004. "*Bittercomix*: Notes from the Post-Apartheid Underground." *South Atlantic Quarterly* 103 (4): 719–54.

Barthes, Roland. 1972. *Mythologies*. New York: Hill and Wang.

Bartholomae, David. 1985. "Inventing the University." In *When A Writer Can't Write: Research on Writer's Block and Other Writing Process Problems*, edited by Mike Rose, 134–65. New York: Guilford.

———. 1989. "Freshman English, Composition, and CCCC." *College Composition and Communication* 40 (1): 38–50.

———. 1995. "Writing with Teachers: A Conversation with Peter Elbow." *College Composition and Communication* 46 (1): 62–71.

Bauman, Zygmunt. 2004. *Wasted Lives: Modernity and Its Outcasts*. Cambridge: Polity.

Bawarshi, Anis. 2003. *Genre and the Invention of the Writer: Reconsidering the Place of Invention in Composition*. Logan: Utah State University Press.

Bazerman, Charles. 1994. "Systems of Genres and the Enactment of Social Institutions." In *Genre and the New Rhetoric*, edited by Aviva Freedman and Peter Medway, 79–101. London: Taylor.

———. 2002. "The Case for Writing Studies as a Major Discipline." In *Rhetoric and Composition as Intellectual Work*, edited by Gary A. Olson, 32–38. Carbondale: Southern Illinois University Press.

Beck, Ulrich. 1992. *Risk Society: Towards a New Modernity*. London: Sage.

Benjamin, Walter. 1986. *Reflections: Essays, Aphorisms, Autobiographical Writings*. Translated by Edmund Jephcott, edited by Peter Demetz. New York: Schocken.

Berkenkotter, Carol, and Thomas N. Huckin. 1995. *Genre Knowledge in Disciplinary Communication: Cognition/Culture/Power*. Hillsdale, NJ: Erlbaum.

——— and John Ackerman. 1991. "Social Context: The Initiation of a Graduate into a Writing Research Community." In *Textual Dynamics of the Professions: Historical and Contemporary Studies of Writing in Professional Communities*, edited by Charles Bazerman and James Paradis, 191–215. Madison: University of Wisconsin Press.

Berlin, James A. 1987. *Rhetoric and Reality: Writing Instruction in American Colleges, 1900–1985*. Carbondale: Southern Illinois University Press.

———. 1988. "Rhetoric and Ideology in the Writing Class." *College English* 50 (5): 477–94.

———. 1996. *Rhetorics, Poetics, and Cultures: Refiguring College English Studies*. Urbana: NCTE.

Berthoff, Ann E. 1971. "The Problem of Problem Solving." *College Composition and Communication* 22 (3): 237–42.

———. 1972. "Response to Janice Lauer, 'Counterstatement.'" *College Composition and Communication* 23 (5): 414–16.

———. 1983. *Forming, Thinking, Writing: The Composing Imagination*. Montclair, NJ: Boynton/Cook Publishers.

Bird, Adrienne. 1984. "The Adult Night School Movements for Blacks on the Witwatersrand 1920–1980." In *Apartheid and Education*, edited by Patrick Kallaway, 192–221. Johannesburg: Ravan.

Bird, Nancy K. 1977. "The Conference on College Composition and Communication: A Historical Study of Its Continuing Education and Professionalization Activities, 1947–1975." Diss. Virginia Polytechnic Institute, 1977.

Bishop, Wendy. 1999. "Places to Stand: The Reflective Writer-Teacher-Writer in Composition." *College Composition and Communication* 51 (1): 9–31.

Bitzer, Lloyd. 1968. "The Rhetorical Situation." *Philosophy and Rhetoric* 1 (1): 1–14.

Bizzell, Patricia. 1992. *Academic Discourse and Critical Consciousness*. Pittsburgh: University of Pittsburgh Press.

———. 1999. "Hybrid Academic Discourses: What, Why, How." *Composition Studies* 27 (2): 7–21.

———. 2000. "Basic Writing and the Issue of Correctness, or What to Do with 'Mixed Forms' of Academic Writing." *Journal of Basic Writing* 19 (4): 4–12.

———. 2002. "The Intellectual Work of 'Mixed' Forms of Academic Discourse." In *Alt Dis: Alternative Discourses and the Academy*, edited by Christopher Schroeder, Helen Fox, and Patricia Bizzell, 1–10. Portsmouth, NH: Boynton/Cook Publishers.

———. 2009. "Composition Studies Saves the World." *College English* 72 (2): 174–87.

——— and Bruce Herzberg, eds. 2000. *The Rhetorical Tradition: Readings from Classical Times to the Present*. Boston: Bedford/St. Martin's.

Bledstein, Burton J. 1976. *The Culture of Professionalism: The Middle Class and the Development of Higher Education in America*. New York: Norton.

Bloom, Allan. 1987. *The Closing of the American Mind*. New York: Simon and Schuster.

Bond, Patrick. 2000. *Elite Transition: From Apartheid to Neoliberalism in South Africa*. Pietermaritzburg: University of Natal Press.

"A Book Is Not a Book Until It Is Read." 1990. *SACHED Journal* 17–19.

Bourdieu, Pierre. 1977. *Outline of a Theory of Practice*. Translated by Richard Nice. Cambridge: Cambridge University Press, 1977.

Bowles, Samuel, and Herbert Gintis. 1976. *Schooling in Capitalist America: Educational Reform and the Contradictions of Economic Life*. New York: Basic.

Bowman, Francis. 1962. "The Chairman Retires." *College Composition and Communication* 13 (1): 55–56.

Brandt, Allan M. 1987. *No Magic Bullet: A Social History of Venereal Disease in the United States Since 1880*. New York: Oxford University Press.

Brody, Jane E. 1997. "Breast Cancer Awareness May Carry Its Own Risks." *New York Times* Oct. 7: F1, F10.

Brown, Brenda Gabioud. 1996. "Elocution." In *Encyclopedia of Rhetoric and Composition*, edited by Theresa Enos. New York: Garland.

Brown, Joshua. 1991. "Every Picture Tells a Story, Don't It?" In *History from South Africa*, edited by Joshua Brown, et al., 379–89. Philadelphia: Temple University Press.

———, Patrick Manning, Karin Shapiro, Jon Wiener, Belinda Bozzoli, and Peter Delius, eds. 1991. *History from South Africa: Alternative Visions and Practices*. Philadelphia: Temple University Press.

Brown, Phil. 1992. "Popular Epidemiology and Toxic Waste Contamination: Lay and Professional Ways of Knowing." *Journal of Health and Social Behavior* 33 (2): 267–81.

Bruffee, Kenneth A. 1972. "The Way Out." *College English* 33 (4): 457–70.

———. 1984. "Collaborative Learning and the 'Conversation of Mankind.'" *College English* 46 (7): 635–52.

_______. 2007. *A Short Course in Writing: Composition, Collaborative Learning, and Constructive Reading*. 4th ed. New York: Longman.

Burke, Kenneth. 1950. *A Rhetoric of Motives*. Berkeley: University of California Press.

Butler, Robert. 2001. "Doin' It Well." *Spill* 3: 40.

Butlin, Henry T. 1892. "Cancer of the Scrotum in Chimney Sweeps and Others: Why Foreign Sweeps Do Not Suffer from Scrotal Cancer." *British Medical Journal* 2 (1): 1–6.

"CCCC: Voices in the Parlor, and Responses." 1988. *Rhetoric Review* 7 (1): 195–213.

Callinicos, Luli. 1981. *A People's History of South Africa*. Vol. 1. *Gold and Workers 1886*. Johannesburg: Ravan.

———. 1987. *A People's History of South Africa*. Vol. 2. *Working Life 1886–1940: Factories, Townships and Popular Culture on the Rand*. Johannesburg: Ravan.

———. 1991. "Popular History in the Eighties." In *History from South Africa*, edited by Joshua Brown, et al. 257–67. Philadelphia: Temple University Press.

———. 1993. *A People's History of South Africa*. Vol. 3. *A Place in the City: The Rand on the Eve of Apartheid*. Johannesburg: Ravan.

Canagarajah, A. Suresh. 2006. "The Place of World Englishes in Composition: Pluralization Continued." *College Composition and Communication* 57 (4): 586–619.

Carter, Michael. 1990. "The Idea of Expertise: An Exploration of Cognitive and Social Dimensions of Writing." *College Composition and Communication* 41 (3): 265.

Christie, Pam. 1985. *The Right to Learn: The Struggle for Education in South Africa*. Johannesburg: Ravan.

Clark, Michael. 1990. "Afterword: A Rhetorical Ethics for Postmodern Pedagogy." In *Reclaiming Pedagogy: The Rhetoric of the Classroom*, edited by Patricia Donahue and Ellen Quandahl, 164–69. Carbondale: Southern Illinois Press.

Cohen, Stanley. 1973. *Folk Devils and Moral Panics: The Creation of Mods and Rockers*. London: Paladin.

Coles, William E., Jr. 1974. *Teaching Composition*. Rochelle Park, NJ: Hayden.

———. 1978. *The Plural I.* New York: Holt.

Collins, Randall. 1979. *The Credential Society: An Historical Sociology of Education and Stratification.* New York: Academic Press.

"Communicating Science to the Public: Whose Job Is It Anyway?" 1998. *Journal of the National Cancer Institute* 90: 1509–11.

"The Composition/Communication Course in General Education Programs." 1959. College Composition and Communication 10 (3): 187–88.

Connors, Robert J. 1991. "Rhetoric in the Modern University: The Creation of an Underclass." In *Politics of Writing Instruction,* edited by Richard Bullock and John Trimbur, 55–84. Portsmouth, NH: Boynton/Cook Publishers.

"Constitution and By-Laws of the Conference on College Composition and Communication." 1952. *College Composition and Communication* 3 (3): 19–24.

"The Conversation Continues: Voices in the Parlor." 1989. *Rhetoric Review* 7 (3): 406–08.

Coontz, Stephanie. 1988. *The Social Origins of Private Life: A History of American Families, 1600–1900.* London: Verso.

Cooper, Linda, Sally Andrew, Jonathan Grossman, and Salim Vally. 2002. "'Schools of Labour' and 'Labour's Schools': Worker Education Under Apartheid." In *History of Education Under Apartheid,* edited by Patrick Kallaway, 111–33. New York: Peter Lang.

Corbett, Edward P. J. 1974. "Statement of Editorial Policy." *College Composition and Communication* 25 (1): 2.

Cornwall, Gareth. 1989. "Towards a History of the South African Committee for Higher Education (SACHED); 1959–1987." M.A. thesis. University of Natal.

Couchman, Gordon W. 1952. "Organization and Administration of the Freshman Communications Course." *College Composition and Communication* 3 (1): 9–11.

Covino, William A. 1991. "Magic, Literacy, and the *National Enquirer.*" In *Contending with Words: Composition and Rhetoric in a Postmodern Age,* edited by Patricia Harkin and John Schilb, 23–37. New York: MLA.

Crowley, Sharon. 1994. *Ancient Rhetorics for Contemporary Students.* New York: Macmillan.

———. 1998. *Composition in the University: Historical and Polemical Essays.* Pittsburgh: University of Pittsburgh Press.

Darnton, Robert. 1982. *The Literary Underground of the Old Regime.* Cambridge, MA: Harvard University Press.

Davenport, Rodney, and Christopher Saunders. 2000. *South Africa: A Modern History.* 5th ed. London: Macmillan.

Dean, Howard H. 1959. "The Communication Course: A Ten-Year Perspective." *College Composition and Communication* 10 (1): 80–85.

De Certeau, Michel. 1984. *The Practice of Everyday Life,* translated by Steven Rendall. Berkeley: University of California Press.

DeKock, Leon. 1996. *Civilising Barbarians: Missionary Narrative and African Textual Response in Nineteenth-Century South Africa*. Johannesburg: Witwatersrand University Press.

Delpit, Lisa. 1988. "The Silenced Dialogue: Power and Pedagogy in Educating Other People's Children." *Harvard Educational Review* 58 (3): 280–98.

Devitt, Amy. 2004. *Writing Genres*. Carbondale: Southern Illinois University Press.

Dewey, John. 1946. *The Public and Its Problems, An Essay in Political Inquiry.* Chicago: Gateway Books.

Downs, Douglas, and Elizabeth Wardle. 2007. "Teaching About Writing, Righting Misconceptions: (Re)Envisioning 'First-Year Composition' as 'Introduction to Writing Studies.'" *College Composition and Communication* 58 (4): 552–84.

Drew, Allison. 2000. *Discordant Comrades: Identities and Loyalties on the South African Left.* Pretoria: Unisa Press.

Durst, Russel K. 1999. *Collision Course: Conflict, Negotiation, and Learning in College Composition*. Urbana: NCTE.

Eagleton, Terry. 1983. *Literary Theory: An Introduction*. Minneapolis: University of Minnesota Press.

Elbow, Peter. 1968. "A Method for Teaching Writing." *College English* 30 (2): 115–25.

———. 1995. "Being a Writer vs. Being an Academic: A Conflict in Goals." *College Composition and Communication* 46 (1): 72–83.

Engels, Friedrich. 1935. Letter to J. Bloch, 1890. *Marx and Engels: Selected Correspondence*. New York: International.

Enos, Theresa. 1990. "Gender and Journals: Conservators or Innovators." *Pre/Text* 9: 209–14.

Enwezor, Okwui. 2006. "*Rapport des Forces*: African Comics and Their Publics." In *Africa Comics*, edited by Samir S. Patel, 17–19. New York: Studio Museum in Harlem.

Epstein, Steven. 1996. *Impure Science: AIDS, Activism, and the Politics of Knowledge*. Berkeley: University of California Press.

Ewald, Helen Rothschild. 1993. "Waiting for Answerability: Bakhtin and Composition Studies." *College Composition and Communication* 44 (3): 331–48.

Faigley, Lester. 1986. "Competing Theories of Process: A Critique and a Proposal." *College English* 48 (6): 527–42.

———. 1992. *Fragments of Rationality: Postmodernity and the Subject of Composition*. Pittsburgh: U of Pittsburgh P.

Fine, Michelle. 1988. "Sexuality, Schooling, and Adolescent Females: The Missing Discourse of Desire." *Harvard Educational Review* 58 (1): 29–53.

Fish, Stanley. 2008. *Save the World on Your Own Time*. New York: Oxford University Press.

Fisher, B. E. 1953. "Problems of Motivation in Junior College Communication Courses." *College Composition and Communication* 4 (1): 43–45.

Fiske, John. 1989. *Understanding Popular Culture.* Boston: Unwin Hyman.

Flower, Linda. 1994. *The Construction of Negotiated Meaning: A Social Cognitive Theory of Writing.* Carbondale: Southern Illinois University Press.

Flower, Linda, and John R. Hayes. 1981. "A Cognitive Process Theory of Writing." *College Composition and Communication* 32 (4): 365–87.

Foucault, Michel. 1979. *Discipline and Punish: The Birth of the Prison.* Translated by Alan Sheridan. New York: Vintage.

———. 1980. *Power/Knowledge: Selected Interviews and Other Writings, 1972–1977,* edited by Colin Gordon. New York: Pantheon.

———. 1984. "What Is Enlightenment?" In *The Foucault Reader,* edited by Paul Rabinow, 32–50. New York: Pantheon.

*Freedom from Below: The Struggle for Trade Unions in South Africa.* 1989. Johannesburg: Skotaville.

Freidson, Eliot. 1986. *Professional Powers: A Study of the Institutionalization of Formal Knowledge.* Chicago: U of Chicago Press.

Freire, Paolo. 1970. *Pedagogy of the Oppressed.* Translated by Myra Ramos. New York: Seabury.

Frost, Karen, Erica Frank, and Edward Maibach. 1977. "Relative Risk in the News Media: A Quantification of Misrepresentations." *American Journal of Public Health* 87: 841–45.

Fulkerson, Richard. 2005. "Composition at the Turn of the Twenty-First Century." *College Composition and Communication* 56 (4): 654–87.

Gardiner, Michael. 1987. "Liberating Language: People's English for the Future." In *People's Education,* 56–62. Bellville: University of the Western Cape, Centre for Adult and Continuing Education.

Geisler, Cheryl. 1994. *Academic Literacy and the Nature of Expertise: Reading, Writing, and Knowing in Academic Philosophy.* Hillsdale, NJ: Erlbaum.

George, Diana. 2002. "From Analysis to Design: Visual Communication in the Teaching of Writing. *College Composition and Communication* 54 (1): 11–39.

Gere, Anne Ruggles. 1994. "Kitchen Tables and Rented Rooms: The Extracurriculum of Composition." *College Composition and Communication* 45 (1): 75–92.

Goggin, Maureen Daly. 1997. "Composing a Discipline: The Role of Scholarly Journals in the Disciplinary Emergence of Rhetoric and Composition Since 1950." *Rhetoric Review* 15 (3): 322–28.

Gorrell, Robert M. 1961. "Philosophy and Structure." *College Composition and Communication* 12 (1): 14–15.

Graff, Harvey. 1991. *The Literacy Myth: Cultural Integration and Social Structure in the Nineteenth Century.* New Brunswick: Transaction.

Green, Jesse. 1996. "Flirting with Suicide." *New York Times Magazine* Sept. 15: 39–45, 54–55, 84–85.

Gregory, Jane, and Steve Miller. 1998. *Science in Public: Communication, Culture, and Credibility*. New York: Plenum.

Grewe, Eugene F. 1961. "A Counter-Proposal Affecting the Future Direction of the CCCC." *College Composition and Communication* 12 (1): 18–22.

Haas-Dyson, Anne. 1994. "Confronting the Split Between 'The Child' and Children: Toward New Curricular Visions of the Child Writer." *English Education* 26 (1): 12–28.

Habermas, Jurgen. 1972. *Knowledge and Human Interests*. Boston: Beacon Press.

———. 1980. "Modernity—An Incomplete Project." In *The Anti-Aesthetic: Essays on Postmodern Culture*, edited by Hal Foster. 3–15. Port Townsend, Washington: Bay Press.

Hairston, Maxine. 1992. "Diversity, Ideology, and Teaching Writing." *College Composition and Communication* 43 (2): 179–93.

Hall, Stuart. 1980. "Encoding/Decoding." *Culture, Media, Language*, edited by Stuart Hall, et al., 128–38. London: Hutchinson.

———. (1983). "The Question of Ideology: Marxism without Guarantees." In *Marx, A Hundred Years On*, edited by Betty Matthews, 57–84. London: Lawrence & Wishart.

———. 1986. "On Postmodernism and Articulation: An Interview with Stuart Hall." Edited by Lawrence Grossberg. *Journal of Communication Inquiry* 10 (2): 45–60.

Halloran, S. Michael. 1983. "Rhetoric in the Modern College Curriculum: The Decline of Public Discourse." *Pre/Text* 3: 245–69.

Harr, Jonathan. 1996. *A Civil Action*. New York: Vintage.

Harries, Patrick. 1994. *Work, Culture, and Identity: Migrant Labourers in Mozambique and South Africa c. 1860–1910*. Johannesburg: Witwatersrand University Press.

Harris, Joseph. 1992. "The Other Reader." *JAC* 12 (1): 27–37.

———. 1997. *A Teaching Subject: Composition Since 1966*. Upper Saddle River, NJ: Prentice.

———. 2010. "Workshop and Seminar." In *Teaching with Student Texts*, edited by Joseph Harris, John D. Miles, and Charles Paine. Logan: Utah State University Press.

Hartshorne, Ken. 1992. *Crisis and Challenge: Black Education 1910–1990*. Cape Town: Oxford University Press.

Heath, Shirley Brice. 1983. *Ways with Words*. Cambridge: Cambridge University Press.

Hebdige, Dick. 1979. *Subculture: The Meaning of Style*. London: Methuen.

Herzberg, Bruce. 1994. "Community Service and Critical Teaching." *College Composition and Communication* 45 (3): 307–19.

Hesse, Doug. 2010. "Response to Cindy Selfe's 'The Movement of Air, the Breath of Meaning: Aurality and Multimodal Composing.'" *College Composition and Communication* 61 (3): 602–05.

Hill, Adams Sherman. 1888. *Our English.* New York: American Book Company.

Hirsch, E. D. 1987. *Cultural Literacy: What Every American Needs to Know.* Boston: Houghton Mifflin.

Hobson, Dorothy. 1982. *Crossroads: The Drama of a Soap Opera.* London: Methuen.

Holbrook, Sue Ellen. 1991. "Women's Work: The Feminizing of Composition." *Rhetoric Review* 9 (2): 201–29.

Horner, Bruce, and Min-Zhan Lu. 2007. "Resisting Monolingualism in 'English': Reading and Writing the Politics of Language." In *Rethinking English in Schools: A New and Constructive Stage,* edited by Viv Ellis, Carol Fox, and Brian Street, 141–57. London: Continuum.

Horner, Bruce, Min-Zhan Lu, Jacqueline Jones Royster, and John Trimbur. 2011. "Language Difference and Writing." *College English* 73 (3): 299–317.

Hunter, David, et al. 1997. "Plasma Organochlorine Levels and the Risk of Breast Cancer." *New England Journal of Medicine* 337: 1253–58.

Hyslop, Jonathan. 1999. *The Classroom Struggle: Policy and Resistance in South Africa 1940–1990.* Pietermartizburg: University of Natal Press.

Irmscher, William. 1961. "Statement of Editorial Policy." *College Composition and Communication* 12 (1): inside front cover.

Jarratt, Susan C. 1991. *Rereading the Sophists: Classical Rhetoric Refigured.* Carbondale: Southern Illinois University Press.

Johnson, Falk S. 1959. "Secretary's Report No. 26." *College Composition and Communication* 10 (2): 128–29.

———. 1960. "Secretary's Report No. 28." *College Composition and Communication* 11 (1): 61–63.

———. 1961. "What Future for CCCC?" *College Composition and Communication* 12 (1): 13–14.

Johnson, Richard. 1979. "'Really Useful Knowledge': Radical Education and Working-Class Culture, 1790–1848." In *Working Class Culture: Studies in History and Theory,* edited by John Clarke, Chas Critcher, and Richard Johnson, 75–102. New York: St. Martin's.

———. 1986–87. "What Is Cultural Studies, Anyway?" *Social Text* 16 (1): 38–80.

Jones, Leroi (Amiri Baraka). 1966. "Expressive Language." *Home.* New York: William Morrow.

Kail, Harvey. 1988. "Narratives of Knowledge: Story and Pedagogy in Four Composition Texts." *Rhetoric* Review 6 (2): 179–89.

Kallaway, Patrick, ed. 1984. *Apartheid and Education: The Education of Black South Africans.* Johannesburg: Ravan.

———, ed. 2002. *The History of Education under Apartheid, 1948–1994: Opening the Doors of Learning and Culture.* New York: Peter Lang.

Kant, Immanuel. 1949. "What Is Enlightenment?" In *The Philosophy of Kant: Immanuel Kant's Moral and Political Writings,* edited by Carl J. Friedrich, 132–39. New York: Modern.

Kirsch, Gesa. 1993. *Women Writing the Academy: Audience, Authority, and Transformation.* Carbondale: Southern Illinois University Press.

Kitzhaber, Albert R. 1963. "4C, Freshman English, and the Future." *College Composition and Communication* 9 (2): 129–38.

Kolata, Gina. 1997. "Study Discounts DDT Role in Breast Cancer." *New York Times* Oct. 30: A19.

Kress, Gunther. 2003. *Literacy in the New Media Age.* London: Routledge.

Kruger, Loren, and Patricia Watson Shariff. 2001. "'Shoo—This Book Makes Me to Think!' Education, Entertainment, and 'Life Skills' Comics in South Africa." *Poetics Today* 22 (4): 474–513.

Larson, Magali Sarfatti. 1977. *The Rise of Professionalism: A Sociological Analysis.* Berkeley: University of California Press.

Lash, Scott, and John Urry. 1987. *The End of Organized Capitalism.* Cambridge: Polity.

Latour, Bruno. 1987. *Science in Action.* Cambridge: Harvard University Press.

Lauer, Janice. 1972. "Response to Ann E. Berthoff, 'The Problem of Problem Solving.'" *College Composition and Communication* 23 (2): 208–10.

Laurence, Leslie. 1997. "How OB-GYNs Fail Women: Read This Before Your Next Check-Up." *Glamour,* Oct.: 292–95.

Lawson, Leslie. 1985. *Working Women in South Africa.* Johannesburg: Ravan Press.

Lazere, Donald. 2009. "Stanley Fish's Tightrope Act." *College English* 71 (5): 528–38.

Leary, Warren E. 1996. "Aspirin Proposed for Suspected Heart Attacks." *New York Times,* June 19: C9.

Leavis, F. R., and Denys Thompson. 1933. *Culture and Environment.* London: Chatto.

Lerman, Caryn, et al. 1996. "BRCA1 Testing in Families with Hereditary Breast-Ovarian Cancer." *JAMA: Journal of the American Medical Association* 275 (24): 1885–92.

Lévi Strauss, Claude. 1977. *Tristes Tropiques.* Translated by John and Doreen Weightman. New York: Pocket Books.

Limpus, Robert. 1954. "The Freshman Program at Western Michigan." *College Composition and Communication* 5 (1): 3–8.

"Literacy Teaching for Workers." 1986. *LACOM News* 2 (November): 10–15.

Lu, Min Zhan, and Bruce Horner. 2009. "Composing in a Global-Local Context: Careers, Mobility, Skills." *College English* 72 (2): 113–33.

Lukács, Georg. 1971. *The Theory of the Novel.* Translated by Anya Bostock. Cambridge: MIT P.

Lunsford, Andrea. 1990. "Composing Ourselves: Politics, Commitment, and the Teaching of Writing." *College Composition and Communication* 41 (1): 71–82.

Lusted, David. 1983. "Feeding the Panic and Breaking the Cycle: 'Popular TV and Schoolchildren.'" *Screen* 24 (6): 81–93.

Lyotard, Jean-François. 1984. *The Postmodern Condition: A Report on Knowledge.* Minneapolis: University of Minnesota Press.

LZB. 1989. "The Conversation Continues: Voices in the Parlor." *Rhetoric Review* 7 (3): 407–08.

Macpherson, C. B. 1962. *The Political Theory of Possessive Individualism.* New York: Oxford University Press.

Macrorie, Ken. 1952. "World's Best Directions Writer." *College English* 13 (3): 275–79.

———. 1960. "Writing's Dying." *College Composition and Communication* 11 (4): 206–10.

———. 1962. "Miscellany." *College Composition and Communication* 13 (1): 57–61.

Malle, Louis, dir. 1981. *My Dinner with André.* Fox Lorber Home Video, 1988. Film.

Marais, Hein. 1998. *South Africa: Limits to Change: The Political Economy of Transformation.* London: Zed Books.

Marx, Karl. 1973. *Grundrisse: Foundations of the Critique of Political Economy.* Translated and Foreword by Martin Nicolau. New York: Penguin.

_______ and Friedrich Engels. 1970. *The German Ideology.* New York: International.

Mashamba, George. 1990. *A Conceptual Critique of the People's Education Discourse.* Johannesburg: University of Witwatersrand.

Mathieu, Paula. 2005. *Tactics of Hope: The Public Turn in English Composition.* Portsmouth, NH: Boynton/Cook Publishers.

Mayers, Tim. 2005. *(Re)Writing Craft: Composition, Creative Writing, and the Future of English Studies.* Pittsburgh: University of Pittsburgh Press.

McCloud, Scott. 1993. *Understanding Comics: The Invisible Art.* New York: Harper.

McComiskey, Bruce. 1997. "Composing Postmodern Subjectivities in the Aporia between Identity and Difference." *Rhetoric Review* 15 (4): 350–64.

McGuigan, Jim. 1992. *Cultural Populism.* London: Routledge.

McQuade, Donald. 1992. "Living In—and On—the Margins." *College Composition and Communication* 43 (1): 11–22.

McRobbie, Angela. 1983. "Jackie: An Ideology of Adolescent Feminity." In *Mass Communication Review Yearbook.* Vol. 4, 251–71. Edited by Ellen Wartella and D. Charles Whitney. Beverley Hills: Sage.

"Media Workshop Held at LACOM/SACHED on 09 June 1990." 1990. Stenciled paper. Historical and Library Papers. Witwatersrand University.

Merton, Robert K. 1973. *The Sociology of Science,* edited by Norman W. Storer. Chicago: University of Chicago Press.

Meyer, Jessica. 2001. "Smoothin' Out the Concrete." *Spill* 3: 4.

Miki, Yoshio, et al. 1994. "A Strong Candidate for the Breast and Ovarian Cancer Susceptibility Gene BRCA1." *Science* 266 (12): 66–71.

Miles, Libby, et al. 2008. "Commenting on Douglas Downs and Elizabeth Wardle's 'Teaching About Writing, Righting Misconceptions.'" *College Composition and Communication* 59 (3): 503–11.

Miller, Carolyn R. 1984. "Genre as Social Action." *Quarterly Journal of Speech* 70 (2): 151–67.

Miller, Susan. 1989. *Rescuing the Subject: A Critical Introduction of Rhetoric and the Writer.* Carbondale: Southern Illinois University Press.

———. 1991. *Textual Carnivals: The Politics of Composition.* Carbondale: Southern Illinois University Press.

———. 1997. "Technologies of Self-Formation." *JAC* 17 (2): 497–500.

———. 2002. "Writing Studies as a Mode of Inquiry." In *Rhetoric and Composition as Intellectual Work,* edited by Gary A. Olson, 41–54. Carbondale: Southern Illinois University Press.

Miller, Thomas P. 1997. *The Formation of College English: Rhetoric and Belles Lettres in the British Cultural Provinces.* Pittsburgh: University of Pittsburgh Press.

Mills, C. Wright. 1958. *The Causes of World War Three.* New York: Simon and Schuster.

Moffett, James. 1988. *Storm in the Mountains: A Case Study of Censorship, Conflict, and Consciousness.* Carbondale: Southern Illinois University Press.

Moore, Marianne. 1982. *The Complete Poems of Marianne Moore.* New York: Penguin.

Morley, Dave. 1980. *The "Nationwide" Audience.* London: British Film Institute.

Mortensen, Peter. 1998. "Going Public." *College Composition and Communication* 50 (2): 182–205.

Motala, Shireen, and Salim Vally. 2002. "People's Education: From People's Power to Tirisano." In *The History of Education Under Apartheid,* edited by Patrick Kallaway, 174–94. New York: Peter Lang.

Myers, Greg. 1990. *Writing Biology: Texts in the Social Construction of Scientific Knowledge.* Madison: University of Wisconsin Press.

Naidoo, Jay. 1987. "Address by Comrade Jay Naidoo." *South African Labour Bulletin* 12 (4): 33–35.

National Advisory Council for Adult Education. 1948. Minutes. Sub-Committee South African Institute of Race Relations. Jan. 18. Historical and Library Papers. Witwatersrand University.

National Science Board. 2010. *Science and Engineering Indicators: 2010.* Arlington, VA: National Science Foundation. www.nsf.gov/statistics/seind10/. Accessed Aug. 17, 2010.

Nekhwevha, Fhulu. 2002. "The Influence of Paolo Freire's 'Pedagogy of Knowing' on the South African Education Struggle in the 1970s and 1980s." In *The History of Education Under Apartheid,* edited by Patrick Kallaway, 134–44. New York: Peter Lang.

Nelkin, Dorothy. 1995. *Selling Science: How the Press Covers Science and Technology*. New York: Freeman.

New London Group. 2000. "A Pedagogy of Multiliteracies: Designing Social Futures." In *Multiliteracies: Literacy Learning and the Design of Social Futures*, edited by Bill Kope and Mary Kalantzis, 9–37. London: Routledge.

"New Techniques in Teaching Composition/Communication Courses." 1959. *College Composition and Communication* 10 (3): 137–39.

North, Stephen. 1987. *The Making of Knowledge in Composition: Portrait of an Emerging Field*. Upper Montclair, NJ: Boynton/Cook Publishers.

"The N.S.S.C. and the C.C.C.C." 1951. *College Composition and Communication* 2 (2): 13–15.

"Obama's 'Restrained' 2011 Budget Would Not Freeze NIH." 2010. *Genome Web Daily News*. Feb. 1. www.genomeweb.com/obamas-restrained-2011-budget-would-not-freeze-nih. Accessed Aug. 17, 2010.

Odell, Lee, and Dixie Goswami. 1982. "Writing in a Non-Academic Setting." *Research in the Teaching of English* 16 (3): 201–23.

Odets, Walt. 1995. *In the Shadow of the Epidemic: Being HIV Negative in the Age of AIDS*. Durham: Duke University Press.

Ohmann, Richard. 1987. "Reading and Writing, Work and Leisure." In *Politics of Letters*, 26–41. Middletown: Wesleyan University Press.

———. 2003. *Politics of Knowledge: The Commercialization of the University, the Professions, and Print Culture*. Middletown: Wesleyan University Press.

Oliphant, Andries Walter, and Ivan Vladislavic, eds. 1988. *Ten Years of Staffrider 1978–1988*. Johannesburg: Ravan.

Olson, Gary A. 2002. "The Death of Composition as an Intellectual Discipline." *Rhetoric and Composition as Intellectual Work*, edited by Gary A. Olson, 23–38. Carbondale, IL: Southern Illinois University Press.

"On the Role of Service Organisations: Some Ideas." 1987. *South African Labour Bulletin* 12 (8): 20–28.

Paine, Charles. 1997. "The Composition Course and Public Discourse." *Rhetoric Review* 15 (3): 282–98.

_______. 1999. *The Resistant Writer: Rhetoric as Immunity, 1850 to the Present*. Albany: State University of New York Press.

Patel, Samir S., ed. 2006. *Africa Comics*. New York: Studio Museum in Harlem.

Peirce, Bronwyn Norton. 1989. "Toward a Pedagogy of Possibility in the Teaching of English Internationally: People's English in South Africa." *TESOL Quarterly* 23 (3): 408–20.

*People's Education: A Collection of Articles*. 1987. Bellville: University of the Western Cape, Centre for Adult and Continuing Education.

"People's Education for All." 1986. *LACOM News* 1 (July): 7–8.

Perl, Sondra. 1980. "Understanding Composing." *College Composition and Communication* 31 (4): 363–69.

Phelps, Louise Wetherbee. 1988. *Composition as a Human Science*. New York: Oxford University Press.

Pound, Ezra. 1935. *Make It New: Essays*. New Haven: Yale University Press.

Prinsloo, Mastin. 1995. "Provision, Acquisition and Culture: Literacy Research in South Africa." *International Journal of Educational Development* 15 (3): 449–60.

Qabala, Alfred Temba, Mi S'Dumo Hlatshwayo, and Nise Malange. 1986. *Black Mamba Rising: South African Worker Poets in Struggle*, edited by Ari Sitas. Durban, South Africa: Worker Resistance and Culture Publications.

Radner, Sanford. 1959. "The Communication Concepts of Harold Innis." *College Composition and Communication* 10 (2): 77–80.

Radway, Janice. 1984. *Reading the Romance: Women, Patriarchy, and Popular Literature*. Chapel Hill: University of North Carolina Press.

Relman, Arnold S. 1998. "A Trip to Stonesville." *New Republic* Dec. 14: 37.

"Responses to Maxine Hairston, 'Diversity, Ideology, and Teaching Writing' [John Trimbur, Robert G. Wood, Ron Strickland, William H. Thelin, William J. Rouster, Toni Mester] and Reply. 1993. *College Composition and Communication* 44 (2): 248–56.

RJC. 1988. "CCCC: Voices in the Parlor, and Responses." *Rhetoric Review* 7 (1): 211–13.

Rodriguez, Richard. 1983. *Hunger of Memory: The Education of Richard Rodriguez: An Autobiography*. Boston: Bantam.

"The Role of the English Literacy Project." 1988. *LACOM News* 6 (September): 1–4.

Rorty, Richard. 1979. *Philosophy and the Mirror of Nature*. Princeton: Princeton University Press.

Rose, Mike. 1990. *Lives on the Boundary*. New York: Penguin.

Ross, Kristin. 1988. *The Emergence of Social Space: Rimbaud and the Paris Commune*. Minneapolis: University of Minnesota Press.

Roux, Eddie. 1942a. "Easy English for Africans." *African Studies* 1 (1): 261–69.

———. 1942b. Letter to Mrs. Rheinallt Jones. Feb. 19. Historical and Library Papers. Witwatersrand University.

———. 1942c. Letter to Mr. von Broembsen. July 20. Historical and Library Papers. Witwatersrand University.

———. 1945. Reply. *African Studies* 2 (3): 164–66.

______. 1964. *Time Longer Than Rope: A History of the Black Man's Struggle for Freedom in South Africa*. Madison: University of Wisconsin Press.

Russell, David R. 1991. *Writing in the Academic Disciplines, 1870–1990: A Curricular History*. Carbondale, IL: Southern Illinois University Press.

———. 1997. "Rethinking Genre in School and Society: An Activity Theory Analysis." *Written Communication* 14 (4): 504–54.

SACHED. *Annual Report.* 1985.

Sartre, Jean Paul. 1965. *What Is Literature?* Translated by Bernard Frechtman. New York: Harper.

Schlesinger, Philip. 1991. *Media, State and Nation: Political Violence and Collective Identities.* London: Sage.

Sheehy, Gail. 1977. Passages: Predictable Crises of Adult Life. New York: Bantam.

Shepherd, Robert H. W. 1940. *Lovedale, South Africa: The Story of a Century 1841–1941.* Lovedale: Lovedale Press.

Smith, Patti. 2010. *Just Kids.* New York: Ecco.

Sommers, Nancy. 1980. "Revision Strategies of Student Writers and Experienced Adult Writers." *College Composition and Communication* 31 (4): 378–88.

______. 1992. "Between the Drafts." *College Composition and Communication* 43 (1): 23–31.

——— and Laurie Saltz. 2004. "The Novice as Expert: Writing the Freshman Year." *College Composition and Communication* 56 (1): 124–49.

Spellmeyer, Kurt. 1993. *Common Ground: Dialogue, Understanding, and the Teaching of Writing.* Englewood Cliffs, NJ: Prentice.

Steedman, Carolyn. 1986. *Landscape for a Good Woman: A Story of Two Lives.* New Brunswick, NJ: Rutgers University Press.

Stout, George. 1954. "The Function of Freshman Composition in General Education." *College Composition and Communication* 4 (2): 95–96.

Strandness, Theodore B. 1956. "Perspective and Personnel in Communication Courses." *College Composition and Communication* 7 (1): 8–12.

Stuckey, J. Elspeth. 1991. *The Violence of Literacy.* Portsmouth, NH: Boynton/Cook Publishers.

Swales, John. 1990. *Genre Analysis: English in Academic and Research Settings.* Cambridge: Cambridge University Press.

Thomas, James C., et al. 1998. "Lay Health Advisors: Sexually Transmitted Disease Prevention Through Community Involvement." *American Journal of Public Health* 88: 1252–53.

Tompkins, Jane. 1988. "Fighting Words: Unlearning to Write the Critical Essay." *Georgia Review* 42 (4): 585–90.

Trimbur, John. 1999a. *The Call to Write.* 1st ed. New York: Addison Wesley Longman.

———. 1999b. "The Problem of Freshman English (Only): Toward Programs of Study in Writing. *WPA: Writing Program Administrator* 22 (3): 9–30.

Vally, Salim. 2004. "From People's Education to Neo-Liberalism in South Africa." *Review of African Political Economy* 34 (1): 39–56.

Varnum, Robin. 1996. *Fencing with Words: A History of Writing Instruction at Amherst College During the Era of Theodore Baird, 1938–1966.* Urbana: NCTE.

Victoria, Anna. 1995. "Banish Arthritis Forever." *Weekly World News* Oct. 24: 8–9.

Villanueva, Victor, Jr. 1997. *Cross-Talk in Comp Theory*. Urbana: NCTE.

von Holdt, Karl. 1986. "Literacy and Liberation: Towards a Workers' School." *South African Labour Bulletin* 11 (7): 67–74.

Wells, Jane. 1998. "Mammography and the Politics of Randomized Controlled Trials." *British Medical Journal* 317: 1228.

Wells, Susan. 1996. "Rogue Cops and Health Care: What Do We Want from Public Writing?" *College Composition and Communication* 47 (4): 325–41.

Williams, Joseph M., and Gregory G. Columb. 1993. "The Case for Explicit Teaching: Why What You Don't Know Can't Help You." *Research in the Teaching of English* 27 (3): 252–64.

Williams, Raymond. 1961. *The Long Revolution*. London: Chatto and Windus.

———. 1962. *Communications*. London: Penguin.

———. 1977. *Marxism and Literature*. Oxford: Oxford University Press.

______. 1979. *Politics and Letters: Interviews with* New Left Review. London: New Left Books.

———. 1983. *Keywords: A Vocabulary of Culture and Society*. Rev. ed. New York: Oxford University Press.

———. 1989a. "Adult Education and Social Change." In *What I Came to Say*, 157–66. London: Hutchinson.

———. 1989b. "The Future of Cultural Studies." In *The Politics of Modernism: Against the New Conformists*, edited by Tony Pinkney, 151–62. London: Verso.

——— and Michael Orrom. 1954. *Preface to Film*. London: Film Drama.

Willis, Paul. 1977. *Learning to Labor: How Working-Class Kids Get Working-Class Jobs*. New York: Columbia University Press.

Wilson, Daphne M. 1991. *Against the Odds: The Struggle of the Cape Town African Night Schools 1945–1967*. Cape Town: Centre for African Studies and Department of Adult Education and Extra Mural Studies, University of Cape Town.

Wilson, Gordon. 1967. "CCCC in Retrospect." *College Composition and Communication* 18 (3): 127–33.

Winsor, Dorothy. 1996. *Writing Like an Engineer: A Rhetorical Education*. New York: Routledge.

Wittgenstein, Ludwig. 1953. *Philosophical Investigations*. Translated by G. E. M. Anscombe. New York: Macmillan.

Witz, Leslie. 1988. *Write Your Own History*. Braamfontein: Ravan.

———. 1991. "The Write Your Own History Project." In *History from South Africa*, edited by Joshua Brown, et al., 368–78. Philadelphia: Temple University Press.

Worsham, Lynn. 1991. "Writing against Writing: The Predicament of Ecriture Feminine in Composition Studies." In *Contending with Words: Composition and Rhetoric in a Postmodern Age,* edited by Patricia Harkin and John Schilb, 82–104. New York: Modern Language Association.

Wright, Richard. 1945. *Black Boy: A Record of Childhood and Youth.* New York: Harper & Brothers.

Wykoff, George. 1950. "Secretary's Report." *College Composition and Communication* 1 (1): 19–21.

———. 1951. "Secretary's Report." *College Composition and Communication* 2 (1): 13–15.

Wynne, Brian. 1996. "Misunderstood Misunderstandings: Social Identities and Public Uptake of Science." In *Misunderstanding Science? The Public Reconstruction of Science and Technology,* edited by Alan Irwin and Brian Wynne, 19–46. Cambridge: Cambridge University Press.

Young, Richard E. 1980. "Arts, Crafts, Gifts, and Knacks: Some Disharmonies in the New Rhetoric." In *Reinventing the Rhetorical Tradition,* edited by Aviva Freedman and Ian Pringle, 53–60. Conway, AR: L&S Books.

———, Alton L. Becker, and Kenneth L. Pike. 1970. *Rhetoric: Discovery and Change.* New York: Harcourt, Brace.

Young, Stephanie. 1997. "Your Pap Smear: A Save-Your-Life Guide." *Glamour* (Aug.): 208–11.

Young, Vershawn Ashanti. 2009. "'Nah, We Straight': An Argument Against Code Switching." *JAC* 29 (1–2): 49–76.

# Index

**Credit lines continued from page ii:**

"Writing Instruction and the Politics of Professionalization" by John Trimbur from *Composition in the Twenty-First Century: Crisis and Change*, edited by Lynn Z. Bloom, Donald A. Daiker, and Edward M. White. Copyright © 1996 by Southern Illinois University Press. Reprinted by permission of the publisher.

"Popularizing Science: At the Boundary of Expert and Lay Biomedical Knowledge" by Lundy Braun and John Trimbur from *Popular Literacy: Studies in Cultural Practices and Poetics*, edited by John Trimbur. Copyright © 2001 by the University of Pittsburgh Press. Reprinted by permission of the publisher.

"Popular Literacy and the Resources of Print Culture: The South African Committee on Higher Education Development" by John Trimbur from *College Composition and Communication* Vol. 61, No. 1, pages 85–108. Copyright © 2009 by the National Council of Teachers of English. Reprinted by permission of the publisher.

"Composition and the Circulation of Writing" by John Trimbur from *College Composition and Communication* Vol. 52, No. 2, pages 188–219. Copyright © 2000 by the National Council of Teachers of English. Reprinted by permission of the publisher.